D1237115

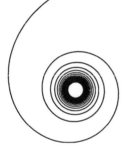

MATLAB *Guide*

MATLAB *Guide*

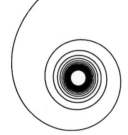

Desmond J. Higham
University of Strathclyde
Glasgow, Scotland

Nicholas J. Higham
University of Manchester
Manchester, England

siam

Society for Industrial and Applied Mathematics
Philadelphia

Copyright © 2000 by the Society for Industrial and Applied Mathematics.

10 9 8 7 6 5 4 3 2

All rights reserved. Printed in the United States of America. No part of this book may be reproduced, stored, or transmitted in any manner without the written permission of the publisher. For information, write to the Society for Industrial and Applied Mathematics, 3600 University City Science Center, Philadelphia, PA 19104-2688.

No warranties, express or implied, are made by the publisher, authors, and their employers that the programs contained in this volume are free of error. They should not be relied on as the sole basis to solve a problem whose incorrect solution could result in injury to person or property. If the programs are employed in such a manner, it is at the user's own risk and the publisher, authors, and their employers disclaim all liability for such misuse.

Trademarked names may be used in this book without the inclusion of a trademark symbol. These names are used in an editorial context only; no infringement of trademark is intended.

Figure 8.26 appears courtesy of Oak Ridge National Laboratories.

Library of Congress Cataloging-in-Publication Data

Higham, D. J. (Desmond J.)
 MATLAB guide / Desmond J. Higham, Nicholas J. Higham.
  p. cm.
 Includes bibliographical references and index.
 ISBN 0-89871-469-9
 ISBN 0-89871-516-4 (pbk.)
  1. MATLAB. 2. Numerical analysis—data processing. I. Higham, Nicholas J., 1961-
 II. Title.

QA297.H5217 2000
519.4'0285—dc21

00-033837

siam is a registered trademark.

To our parents

Contents

List of Figures

List of Tables

List of M-Files

Preface

MATLAB[1] is an interactive system for numerical computation. Numerical analyst Cleve Moler wrote the initial Fortran version of MATLAB in the late 1970s as a teaching aid. It became popular for both teaching and research and evolved into a commercial software package written in C. For many years now, MATLAB has been widely used in universities and industry.

MATLAB has several advantages over more traditional means of numerical computing (e.g., writing Fortran or C programs and calling numerical libraries):

- It allows quick and easy coding in a very high-level language.

- Data structures require minimal attention; in particular, arrays need not be declared before first use.

- An interactive interface allows rapid experimentation and easy debugging.

- High-quality graphics and visualization facilities are available.

- MATLAB M-files are completely portable across a wide range of platforms.

- Toolboxes can be added to extend the system, giving, for example, specialized signal processing facilities and a symbolic manipulation capability.

- A wide range of user-contributed M-files is freely available on the Internet.

Furthermore, MATLAB is a modern programming language and problem solving environment: it has sophisticated data structures, contains built-in debugging and profiling tools, and supports object-oriented programming. These factors make MATLAB an excellent language for teaching and a powerful tool for research and practical problem solving. Being interpreted, MATLAB inevitably suffers some loss of efficiency compared with compiled languages, but this can be mitigated by using the MATLAB Compiler or by linking to compiled Fortran or C code using MEX files.

This book has two purposes. First, it aims to give a lively introduction to the most popular features of MATLAB, covering all that most users will ever need to know. We assume no prior knowledge of MATLAB, but the reader is expected to be familiar with the basics of programming and with the use of the operating system under which MATLAB is being run. We describe how and why to use MATLAB functions but do not explain the mathematical theory and algorithms underlying them; instead, references are given to the appropriate literature.

The second purpose of the book is to provide a compact reference for all MATLAB users. The scope of MATLAB has grown dramatically as the package has been developed (see Table 0.1), and even experienced MATLAB users may be unaware of some of the functionality of the latest version. Indeed the documentation provided

---

[1]MATLAB is a registered trademark of The MathWorks, Inc.

Table 0.1. *Versions of MATLAB.*

Year	Version	Notable features
1978	Classic MATLAB	Original Fortran version.
1984	MATLAB 1	Rewritten in C.
1985	MATLAB 2	30% more commands and functions, typeset documentation.
1987	MATLAB 3	Faster interpreter, color graphics, high-resolution graphics hard copy.
1992	MATLAB 4	Sparse matrices, animation, visualization, user interface controls, debugger, Handle Graphics,* Microsoft Windows support.
1997	MATLAB 5	Profiler, object-oriented programming, multidimensional arrays, cell arrays, structures, more sparse linear algebra, new ordinary differential equation solvers, browser-based help.
2000	MATLAB 6	MATLAB desktop including Help Browser, matrix computations based on LAPACK with optimized BLAS, function handles, `eigs` interface to ARPACK, boundary value problem and partial differential equation solvers, graphics object transparency, Java support.

* Handle Graphics is a registered trademark of The MathWorks, Inc.

with MATLAB has grown to such an extent that the introductory *Using MATLAB* [56] greatly exceeds this book in page length. Hence we believe that there is a need for a manual that is wide-ranging yet concise. We hope that our approach of focusing on the most important features of MATLAB, combined with the book's logical organization and detailed index, will make *MATLAB Guide* a useful reference.

The book is intended to be used by students, researchers and practitioners alike. Our philosophy is to teach by giving informative examples rather than to treat every function comprehensively. Full documentation is available in MATLAB's online help and we pinpoint where to look for further details.

Our treatment includes many "hidden" or easily overlooked features of MATLAB and we provide a wealth of useful tips, covering such topics as customizing graphics, M-file style, code optimization and debugging.

The main subject omitted is object-oriented programming. Every MATLAB user benefits, perhaps unknowingly, from its object-oriented nature, but we think that the typical user does not need to program in an object-oriented fashion. Other areas not covered include Graphical User Interface tools, MATLAB's Java interface, and some of the more advanced visualization features.

We have not included exercises; MATLAB is often taught in conjunction with particular subjects, and exercises are best tailored to the context.

We have been careful to show complete, undoctored MATLAB output and to test every piece of MATLAB code listed. The only editing we have done of output has been to break over-long lines that continued past our right margin—in these cases we have manually inserted the continuation periods "..." at the line break.

MATLAB runs on several operating systems and we concentrate on features common to all. We do not describe how to install or run MATLAB, or how to customize it—the manuals, available in both printed and online form, should be consulted for this system-specific information.

A Web page has been created for the book, at

http://www.siam.org/books/ot75

It includes

- All the M-files used as examples in the book.

- Updates relating to material in the book.

- Links to various MATLAB-related Web resources.

What This Book Describes

This book describes MATLAB 6 (Release 12), although most of the examples work with at most minor modification in MATLAB 5.3 (Release 11). If you are not sure which version of MATLAB you are using type ver or version at the MATLAB prompt. The book is based on a prerelease version of MATLAB 6, and it is possible that some of what we say does not fully reflect the release version; any corrections and additions will be posted on the Web site mentioned above.

All the output shown was generated on a Pentium III machine running MATLAB under Windows 98.

How This Book Is Organized

The book begins with a tutorial that provides a quick tour of MATLAB. The rest of the book is independent of the tutorial, so the tutorial can be skipped—for example, by readers already familiar with MATLAB.

The chapters are ordered so as to introduce topics in a logical fashion, with the minimum of forward references. A principal aim was to cover M-files and graphics as early as possible, subject to being able to provide meaningful examples. Later chapters contain material that is more advanced or less likely to be needed by the beginner.

Using the Book

Readers new to MATLAB should begin by working through the tutorial in Chapter 1. Although it is designed to be read sequentially, with most chapters building on material from earlier ones, the book can be read in a nonsequential fashion by following cross-references and making use of the index. It is difficult to do serious MATLAB computation without a knowledge of arithmetic, matrices, the colon notation, operators, flow control and M-files, so Chapters 4–7 contain information essential for all users.

Experienced MATLAB users who are upgrading from versions earlier than version 6 should refer to Appendix A, which lists some of the main changes in recent releases.

Acknowledgments

We are grateful to a number of people who offered helpful advice and comments during the preparation of the book:

Penny Anderson, Christian Beardah, Tom Bryan, Brian Duffy, Cleve Moler, Damian Packer, Harikrishna Patel, Larry Shampine, Françoise Tisseur, Nick Trefethen, Jack Williams.

Once again we enjoyed working with the SIAM staff, and we thank particularly Vickie Kearn, Michelle Montgomery, Deborah Poulson, Lois Sellers, Kelly Thomas, Marianne Will, and our copy editor, Beth Gallagher.

For those of you that have not experienced MATLAB, we would like to try to show you what everybody is excited about . . . The best way to appreciate PC-MATLAB is, of course, to try it yourself.
— JOHN LITTLE and CLEVE MOLER, *A Preview of PC-MATLAB* (1985)

In teaching, writing and research, there is no greater clarifier than a well-chosen example.
— CHARLES F. VAN LOAN, *Using Examples to Build Computational Intuition* (1995)

Chapter 1
A Brief Tutorial

The best way to learn MATLAB is by trying it yourself, and hence we begin with a whirlwind tour. Working through the examples below will give you a quick feel for the way that MATLAB operates and an appreciation of its power and flexibility.

The tutorial is entirely independent of the rest of the book—all the MATLAB features introduced are discussed in greater detail in the subsequent chapters. Indeed, in order to keep this chapter brief, we have not explained all the functions used here. You can use the index to find out more about particular topics that interest you.

The tutorial contains commands for you to type at the command line. In the last part of the tutorial we give examples of script and function files—MATLAB's versions of programs and functions, subroutines, or procedures in other languages. These files are short, so you can type them in quickly. Alternatively, you can download them from the Web site mentioned in the preface on p. xxi. You should experiment as you proceed, keeping the following points in mind.

- Upper and lower case characters are not equivalent (MATLAB is case sensitive).

- Typing the name of a variable will cause MATLAB to display its current value.

- A semicolon at the end of a command suppresses the screen output.

- MATLAB uses both parentheses, (), and square brackets, [], and these are not interchangeable.

- The up arrow and down arrow keys can be used to scroll through your previous commands. Also, an old command can be recalled by typing the first few characters followed by up arrow.

- You can type `help topic` to access online help on the command, function or symbol `topic`.

- You can quit MATLAB by typing `exit` or `quit`.

Having entered MATLAB, you should work through this tutorial by typing in the text that appears after the MATLAB prompt, >>, in the Command Window. After showing you what to type, we display the output that is produced. We begin with

```
>> a = [1 2 3]

a =

     1     2     3
```

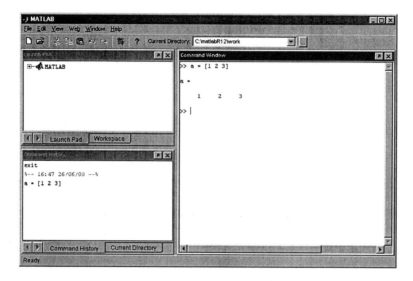

Figure 1.1. *MATLAB desktop at start of tutorial.*

This means that you are to type "a = [1 2 3]", after which you will see MATLAB's output "a =" and "1   2   3" on separate lines separated by a blank line. See Figure 1.1. (To save space we will subsequently omit blank lines in MATLAB's output. You can tell MATLAB to suppress blank lines by typing format compact.) This example sets up a 1-by-3 array a (a row vector). In the next example, semicolons separate the entries:

```
>> c = [4; 5; 6]
c =
     4
     5
     6
```

A semicolon tells MATLAB to start a new row, so c is 3-by-1 (a column vector). Now you can multiply the arrays a and c:

```
>> a*c
ans =
    32
```

Here, you performed an inner product: a 1-by-3 array multiplied into a 3-by-1 array. MATLAB automatically assigned the result to the variable ans, which is short for answer. An alternative way to compute an inner product is with the dot function:

```
>> dot(a,c)
ans =
    32
```

Inputs to MATLAB functions are specified after the function name and within parentheses. You may also form the outer product:

```
>> A = c*a
```

```
A =
     4      8     12
     5     10     15
     6     12     18
```

Here, the answer is a 3-by-3 matrix that has been assigned to A.

The product a*a is not defined, since the dimensions are incompatible for matrix multiplication:

```
>> a*a
??? Error using ==> *
Inner matrix dimensions must agree.
```

Arithmetic operations on matrices and vectors come in two distinct forms. Matrix sense operations are based on the normal rules of linear algebra and are obtained with the usual symbols +, -, *, / and ^. Array sense operations are defined to act elementwise and are generally obtained by preceding the symbol with a dot. Thus if you want to square each element of a you can write

```
>> b = a.^2
b =
     1      4      9
```

Since the new vector b is 1-by-3, like a, you can form the array product of it with a:

```
>> a.*b
ans =
     1      8     27
```

MATLAB has many mathematical functions that operate in the array sense when given a vector or matrix argument. For example,

```
>> exp(a)
ans =
    2.7183     7.3891    20.0855

>> log(ans)
ans =
     1      2      3

>> sqrt(a)
ans =
    1.0000     1.4142     1.7321
```

MATLAB displays floating point numbers to 5 decimal digits, by default, but always stores numbers and computes to the equivalent of 16 decimal digits. The output format can be changed using the format command:

```
>> format long

>> sqrt(a)
ans =
    1.00000000000000     1.41421356237310     1.73205080756888

>> format
```

The last command reinstates the default output format of 5 digits. Large or small numbers are displayed in exponential notation, with a power of 10 scale factor preceded by e:

```
>> 2^(-24)
ans =
   5.9605e-008
```

Various data analysis functions are also available:

```
>> sum(b), mean(c)
ans =
     14
ans =
     5
```

As this example shows, you may include more than one command on the same line by separating them with commas. If a command is followed by a semicolon then MATLAB suppresses the output:

```
>> pi
ans =
   3.1416

>> y = tan(pi/6);
```

The variable pi is a permanent variable with value π. The variable ans always contains the most recent unassigned expression evaluated without a semicolon, so after the assignment to y, ans still holds the value π.

You may set up a two-dimensional array by using spaces to separate entries within a row and semicolons to separate rows:

```
>> B = [-3 0 1; 2 5 -7; -1 4 8]
B =
    -3      0      1
     2      5     -7
    -1      4      8
```

At the heart of MATLAB is a powerful range of linear algebra functions. For example, recalling that c is a 3-by-1 vector, you may wish to solve the linear system B*x = c. This can be done with the backslash operator:

```
>> x = B\c
x =
   -1.3717
    1.3874
   -0.1152
```

You can check the result by computing the Euclidean norm of the residual:

```
>> norm(B*x-c)
ans =
   8.8818e-016
```

The eigenvalues of B can be found using `eig`:

```
>> e = eig(B)
e =
  -2.8601
   6.4300 + 5.0434i
   6.4300 - 5.0434i
```

Here, i is the imaginary unit, $\sqrt{-1}$. You may also specify two output arguments for the function `eig`:

```
>> [V,D] = eig(B)
V =
     0.9823          0.0400 + 0.0404i    0.0400 - 0.0404i
    -0.1275         -0.7922             -0.7922
     0.1374          0.1733 + 0.5823i    0.1733 - 0.5823i
D =
    -2.8601                0                    0
          0          6.4300 + 5.0434i          0
          0                0            6.4300 - 5.0434i
```

In this case the columns of V are eigenvectors of B and the diagonal elements of D are the corresponding eigenvalues.

The colon notation is useful for constructing vectors of equally spaced values. For example,

```
>> v = 1:6
v =
     1     2     3     4     5     6
```

Generally, m:n generates the vector with entries m, m+1, ..., n. Nonunit increments can be specified with m:s:n, which generates entries that start at m and increase (or decrease) in steps of s as far as n:

```
>> w = 2:3:10, y = 1:-0.25:0
w =
     2     5     8
y =
     1.0000    0.7500    0.5000    0.2500         0
```

You may construct big matrices out of smaller ones by following the conventions that (a) square brackets enclose an array, (b) spaces or commas separate entries in a row and (c) semicolons separate rows:

```
>> C = [A,[8;9;10]], D = [B;a]
C =
     4     8    12     8
     5    10    15     9
     6    12    18    10

D =
    -3     0     1
     2     5    -7
    -1     4     8
     1     2     3
```

The element in row i and column j of the matrix C (where i and j always start at 1) can be accessed as C(i,j):

```
>> C(2,3)
ans =
    15
```

More generally, C(i1:i2,j1:j2) picks out the submatrix formed by the intersection of rows i1 to i2 and columns j1 to j2:

```
>> C(2:3,1:2)
ans =
     5    10
     6    12
```

You can build certain types of matrix automatically. For example, identities and matrices of 0s and 1s can be constructed with eye, zeros and ones:

```
>> I3 = eye(3,3), Y = zeros(3,5), Z = ones(2)
I3 =
     1    0    0
     0    1    0
     0    0    1
Y =
     0    0    0    0    0
     0    0    0    0    0
     0    0    0    0    0
Z =
     1    1
     1    1
```

Note that for these functions the first argument specifies the number of rows and the second the number of columns; if both numbers are the same then only one need be given. The functions rand and randn work in a similar way, generating random entries from the uniform distribution over $[0, 1]$ and the normal $(0, 1)$ distribution, respectively. If you want to make your experiments repeatable, you should set the state of the two random number generators. Here, they are set to 20:

```
>> rand('state',20), randn('state',20)
>> F = rand(3), G = randn(1,5)
F =
    0.7062    0.3586    0.8468
    0.5260    0.8488    0.3270
    0.2157    0.0426    0.5541
G =
    1.4051    1.1780   -1.1142    0.2474   -0.8169
```

Single (closing) quotes act as string delimiters, so 'state' is a string. Many MATLAB functions take string arguments.

By this point several variables have been created in the workspace. You can obtain a list with the who command:

```
>> who

Your variables are:

A          F          Y          b          w
B          G          Z          c          x
C          I3         a          e          y
D          V          ans        v
```

Alternatively, type **whos** for a more detailed list showing the size and class of each variable, too.

Like most programming languages, MATLAB has loop constructs. The following example uses a **for** loop to evaluate the continued fraction

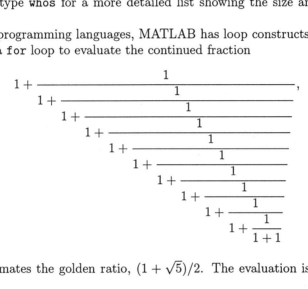

which approximates the golden ratio, $(1 + \sqrt{5})/2$. The evaluation is done from the bottom up:

```
>> g = 2;
>> for k=1:10, g = 1 + 1/g; end
>> g
g =
    1.6181
```

Loops involving **while** can be found later in this tutorial.

The **plot** function produces two-dimensional (2D) pictures:

```
>> t = 0:0.005:1; z = exp(10*t.*(t-1)).*sin(12*pi*t);
>> plot(t,z)
```

Here, **plot(t,z)** joins the points **t(i),z(i)** using the default solid linetype. MATLAB opens a figure window in which the picture is displayed. Figure 1.2 shows the result.

You can produce a histogram with the function **hist**:

```
>> hist(randn(1000,1))
```

Here, **hist** is given 1000 points from the normal $(0,1)$ random number generator. The result is shown in Figure 1.3.

You are now ready for more challenging computations. A random Fibonacci sequence $\{x_n\}$ is generated by choosing x_1 and x_2 and setting

$$x_{n+1} = x_n \pm x_{n-1}, \quad n \geq 2.$$

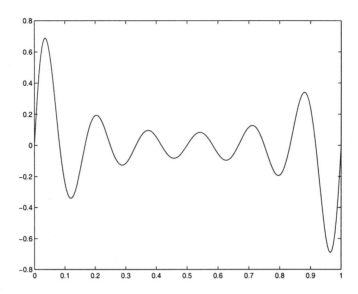

Figure 1.2. *Basic 2D picture produced by* plot.

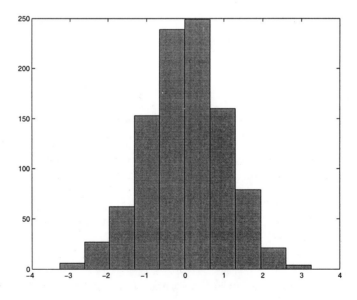

Figure 1.3. *Histogram produced by* hist.

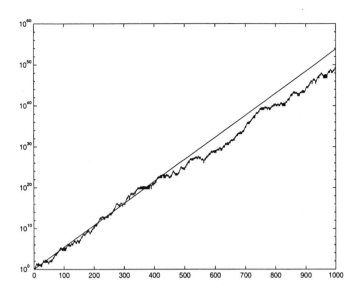

Figure 1.4. *Growth of a random Fibonacci sequence.*

Here, the $\pm$ indicates that $+$ and $-$ must have equal probability of being chosen. Viswanath [82] analyzed this recurrence and showed that, with probability 1, for large n the quantity $|x_n|$ increases like a multiple of c^n, where $c = 1.13198824\ldots$ (see also [17]). You can test Viswanath's result as follows:

```
>> clear
>> rand('state',100)
>> x = [1 2];
>> for n = 2:999, x(n+1) = x(n) + sign(rand-0.5)*x(n-1); end
>> semilogy(1:1000,abs(x))
>> c = 1.13198824;
>> hold on
>> semilogy(1:1000,c.^[1:1000])
>> hold off
```

Here, `clear` removes all variables from the workspace. The `for` loop stores a random Fibonacci sequence in the array `x`; MATLAB automatically extends `x` each time a new element `x(n+1)` is assigned. The `semilogy` function then plots `n` on the x-axis against `abs(x)` on the y-axis, with logarithmic scaling for the y-axis. Typing `hold on` tells MATLAB to superimpose the next picture on top of the current one. The second `semilogy` plot produces a line of slope `c`. The overall picture, shown in Figure 1.4, is consistent with Viswanath's theory.

The MATLAB commands to generate Figure 1.4 stretched over several lines. This is inconvenient for a number of reasons, not least because if a change is made to the experiment then it is necessary to reenter all the commands. To avoid this difficulty you can employ a script M-file. Create an ASCII file named `rfib.m` identical to Listing 1.1 in your current directory. (Typing `edit` calls up MATLAB's Editor/Debugger; `pwd` displays the current directory and `ls` or `dir` lists its contents.) Now type

```
>> rfib
```

Listing 1.1. *Script M-file* rfib.m.

```
%RFIB                    Random Fibonacci sequence.

rand('state',100)        % Set random number state.
m = 1000;                % Number of iterations.

x = [1 2];               % Initial conditions.
for n = 2:m-1            % Main loop.
    x(n+1) = x(n) + sign(rand-0.5)*x(n-1);
end

semilogy(1:m,abs(x))
c = 1.13198824;          % Viswanath's constant.
hold on
semilogy(1:m,c.^(1:m))
hold off
```

at the command line. This will reproduce the picture in Figure 1.4. Running rfib in this way is essentially the same as typing the commands in the file at the command line, in sequence. Note that in Listing 1.1 blank lines and indentation are used to improve readability, and we have made the number of iterations a variable, m, so that it can be more easily changed. The script also contains helpful comments— all text on a line after the % character is ignored by MATLAB. Having set up these commands in an M-file you are now free to experiment further. For example, changing rand('state',100) to rand('state',101) generates a different random Fibonacci sequence, and adding the line title('Random Fibonacci Sequence') at the end of the file will put a title on the graph.

Our next example involves the Collatz iteration, which, given a positive integer x_1, has the form $x_{k+1} = f(x_k)$, where

$$f(x) = \begin{cases} 3x + 1, & \text{if } x \text{ is odd,} \\ x/2, & \text{if } x \text{ is even.} \end{cases}$$

In words: if x is odd, replace it by $3x + 1$, and if x is even, halve it. It has been conjectured that this iteration will always lead to a value of 1 (and hence thereafter cycle between 4, 2 and 1) whatever starting value x_1 is chosen. There is ample computational evidence to support this conjecture, which is variously known as the Collatz problem, the $3x + 1$ problem, the Syracuse problem, Kakutani's problem, Hasse's algorithm, and Ulam's problem. However, a rigorous proof has so far eluded mathematicians. For further details, see [47] or type "Collatz problem" into your favorite Web search engine. You can investigate the conjecture by creating the script M-file collatz.m shown in Listing 1.2. In this file a while loop and an if statement are used to implement the iteration. The input command prompts you for a starting value. The appropriate response is to type an integer and then hit return or enter:

```
>> collatz
Enter an integer bigger than 2:   27
```

Here, the starting value 27 has been entered. The iteration terminates and the resulting picture is shown in Figure 1.5.

Listing 1.2. *Script M-file* `collatz.m`.

```
%COLLATZ                Collatz iteration.

n = input('Enter an integer bigger than 2:    ');
narray = n;

count = 1;
while n ~= 1
  if rem(n,2) == 1    % Remainder modulo 2.
     n = 3*n+1;
  else
     n = n/2;
  end
  count = count + 1;
  narray(count) = n; % Store the current iterate.
end

plot(narray,'*-')     % Plot with * marker and solid line style.
title(['Collatz iteration starting at ' int2str(narray(1))],'FontSize',16)
```

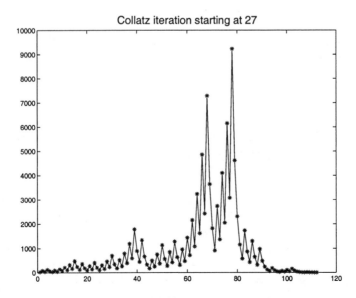

Figure 1.5. *Plot produced by* `collatz.m`.

To investigate the Collatz problem further, the script `collbar` in Listing 1.3 plots a bar graph of the number of iterations required to reach the value 1, for starting values $1, 2, \ldots, 29$. The result is shown in Figure 1.6. For this picture, the function `grid` adds grid lines that extend from the axis tick marks, and `title`, `xlabel` and `ylabel` add further information.

The well-known and much studied Mandelbrot set can be approximated graphically in just a few lines of MATLAB. It is defined as the set of points c in the complex plane for which the sequence generated by the map $z \mapsto z^2 + c$, starting with $z = c$, remains bounded [65, Chap. 14]. The script `mandel` in Listing 1.4 produces the plot of the Mandelbrot set shown in Figure 1.7. The script contains calls to `linspace` of the form `linspace(a,b,n)`, which generate an equally spaced vector of n values between a and b. The `meshgrid` and `complex` functions are used to construct a matrix C that represents the rectangular region of interest in the complex plane. The `waitbar` function plots a bar showing the progress of the computation and illustrates MATLAB's Handle Graphics (the variable h is a "handle" to the bar). The plot itself is produced by `contourf`, which plots a filled contour. The expression `abs(Z)<Z_max` in the call to `contourf` detects points that have not exceeded the threshold `Z_max` and which are therefore assumed to lie in the Mandelbrot set. You can experiment with `mandel` by changing the region that is plotted, via the `linspace` calls, the number of iterations `it_max`, and the threshold `Z_max`.

Next we solve the ordinary differential equation (ODE) system

$$\frac{d}{dt}y_1(t) = 10(y_2(t) - y_1(t)),$$

$$\frac{d}{dt}y_2(t) = 28y_1(t) - y_2(t) - y_1(t)y_3(t),$$

$$\frac{d}{dt}y_3(t) = y_1(t)y_2(t) - 8y_3(t)/3.$$

This is an example from the Lorenz equations family; see [74]. We take initial conditions $y(0) = [0, 1, 0]^T$ and solve over $0 \le t \le 50$. The M-file `lorenzde` in Listing 1.5 is an example of a MATLAB function. Given t and y, this function returns the right-hand side of the ODE as the vector `yprime`. This is the form required by MATLAB's ODE solving functions. The script `lrun` in Listing 1.6 uses the MATLAB function `ode45` to solve the ODE numerically and then produces the (y_1, y_3) phase plane plot shown in Figure 1.8. You can see an animated plot of the solution by typing `lorenz`, which calls one of MATLAB's demonstrations (type `help demos` for the complete list).

Now we give an example of a recursive function, that is, a function that calls itself. The Sierpinski gasket [64, Sec. 2.2] is based on the following process. Given a triangle with vertices P_a, P_b and P_c, we remove the triangle with vertices at the midpoints of the edges, $(P_a + P_b)/2$, $(P_b + P_c)/2$ and $(P_c + P_a)/2$. This removes the "middle quarter" of the triangle, as illustrated in Figure 1.9. Effectively, we have replaced the original triangle with three "subtriangles". We can now apply the middle quarter removal process to each of these subtriangles to generate nine subsubtriangles, and so on. The Sierpinski gasket is the set of all points that are never removed by repeated application of this process. The function `gasket` in Listing 1.7 implements the removal process. The input arguments Pa, Pb and Pc define the vertices of the triangle and `level` specifies how many times the process is to be applied. If `level` is nonzero then `gasket` calls itself three times with `level` reduced by 1, once for each

Listing 1.3. *Script M-file* `collbar.m`.

```
%COLLBAR                  Collatz iteration bar graph.

N = 29;                % Use starting values 1,2,...,N.
niter = zeros(N,1);    % Preallocate array.
for i = 1:N
    count = 0;
    n = i;
    while n ~= 1
        if rem(n,2) == 1
            n = 3*n+1;
        else
            n = n/2;
        end
        count = count + 1;
    end
    niter(i) = count;
end
bar(niter)    % Bar graph.
grid          % Add horizontal and vertical grid lines.
title('Collatz iteration counts','FontSize',16)
xlabel('Starting value','FontSize',16)        % Label x axis.
ylabel('Number of iterations','FontSize',16)  % Label y axis.
```

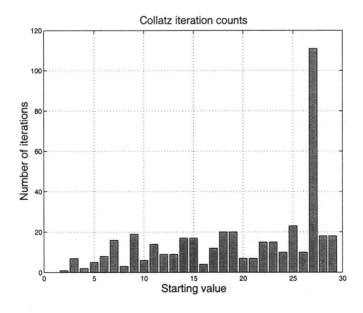

Figure 1.6. *Plot produced by* `collbar.m`.

Listing 1.4. *Script M-file* mandel.m.

```
%MANDEL       Mandelbrot set.

h = waitbar(0,'Computing...');
x = linspace(-2.1,0.6,301);
y = linspace(-1.1,1.1,301);
[X,Y] = meshgrid(x,y);
C = complex(X,Y);

Z_max = 1e6; it_max = 50;
Z = C;
for k = 1:it_max
    Z = Z.^2 + C;
    waitbar(k/it_max)
end
close(h)

contourf(x,y,abs(Z)<Z_max,1)
title('Mandelbrot Set','FontSize',16)
```

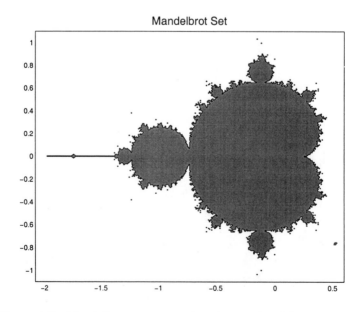

Figure 1.7. *Mandelbrot set approximation produced by* mandel.m.

Listing 1.5. *Function M-file* `lorenzde.m`.

```
function yprime = lorenzde(t,y)
%LORENZDE    Lorenz equations.
%            YPRIME  = LORENZDE(T,Y).

yprime = [10*(y(2)-y(1))
          28*y(1)-y(2)-y(1)*y(3)
          y(1)*y(2)-8*y(3)/3];
```

Listing 1.6. *Script M-file* `lrun.m`.

```
%LRUN       ODE solving example: Lorenz.

tspan = [0 50];                         % Solve for 0 <= t <= 50.
yzero = [0;1;0];                        % Initial conditions.
[t,y] = ode45(@lorenzde,tspan,yzero);
plot(y(:,1),y(:,3))                     % (y_1,y_3) phase plane.
xlabel('y_1','FontSize',14)
ylabel('y_3 ','FontSize',14,'Rotation',0,'HorizontalAlignment','right')
title('Lorenz equations','FontSize',16)
```

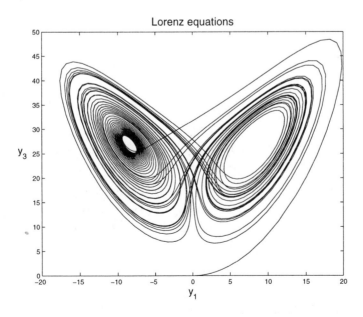

Figure 1.8. *Phase plane plot from* `ode45`.

Listing 1.7. *Function M-file* gasket.m.

```
function gasket(Pa,Pb,Pc,level)
%GASKET  Recursively generated Sierpinski gasket.
%        GASKET(PA, PB, PC, LEVEL) generates an approximation to
%        the Sierpinski gasket, where the 2-vectors PA, PB and PC
%        define the triangle vertices.
%        LEVEL is the level of recursion.

if level == 0
  % Fill the triangle with vertices Pa, Pb, Pc.
  fill([Pa(1),Pb(1),Pc(1)],[Pa(2),Pb(2),Pc(2)],[0.5 0.5 0.5]);
  hold on
else
  % Recursive calls for the three subtriangles.
  gasket(Pa,(Pa+Pb)/2,(Pa+Pc)/2,level-1)
  gasket(Pb,(Pb+Pa)/2,(Pb+Pc)/2,level-1)
  gasket(Pc,(Pc+Pa)/2,(Pc+Pb)/2,level-1)
end
```

of the three subtriangles. When level finally reaches zero, the appropriate triangle is drawn. The following code generates Figure 1.10.

```
>> level = 5;
>> Pa = [0;0];
>> Pb = [1;0];
>> Pc = [0.5;sqrt(3)/2];
>> gasket(Pa,Pb,Pc,level)
>> hold off
>> title(['Gasket level = ' num2str(level)],'FontSize',16)
>> axis('equal','off')
```

(Figure 1.9 was generated in the same way with level = 1.) In the last line, the call to axis makes the units of the x- and y-axes equal and turns off the axes and their labels. You should experiment with different initial vertices Pa, Pb and Pc, and different levels of recursion, but keep in mind that setting level bigger than 8 may overstretch either your patience or your computer's resources.

The Sierpinski gasket can also be generated by playing Barnsley's "chaos game" [64, Sec. 1.3]. We choose one of the vertices of a triangle as a starting point. Then we pick one of the three vertices at random, take the midpoint of the line joining this vertex with the starting point and plot this new point. Then we take the midpoint of this point and a randomly chosen vertex as the next point, which is plotted, and the process continues. The script barnsley in Listing 1.8 implements the game. Figure 1.11 shows the result of choosing 1000 iterations:

```
>> barnsley
Enter number of points (try 1000) 1000
```

Try experimenting with the number of points, n, the type and size of marker in the plot command, and the location of the starting point.

Gasket level = 1

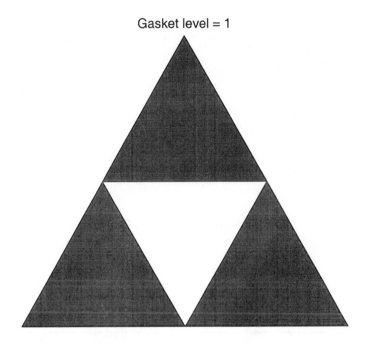

Figure 1.9. *Removal process for the Sierpinski gasket.*

Gasket level = 5

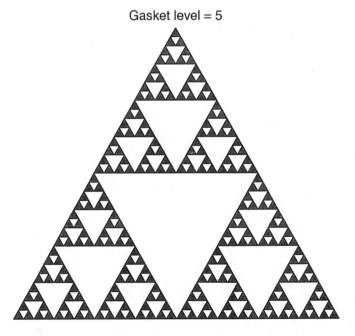

Figure 1.10. *Level 5 Sierpinski gasket approximation from* `gasket.m`.

Listing 1.8. *Script M-file* barnsley.m.

```
%BARNSLEY             Barnsley's game to compute Sierpinski gasket.

rand('state',1)                    % Set random number state.
V = [0, 1, 0.5; 0, 0, sqrt(3)/2]; % Columns give triangle vertices.

point = V(:,1);                    % Start at a vertex.
n = input('Enter number of points (try 1000) ');

for k = 1:n
    node = ceil(3*rand);           % node is 1, 2 or 3 with equal prob.
    point = (V(:,node) + point)/2;
    plot(point(1),point(2),'.','MarkerSize',15)
    hold on
end

axis('equal','off')
hold off
```

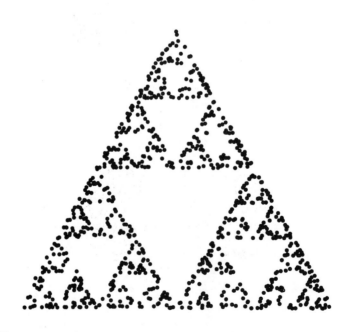

Figure 1.11. *Sierpinski gasket approximation from* barnsley.m.

Listing 1.9. *Script M-file* sweep.m.

```
%SWEEP          Generates a volume-swept 3D object.

N = 10;                      % Number of increments - try increasing.

z   = linspace(-5,5,N)';
radius = sqrt(1+z.^2);       % Try changing SQRT to some other function.
theta = 2*pi*linspace(0,1,N);
X = radius*cos(theta);
Y = radius*sin(theta);
Z = z(:,ones(1,N));

surf(X,Y,Z)
axis equal
```

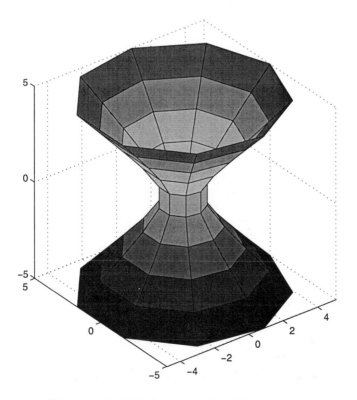

Figure 1.12. *3D picture produced by* sweep.m.

We finish with the script sweep in Listing 1.9, which generates a volume-swept three-dimensional (3D) object; see Figure 1.12. Here, the command surf(X,Y,Z) creates a 3D surface where the height Z(i,j) is specified at the point (X(i,j),Y(i,j)) in the x-y plane. The script is not written in the most obvious fashion, which would use two nested for loops. Instead it is vectorized. To understand how it works you will need to be familiar with Chapter 5 and Section 21.4. You can experiment with the script by changing the parameter N and the function that determines the variable radius: try replacing sqrt by other functions, such as log, sin or abs.

If you are one of those experts who wants to see something from MATLAB right now and would rather read the instructions later, this page is for you.

— 386-MATLAB User's Guide (1989)

Do not be too timid and squeamish about your actions. All life is an experiment. The more experiments you make the better.

— RALPH WALDO EMERSON

Chapter 2
Basics

2.1. Interaction and Script Files

MATLAB is an interactive system. You type commands at the prompt (>>) in the Command Window and computations are performed when you press the enter or return key. At its simplest level, MATLAB can be used like a pocket calculator:

```
>> (1+sqrt(5))/2
ans =
     1.6180

>> 2^(-53)
ans =
   1.1102e-016
```

The first example computes $(1 + \sqrt{5})/2$ and the second 2^{-53}. Note that the second result is displayed in exponential notation: it represents 1.1102×10^{-16}. The variable ans is created (or overwritten, if it already exists) when an expression is not assigned to a variable. It can be referenced later, just like any other variable. Unlike in most programming languages, variables are not declared prior to use but are created by MATLAB when they are assigned:

```
>> x = sin(22)
x =
    -0.0089
```

Here we have assigned to x the sine of 22 radians. The printing of output can be suppressed by appending a semicolon. The next example assigns a value to y without displaying the result:

```
>> y = 2*x + exp(-3)/(1+cos(.1));
```

Commas or semicolons are used to separate statements that appear on the same line:

```
>> x = 2, y = cos(.3), z = 3*x*y
x =
     2
y =
    0.9553
z =
    5.7320

>> x = 5; y = cos(.5); z = x*y^2
```

21

```
z =
    3.8508
```

Note again that the semicolon causes output to be suppressed.

MATLAB is case sensitive. This means, for example, that x and X are distinct variables.

To perform a sequence of related commands, you can write them into a script M-file, which is a text file with a .m filename extension. For example, suppose you wish to process a set of exam marks using the MATLAB functions sort, mean, median and std, which, respectively, sort into increasing order and compute the arithmetic mean, the median and the standard deviation. You can create a file, say marks.m, of the form

```
%MARKS
exmark = [12 0 5 28 87 3 56];
exsort = sort(exmark)
exmean = mean(exmark)
exmed  = median(exmark)
exstd  = std(exmark)
```

The % denotes a comment line. Typing

```
>> marks
```

at the command line then produces the output

```
exsort =
     0     3     5    12    28    56    87
exmean =
   27.2857
exmed =
    12
exstd =
   32.8010
```

Note that calling marks is entirely equivalent to typing each of the individual commands in sequence at the command line. More details on creating and using script files can be found in Chapter 7.

Throughout this book, unless otherwise indicated, the prompt >> signals an example that has been typed at the command line and it is immediately followed by MATLAB's output (if any). A sequence of MATLAB commands without the prompt should be interpreted as forming a script file (or part of one).

To quit MATLAB type exit or quit.

2.2. More Fundamentals

MATLAB has many useful functions in addition to the usual ones found on a pocket calculator. For example, you can set up a random matrix of order 3 by typing

```
>> A = rand(3)
A =
    0.9501    0.4860    0.4565
    0.2311    0.8913    0.0185
    0.6068    0.7621    0.8214
```

Here each entry of A is chosen independently from the uniform distribution on the interval $[0, 1]$. The inv command inverts A:

```
>> inv(A)
ans =
      1.6740    -0.1196    -0.9276
     -0.4165     1.1738     0.2050
     -0.8504    -1.0006     1.7125
```

The inverse has the property that its product with the matrix is the identity matrix. We can check this property for our example by typing

```
>> ans*A
ans =
      1.0000     0.0000    -0.0000
      0.0000     1.0000     0.0000
      0.0000    -0.0000     1.0000
```

The product has 1s on the diagonal, as expected. The off-diagonal elements, displayed as plus or minus 0.0000, are, in fact, not exactly zero. MATLAB stores numbers and computes to a relative precision of about 16 decimal digits. By default it displays numbers in a 5-digit fixed point format. While concise, this is not always the most useful format. The format command can be used to set a 5-digit floating point format (also known as scientific or exponential notation):

```
>> format short e
>> ans
ans =
   1.0000e+000   7.4485e-017  -8.9772e-017
   1.3986e-017   1.0000e+000   9.7172e-018
   7.4159e-017  -7.9580e-017   1.0000e+000
```

Now we see that the off-diagonal elements of the product are nonzero but tiny— the result of rounding errors. The default format can be reinstated by typing format short, or simply format. The format command has many options, which can be seen by typing help format. See Table 2.1 for some examples. All the MATLAB output shown in this book was generated with format compact in effect, which suppresses blank lines.

Generally, help foo displays information on the command or function named foo. For example:

```
>> help sqrt

 SQRT   Square root.
    SQRT(X) is the square root of the elements of X. Complex
    results are produced if X is not positive.

    See also SQRTM.
```

Note that it is a convention that function names are capitalized within help lines, in order to make them easy to identify. The names of all functions that are part of MATLAB or one of its toolboxes should be typed in lower case, however. On Unix systems the names of user-written M-files should be typed to match the case of the

Table 2.1. `10*exp(1)` *displayed in several output formats.*

format short	27.1828
format long	27.18281828459045
format short e	2.7183e+001
format long e	2.718281828459045e+001
format short g	27.183
format long g	27.1828182845905
format hex	403b2ecd2dd96d44
format bank	27.18
format rat	2528/93

name of the .m file, since Unix filenames are case sensitive (Windows filenames are not).

Typing `help` by itself produces the list of directories shown in Table 2.2 (extra directories will be shown for any toolboxes that are available, and if you have added your own directories to the path they will be shown as well). This list provides an overview of how MATLAB functions are organized. Typing `help` followed by a directory name (e.g., `help general`) gives a list of functions in that directory. Type `help help` for further details on the `help` command.

The most comprehensive documentation is available in the Help Browser (see Figure 2.1), which provides help for all MATLAB functions, release and upgrade notes, and online versions of the complete MATLAB documentation in html and PDF format. The Help Browser includes a Help Navigator pane containing tabs for a Contents listing, an Index listing, a Search facility, and Favorites. The attached display pane displays html documentation containing links to related subjects and allows you to move back or forward a page, to search the current page, and to add a page to the list of favorites. The Help Browser is accessed by clicking the "?" icon on the toolbar of the MATLAB desktop, by selecting Help from the Help menu, or by typing `helpbrowser` at the command line prompt. You can type `doc foo` to call up help on function `foo` directly in the Help Browser. Typing `helpwin` calls up the Help Browser with the same list of directories produced by `help`; clicking on a directory takes you to a list of M-files in that directory and you can click on an M-file name to obtain help on that M-file.

A useful search facility is provided by the `lookfor` command. Type `lookfor keyword` to search for functions relating to the keyword. Example:

```
>> lookfor elliptic
ELLIPJ Jacobi elliptic functions.
ELLIPKE Complete elliptic integral.
PDEPE  Solve initial-boundary value problems for parabolic-elliptic
       PDEs in 1-D.
```

If you make an error when typing at the prompt you can correct it using the arrow keys and the backspace or delete keys. Previous command lines can be recalled using the up arrow key, and the down arrow key takes you forward through the command list. If you type a few characters before hitting up arrow then the most recent command line beginning with those characters is recalled. A number of the

Table 2.2. *MATLAB directory structure (under Windows).*

```
>> help

HELP topics:

matlab\general      -  General purpose commands.
matlab\ops          -  Operators and special characters.
matlab\lang         -  Programming language constructs.
matlab\elmat        -  Elementary matrices and matrix manipulation.
matlab\elfun        -  Elementary math functions.
matlab\specfun      -  Specialized math functions.
matlab\matfun       -  Matrix functions - numerical linear algebra.
matlab\datafun      -  Data analysis and Fourier transforms.
matlab\audio        -  Audio support.
matlab\polyfun      -  Interpolation and polynomials.
matlab\funfun       -  Function functions and ODE solvers.
matlab\sparfun      -  Sparse matrices.
matlab\graph2d      -  Two dimensional graphs.
matlab\graph3d      -  Three dimensional graphs.
matlab\specgraph    -  Specialized graphs.
matlab\graphics     -  Handle Graphics.
matlab\uitools      -  Graphical user interface tools.
matlab\strfun       -  Character strings.
matlab\iofun        -  File input/output.
matlab\timefun      -  Time and dates.
matlab\datatypes    -  Data types and structures.
matlab\verctrl      -  (No table of contents file)
matlab\winfun       -  Windows Operating System Interface Files
                       (DDE/ActiveX)
matlab\demos        -  Examples and demonstrations.
toolbox\local       -  Preferences.
matlabr12\work      -  (No table of contents file)

For more help on directory/topic, type "help topic".
```

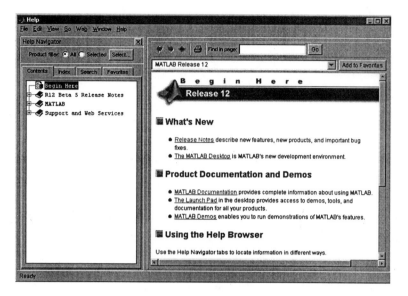

Figure 2.1. *Help Browser.*

Emacs control key commands for cursor movement are also supported. Table 2.3 summarizes the command line editing keypresses. You can scroll through commands previously typed in the current and past sessions in the Command History window. Double-clicking on a command in this window executes it.

Type `clc` to clear the Command Window.

A MATLAB computation can be aborted by pressing ctrl-c (holding down the control key and pressing the "c" key). If MATLAB is executing a built-in function it may take some time to respond to this keypress.

A line can be terminated with three periods (. . .), which causes the next line to be a continuation line:

```
>> x = 1 + 1/2 + 1/3 + 1/4 + 1/5 + ...
      1/6 + 1/7 + 1/8 + 1/9 + 1/10
x =
    2.9290
```

The value of x illustrates the fact that, unlike in some other programming languages, there is no separate type and arithmetic for integers, so all computations are done in floating point arithmetic and can be written in the natural way.

Several functions provide special values:

- pi is $\pi = 3.14159\ldots$;

- i is the imaginary unit, $\sqrt{-1}$, as is j. Complex numbers are entered as, for example, `2-3i`, `2-3*i`, `2-3*sqrt(-1)`, or `complex(2,-3)`. Note that the form `2-3*i` may not produce the intended results if i is being used as a variable, so the other forms are generally preferred.

Functions generating constants related to floating point arithmetic are described in Chapter 4. It is possible to override existing variables and functions by creating

Table 2.3. *Command line editing keypresses.*

Key	Control equivalent	Operation
Up arrow	Ctrl-p	Recall previous line
Down arrow	Ctrl-n	Recall next line
Left arrow	Ctrl-b	Back one character
Right arrow	Ctrl-f	Forward one character
Ctrl left arrow	Ctrl-l	Left one word
Ctrl right arrow	Ctrl-r	Forward one word
Home	Ctrl-a	Beginning of line
Esc	Ctrl-u	Clear line
End	Ctrl-e	End of line
Del	Ctrl-d	Delete character under cursor
Backspace	Ctrl-h	Delete previous character
	Ctrl-k	Delete (kill) to end of line
	Ctrl-t	Toggle insert mode (Unix only)

new ones with the same names. This practice should be avoided, as it can lead to confusion. However, the use of i and j as counting variables is widespread.

MATLAB fully supports complex arithmetic. For example,

```
>> w = (-1)^0.25
w =
   0.7071 + 0.7071i

>> exp(i*pi)
ans =
   -1.0000 + 0.0000i
```

Variable names are case sensitive and can be up to 31 characters long, consisting of a letter followed by any combination of letters, digits and underscores.

A list of variables in the workspace can be obtained by typing who, while whos shows the size and class of each variable as well. For example, after executing the commands so far in this chapter, whos produces

```
Name        Size         Bytes  Class

A           3x3             72  double array
ans         1x1             16  double array (complex)
exmark      1x7             56  double array
exmean      1x1              8  double array
exmed       1x1              8  double array
exsort      1x7             56  double array
exstd       1x1              8  double array
w           1x1             16  double array (complex)
x           1x1              8  double array
y           1x1              8  double array
z           1x1              8  double array

Grand total is 31 elements using 264 bytes
```

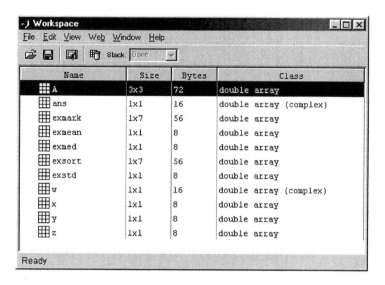

Figure 2.2. *Workspace Browser.*

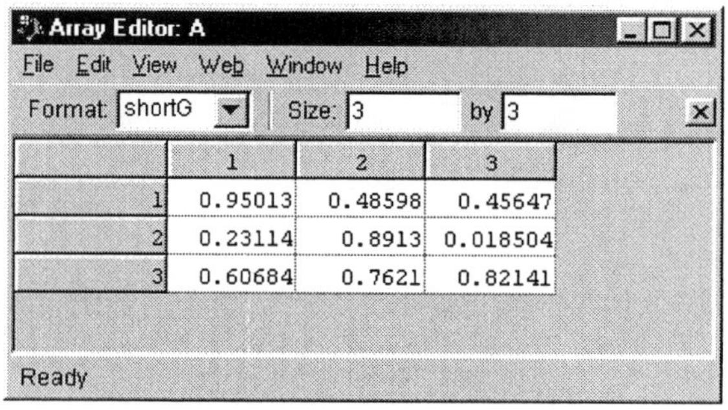

Figure 2.3. *Array Editor.*

An existing variable `var` can be removed from the workspace by typing `clear var`, while `clear` clears all existing variables.

The workspace can also be examined via the Workspace Browser (see Figure 2.2), which is invoked by the View-Workspace menu option or by typing `workspace`. A variable, `A`, say, can be edited interactively in spreadsheet format in the Array Editor by double-clicking on the variable name (see Figure 2.3); alternatively, typing `openvar('A')` calls up the Array Editor on `A`.

To save variables for recall in a future MATLAB session type `save filename`; all variables in the workspace are saved to `filename.mat`. Alternatively,

```
save filename A x
```

saves just the variables `A` and `x`. The command `load filename` loads in the variables from `filename.mat`, and individual variables can be loaded using the same syntax as for `save`. The default is to save and load variables in binary form, but options allow ASCII form to be specified. MAT-files can be ported between MATLAB implementations running on different computer systems. An Import Wizard, accessible from the

Table 2.4. *Information and demonstrations.*

bench	Benchmarks to test the speed of your computer
demo	A collection of demonstrations
info	Contact information for The MathWorks
intro	A "slideshow" giving a brief introduction to MATLAB
ver	Version number and release dates of MATLAB and toolboxes
version	Version number and release dates of MATLAB.
whatsnew	whatsnew brings up the Release Notes in the Help Browser. whatsnew matlab displays the readme file for MATLAB, which explains the new features introduced in the most recent version. whatsnew toolbox displays the readme file for the specified toolbox

File-Import Data menu option, provides a graphical interface to MATLAB's import functions.

Often you need to capture MATLAB output for incorporation into a report. This is most conveniently done with the `diary` command. If you type `diary filename` then all subsequent input and (most) text output is copied to the specified file; `diary off` turns off the diary facility. After typing `diary off` you can later type `diary on` to cause subsequent output to be appended to the same diary file.

To print the value of a variable or expression without the name of the variable or `ans` being displayed, you can use `disp`:

```
>> A = eye(2); disp(A)
     1     0
     0     1

>> disp('Result:'), disp(1/7)
Result:
    0.1429
```

Commands are available for interacting with the operating system, including `cd` (change directory), `copyfile` (copy file), `mkdir` (make directory), `pwd` (print working directory), `dir` or `ls` (list directory), and `delete` (delete file). A command can be issued to the operating system by preceding it with an exclamation mark, `!`. For example, you might type `!emacs myscript.m` to edit `myscript` with the Emacs editor.

Some MATLAB commands giving access to information and demonstrations are listed in Table 2.4.

Help!
— Title of a song by LENNON and MCCARTNEY (1965)

If ifs and ans were pots and pans,
there'd be no trade for tinkers.
— Proverb

Chapter 3
Distinctive Features of MATLAB

MATLAB has three features that distinguish it from most other modern programming languages and problem solving environments. We introduce them in this chapter and elaborate on them later in the book.

3.1. Automatic Storage Allocation

As we saw in Chapter 2, variables need not be declared prior to being assigned. This applies to arrays as well as scalars. Moreover, MATLAB automatically expands the dimensions of arrays in order for assignments to make sense. Thus, starting with an empty workspace, we can set up a 1-by-3 vector x of zeros with

```
>> x(3) = 0
x =
     0     0     0
```

and then expand it to length 6 with

```
>> x(6) = 0
x =
     0     0     0     0     0     0
```

MATLAB's automatic allocation of storage is one of its most convenient and distinctive features.

3.2. Functions with Variable Arguments Lists

MATLAB contains a large (and user-extendible) collection of functions. They take zero or more input arguments and return zero or more output arguments. MATLAB enforces a clear distinction between input and output: input arguments appear on the right of the function name, within parentheses, and output arguments appear on the left, within square brackets. Functions can support a variable number of input and output arguments, so that on a given call not all arguments need be supplied. Functions can even vary their behavior depending on the precise number and type of arguments supplied. We illustrate with some examples.

The norm function computes the Euclidean norm, or 2-norm, of a vector (the square root of the sum of squares of the absolute values of the elements):

```
>> x = [3 4];
```

```
>> norm(x)
```

```
ans =
     5
```

A different norm can be obtained by supplying `norm` with a second input argument. For example, the 1-norm (the sum of the absolute values of the elements) is obtained with

```
>> norm(x,1)
ans =
     7
```

If the second argument is not specified then it defaults to 2, giving the 2-norm. The `max` function has a variable number of output arguments. With one output argument it returns the largest element of the input vector:

```
>> m = max(x)
m =
     4
```

If a second output argument is supplied then the index of the largest element is assigned to it:

```
>> [m,k] = max(x)
m =
     4
k =
     2
```

As a final illustration of the versatility of MATLAB functions consider `size`, which returns the dimensions of an array. In the following example we set up a 5-by-3 random matrix and then request its dimensions:

```
>> A = rand(5,3);

>> s = size(A)
s =
     5     3
```

With one output argument, `size` returns a 1-by-2 vector with first element the number of rows of the input argument and second element the number of columns. However, `size` can also be given two output arguments, in which case it sets them to the number of rows and columns individually:

```
>> [m,n] = size(A)
m =
     5
n =
     3
```

3.3. Complex Arrays and Arithmetic

The fundamental data type in MATLAB is a multidimensional array of complex numbers, with real and imaginary parts stored in double precision floating point arithmetic. Important special cases are matrices (two-dimensional arrays), vectors and scalars. All computation in MATLAB is performed in floating point arithmetic, and complex arithmetic is used automatically when the data is complex. There is no separate real data type (though for reals the imaginary part is not stored). This can be contrasted with Fortran, in which different data types are used for real and complex numbers, and with C, C++ and Java, which support only real numbers and real arithmetic.

There are some integer data types, but they are used for memory-efficient storage only, not for computation; see `help datatypes`.

The guts of MATLAB are written in C.
Much of MATLAB is also written in MATLAB,
because it's a programming language.

— CLEVE MOLER, *Putting Math to Work* (1999)

In some ways, MATLAB resembles SPEAKEASY and, to a lesser extent, APL.
All are interactive terminal languages that ordinarily
accept single-line commands or statements,
process them immediately,
and print the results.
All have arrays as the principal data type.

— CLEVE B. MOLER, *Demonstration of a Matrix Laboratory* (1982)

Chapter 4
Arithmetic

4.1. IEEE Arithmetic

MATLAB carries out all its arithmetic computations in double precision floating point arithmetic, conforming to the IEEE standard [32]. The logical function `isieee` returns a result of 1 (true) if MATLAB is using IEEE arithmetic and 0 (false) if not. For MATLAB 6 `isieee` is always true, but earlier versions of MATLAB were available for certain machines that did not support IEEE arithmetic. The function `computer` returns the type of computer on which MATLAB is running. The machine used to produce all the output shown in this book gives

```
>> computer
ans =
PCWIN

>> isieee
ans =
     1
```

In MATLAB's `double` data type each number occupies a 64-bit word. Nonzero numbers range in magnitude between approximately 10^{-308} and 10^{+308} and the unit roundoff is $2^{-53} \approx 1.11 \times 10^{-16}$. (See [30, Chap. 2] for a detailed explanation of floating point arithmetic.) The significance of the unit roundoff is that it is a bound for the relative error in converting a real number to floating point form and also a bound for the relative error in adding, subtracting, multiplying or dividing two floating point numbers or taking the square root of a floating point number. In simple terms, MATLAB stores floating point numbers and carries out elementary operations to an accuracy of about 16 significant decimal digits.

The function `eps` returns the distance from 1.0 to the next larger floating point number:

```
>> eps
ans =
   2.2204e-016
```

This distance, 2^{-52}, is *twice* the unit roundoff.

Because MATLAB implements the IEEE standard, every computation produces a floating point number, albeit possibly one of a special type. If the result of a computation is larger than the value returned by the function `realmax` then overflow occurs and the result is `Inf` (also written `inf`), representing infinity. Similarly, a result more negative than `−realmax` produces `−inf`. Example:

```
>> realmax
ans =
   1.7977e+308

>> -2*realmax
ans =
   -Inf

>> 1.1*realmax
ans =
   Inf
```

A computation whose result is not mathematically defined produces a NaN, standing for Not a Number. A NaN (also written nan) is generated by expressions such as $0/0$, inf/inf and $0 * \text{inf}$:

```
>> 0/0
Warning: Divide by zero.
ans =
   NaN

>> inf/inf
ans =
   NaN

>> inf-inf
ans =
   NaN
```

Once generated, a NaN propagates through all subsequent computations:

```
>> NaN-NaN
ans =
   NaN

>> 0*NaN
ans =
   NaN
```

The function realmin returns the smallest positive normalized floating point number. Any computation whose result is smaller than realmin either underflows to zero if it is smaller than eps*realmin or produces a subnormal number—one with leading zero bits in its mantissa. To illustrate:

```
>> realmin
ans =
   2.2251e-308

>> realmin*eps
ans =
   4.9407e-324
```

Table 4.1. *Arithmetic operator precedence.*

Precedence level	Operator
1 (highest)	Exponentiation (^)
2	Unary plus (+), unary minus (-)
3	Multiplication (*), division (/)
4 (lowest)	Addition (+), subtraction (-)

```
>> realmin*eps/2
ans =
     0
```

To obtain further insight, repeat all the above computations after typing `format hex`, which displays the binary floating point representation of the numbers in hexadecimal format.

4.2. Precedence

MATLAB's arithmetic operators obey the same precedence rules as those in most calculators and computer languages. The rules are shown in Table 4.1. (For a more complete table, showing the precedence of all MATLAB operators, see Table 6.2.) For operators of equal precedence evaluation is from left to right. Parentheses can always be used to overrule priority, and their use is recommended to avoid ambiguity. Examples:

```
>> 2^10/10
ans =
   102.4000

>> 2 + 3*4
ans =
    14

>> -2 - 3*4
ans =
   -14

>> 1 + 2/3*4
ans =
    3.6667

>> 1 + 2/(3*4)
ans =
    1.1667
```

Table 4.2. *Elementary and special mathematical functions ("fun*" indicates that more than one function name begins "fun").*

cos, sin, tan, csc, sec, cot	Trigonometric
acos, asin, atan, atan2, asec, acsc, acot	Inverse trigonometric
cosh, sinh, tanh, sech, csch, coth	Hyperbolic
acosh, asinh, atanh, asech, acsch, acoth	Inverse hyperbolic
log, log2, log10, exp, pow2, nextpow2	Exponential
ceil, fix, floor, round	Rounding
abs, angle, conj, imag, real	Complex
mod, rem, sign	Remainder, sign
airy, bessel*, beta*, erf*, expint, gamma*, legendre	Mathematical
factor, gcd, isprime, lcm, primes, nchoosek, perms, rat, rats	Number theoretic
cart2sph, cart2pol, pol2cart, sph2cart	Coordinate transforms

4.3. Mathematical Functions

MATLAB contains a large set of mathematical functions. Typing help elfun and help specfun calls up full lists of elementary and special functions. A selection is listed in Table 4.2. The trigonometric functions take arguments in radians.

The Airy and Bessel functions are evaluated using a MEX interface to a library of Amos [2]. (You can view the Fortran source in the file specfun\besselmx.f.)

Round numbers are always false.
— SAMUEL JOHNSON, Boswell's *Life of Johnson* (1791)

Minus times minus is plus.
The reason for this we need not discuss.
— W. H. AUDEN, *A Certain World* (1971)

The only feature of classic MATLAB that is
not present in modern MATLAB is the "chop" function
which allows the simulation of shorter precision arithmetic.
It is an interesting curiosity,
but it is no substitute for roundoff error analysis
and it makes execution very slow, even when it isn't used.
— CLEVE B. MOLER, *MATLAB Digest Volume 3, Issue 1* (1991)

Chapter 5
Matrices

An m-by-n matrix is a two-dimensional array of numbers consisting of m rows and n columns. Special cases are a column vector ($n = 1$) and a row vector ($m = 1$).

Matrices are fundamental to MATLAB, and even if you are not intending to use MATLAB for linear algebra computations you need to become familiar with matrix generation and manipulation. In versions 3 and earlier of MATLAB there was only one data type: the complex matrix.[2] Nowadays MATLAB has several data types (see Chapter 18) and matrices are special cases of a `double`: a double precision multidimensional array.

5.1. Matrix Generation

Matrices can be generated in several ways. Many elementary matrices can be constructed directly with a MATLAB function; see Table 5.1. The matrix of zeros, the matrix of ones and the identity matrix (which has ones on the diagonal and zeros elsewhere) are returned by the functions `zeros`, `ones` and `eye`, respectively. All have the same syntax. For example, `zeros(m,n)` or `zeros([m,n])` produces an m-by-n matrix of zeros, while `zeros(n)` produces an n-by-n matrix. Examples:

```
>> zeros(2)
ans =
      0     0
      0     0

>> ones(2,3)
ans =
      1     1     1
      1     1     1

>> eye(3,2)
ans =
      1     0
      0     1
      0     0
```

A common requirement is to set up an identity matrix whose dimensions match those of a given matrix A. This can be done with `eye(size(A))`, where `size` is the function introduced in Section 3.2. Related to `size` is the `length` function: `length(A)` is the larger of the two dimensions of A. Thus for an n-by-1 or 1-by-n vector x, `length(x)` returns n.

---

[2] Cleve Moler used to joke that "MATLAB is a strongly typed language: it only has one data type!"

Table 5.1. *Elementary matrices.*

`zeros`	Zeros array
`ones`	Ones array
`eye`	Identity matrix
`repmat`	Replicate and tile array
`rand`	Uniformly distributed random numbers
`randn`	Normally distributed random numbers
`linspace`	Linearly spaced vector
`logspace`	Logarithmically spaced vector
`meshgrid`	X and Y arrays for 3D plots
`:`	Regularly spaced vector and index into matrix

Two other very important matrix generation functions are **rand** and **randn**, which generate matrices of (pseudo-)random numbers using the same syntax as **eye**. The function **rand** produces a matrix of numbers from the uniform distribution over the interval $[0,1]$. For this distribution the proportion of numbers in an interval $[a,b]$ with $0 < a < b < 1$ is $b - a$. The function **randn** produces a matrix of numbers from the standard normal (0,1) distribution. Called without any arguments, both functions produce a single random number.

```
>> rand
ans =
    0.9528

>> rand(3)
ans =
    0.7041    0.8407    0.5187
    0.9539    0.4428    0.0222
    0.5982    0.8368    0.3759
```

In carrying out experiments with random numbers it is often important to be able to regenerate the same numbers on a subsequent occasion. The numbers produced by a call to **rand** depend on the state of the generator. The state can be set using the command **rand('state',j)**. For j=0 the **rand** generator is set to its initial state (the state it has when MATLAB starts). For a nonzero integer j, the generator is set to its jth state. The state of **randn** is set in the same way. The periods of **rand** and **randn**, that is, the number of terms generated before the sequences start to repeat, exceed $2^{1492} \approx 10^{449}$.

Matrices can be built explicitly using the square bracket notation. For example, a 3-by-3 matrix comprising the first 9 primes can be set up with the command

```
>> A = [2  3  5
        7  11 13
        17 19 23]
A =
     2     3     5
     7    11    13
    17    19    23
```

The end of a row can be specified by a semicolon instead of a carriage return, so a more compact command with the same effect is

```
>> A = [2 3 5; 7 11 13; 17 19 23]
```

Within a row, elements can be separated by spaces or by commas. In the former case, if numbers are specified with a plus or minus sign take care not to leave a space after the sign, else MATLAB will interpret the sign as an addition or subtraction operator. To illustrate with vectors:

```
>> v = [-1 2 -3 4]
v =
     -1      2     -3      4

>> w = [-1, 2, -3, 4]
w =
     -1      2     -3      4

>> x = [-1 2 - 3 4]
x =
     -1     -1      4
```

Matrices can be constructed in block form. With B defined by B = [1 2; 3 4], we may create

```
>> C = [B         zeros(2)
        ones(2)   eye(2)]
C =
     1      2      0      0
     3      4      0      0
     1      1      1      0
     1      1      0      1
```

Block diagonal matrices can be defined using the function blkdiag, which is easier than using the square bracket notation. Example:

```
>> A = blkdiag(2*eye(2),ones(2))
A =
     2      0      0      0
     0      2      0      0
     0      0      1      1
     0      0      1      1
```

Useful for constructing "tiled" block matrices is repmat: repmat(A,m,n) creates a block m-by-n matrix in which each block is a copy of A. If m is omitted, it defaults to n. Example:

```
>> A = repmat(eye(2),2)
A =
     1      0      1      0
     0      1      0      1
     1      0      1      0
     0      1      0      1
```

Table 5.2. *Special matrices.*

compan	Companion matrix
gallery	Large collection of test matrices
hadamard	Hadamard matrix
hankel	Hankel matrix
hilb	Hilbert matrix
invhilb	Inverse Hilbert matrix
magic	Magic square
pascal	Pascal matrix
rosser	Classic symmetric eigenvalue test problem
toeplitz	Toeplitz matrix
vander	Vandermonde matrix
wilkinson	Wilkinson's eigenvalue test matrix

MATLAB provides a number of special matrices; see Table 5.2. These matrices have interesting properties that make them useful for constructing examples and for testing algorithms. One of the most famous is the Hilbert matrix, whose (i, j) element is $1/(i + j - 1)$. The matrix is generated by hilb and its inverse (which has integer entries) by invhilb. The function magic generates magic squares, which are fun to investigate using MATLAB [60].

The function gallery provides access to a large collection of test matrices created by N. J. Higham [29] (an earlier version of the collection was published in [28]). Table 5.3 lists the matrices; more information is obtained by typing help private/matrix_name. As indicated in the table some of the matrices in gallery are returned in the sparse data type—see Chapter 15. Example:

```
>> help private/moler

  MOLER  Moler matrix (symmetric positive definite).
     A = GALLERY('MOLER',N,ALPHA) is the symmetric positive definite
     N-by-N matrix U'*U, where U = GALLERY('TRIW',N,ALPHA).

     For the default ALPHA = -1, A(i,j) = MIN(i,j)-2, and A(i,i) = i.
     One of the eigenvalues of A is small.

>> A = gallery('moler',5)
A =
      1    -1    -1    -1    -1
     -1     2     0     0     0
     -1     0     3     1     1
     -1     0     1     4     2
     -1     0     1     2     5
```

Table 5.4 lists matrices from Tables 5.2 and 5.3 having certain properties; in most cases the matrix has the property for the default arguments, but in some cases, such as for gallery's randsvd, the arguments must be suitably chosen. For definitions of these properties see Chapter 9 and the textbooks listed at the start of that chapter.

Another way to generate a matrix is to load it from a file using the `load` command (see p. 28).

Table 5.3. *Matrices available through* `gallery`.

cauchy	Cauchy matrix
chebspec	Chebyshev spectral differentiation matrix
chebvand	Vandermonde-like matrix for the Chebyshev polynomials
chow	Chow matrix—a singular Toeplitz lower Hessenberg matrix
circul	Circulant matrix
clement	Clement matrix—tridiagonal with zero diagonal entries
compar	Comparison matrices
condex	Counter-examples to matrix condition number estimators
cycol	Matrix whose columns repeat cyclically
dorr	Dorr matrix—diagonally dominant, ill-conditioned, tridiagonal (one or three output arguments, `sparse`)
dramadah	Matrix of 1s and 0s whose inverse has large integer entries
fiedler	Fiedler matrix—symmetric
forsythe	Forsythe matrix—a perturbed Jordan block
frank	Frank matrix—ill-conditioned eigenvalues
gearmat	Gear matrix
grcar	Grcar matrix—a Toeplitz matrix with sensitive eigenvalues
hanowa	Matrix whose eigenvalues lie on a vertical line in the complex plane
house	Householder matrix (two output arguments)
invhess	Inverse of an upper Hessenberg matrix
invol	Involutory matrix
ipjfact	Hankel matrix with factorial elements (two output arguments)
jordbloc	Jordan block matrix
kahan	Kahan matrix—upper trapezoidal
kms	Kac–Murdock–Szego Toeplitz matrix
krylov	Krylov matrix
lauchli	Läuchli matrix—rectangular
lehmer	Lehmer matrix—symmetric positive definite
lesp	Tridiagonal matrix with real, sensitive eigenvalues
lotkin	Lotkin matrix
minij	Symmetric positive definite matrix $\min(i, j)$
moler	Moler matrix—symmetric positive definite
neumann	Singular matrix from the discrete Neumann problem (`sparse`)
orthog	Orthogonal and nearly orthogonal matrices
parter	Parter matrix—a Toeplitz matrix with singular values near π
pei	Pei matrix
poisson	Block tridiagonal matrix from Poisson's equation (`sparse`)
prolate	Prolate matrix—symmetric, ill-conditioned Toeplitz matrix
randcolu	Random matrix with normalized columns and specified singular values
randcorr	Random correlation matrix with specified eigenvalues
randhess	Random, orthogonal upper Hessenberg matrix
rando	Random matrix with elements -1, 0 or 1

Table 5.3. (*continued*)

`randsvd`	Random matrix with preassigned singular values and specified bandwidth
`redheff`	Matrix of 0s and 1s of Redheffer
`riemann`	Matrix associated with the Riemann hypothesis
`ris`	Ris matrix—a symmetric Hankel matrix
`smoke`	Smoke matrix—complex, with a "smoke ring" pseudospectrum
`toeppd`	Symmetric positive definite Toeplitz matrix
`toeppen`	Pentadiagonal Toeplitz matrix (`sparse`)
`tridiag`	Tridiagonal matrix (`sparse`)
`triw`	Upper triangular matrix discussed by Wilkinson and others
`wathen`	Wathen matrix—a finite element matrix (`sparse`, random entries)
`wilk`	Various specific matrices devised/discussed by Wilkinson (two output arguments)
`gallery(3)`	Badly conditioned 3-by-3 matrix
`gallery(5)`	Interesting eigenvalue problem

Table 5.4. *Matrices classified by property. Most of the matrices listed here are accessed through* `gallery`.

Defective	`chebspec, gallery(5), gearmat, jordbloc, triw`
Hankel	`hilb, ipjfact, ris`
Hessenberg	`chow, frank, grcar, randhess, randsvd`
Idempotent	`invol`
Inverse of tridiagonal matrix	`kms, lehmer, minij`
Involutary	`invol, orthog, pascal`
Nilpotent	`chebspec, gallery(5)`
Normal*	`circul`
Orthogonal	`hadamard, orthog, randhess, randsvd`
Rectangular	`chebvand, cycol, kahan, krylov, lauchli, rando, randsvd, triw`
Symmetric indefinite	`clement, fiedler`
Symmetric positive definite	`hilb, invhilb, ipjfact, kms, lehmer, minij, moler, pascal, pei, poisson, prolate, randsvd, toeppd, tridiag, wathen`
Toeplitz	`chow, dramadah, grcar, kms, parter, prolate, toeppd, toeppen`
Totally positive/nonnegative	`cauchy,`[†] `hilb, lehmer, pascal`
Tridiagonal	`clement, dorr, lesp, randsvd, tridiag, wilk, wilkinson`
Triangular	`dramadah, jordbloc, kahan, pascal, triw`

* But not symmetric or orthogonal.

[†] `cauchy(x,y)` is totally positive if $0 < x_1 < \cdots < x_n$ and $0 < y_1 < \cdots < y_n$ [30].

5.2. Subscripting and the Colon Notation

To enable access and assignment to submatrices MATLAB has a powerful notation based on the colon character. The colon is used to define vectors that can act as subscripts. For integers i and j, i:j denotes the row vector of integers from i to j (in steps of 1). A nonunit step (or stride) s is specified as i:s:j. This notation is valid even for noninteger i, j and s. Examples:

```
>> 1:5
ans =
      1    2    3    4    5

>> 4:-1:-2
ans =
      4    3    2    1    0   -1   -2

>> 0:.75:3
ans =
      0    0.7500    1.5000    2.2500    3.0000
```

Single elements of a matrix are accessed as A(i,j), where i ≥ 1 and j ≥ 1 (zero or negative subscripts are not supported in MATLAB). The submatrix comprising the intersection of rows p to q and columns r to s is denoted by A(p:q,r:s). As a special case, a lone colon as the row or column specifier covers all entries in that row or column; thus A(:,j) is the jth column of A and A(i,:) the ith row. The keyword end used in this context denotes the last index in the specified dimension; thus A(end,:) picks out the last row of A. Finally, an arbitrary submatrix can be selected by specifying the individual row and column indices. For example, A([i j k],[p q]) produces the submatrix given by the intersection of rows i, j and k and columns p and q. Here are some examples, using the matrix of primes set up above:

```
>> A
A =
      2    3    5
      7   11   13
     17   19   23

>> A(2,1)
ans =
      7

>> A(2:3,2:3)
ans =
     11   13
     19   23

>> A(:,1)
ans =
      2
      7
     17
```

```
>> A(2,:)
ans =
     7      11      13

>> A([1 3],[2 3])
ans =
     3       5
    19      23
```

A further special case is `A(:)`, which denotes a vector comprising all the elements of A taken down the columns from first to last:

```
>> B = A(:)
B =
     2
     7
    17
     3
    11
    19
     5
    13
    23
```

When placed on the left side of an assignment statement `A(:)` fills A, preserving its shape. Using this notation, another way to define our 3-by-3 matrix of primes is

```
>> A = zeros(3); A(:) = primes(23); A = A'
A =
     2       3       5
     7      11      13
    17      19      23
```

The function `primes` returns a vector of the prime numbers less than or equal to its argument. The transposition `A = A'` (see the next section) is necessary to reorder the primes across the rows rather than down the columns.

Related to the colon notation for generating vectors of equally spaced numbers is the function `linspace`, which accepts the number of points rather than the increment: `linspace(a,b,n)` generates n equally spaced points between a and b. If n is omitted it defaults to 100. Example:

```
>> linspace(-1,1,9)
ans =
  Columns 1 through 7
   -1.0000    -0.7500    -0.5000    -0.2500         0    0.2500    0.5000
  Columns 8 through 9
    0.7500     1.0000
```

The notation [] denotes an empty, 0-by-0 matrix. Assigning [] to a row or column is one way to delete that row or column from a matrix:

Table 5.5. *Elementary matrix and array operations.*

Operation	Matrix sense	Array sense
Addition	+	+
Subtraction	−	−
Multiplication	*	.*
Left division	\	.\
Right division	/	./
Exponentiation	^	.^

```
>> A(2,:) = []
A =
     2     3     5
    17    19    23
```

In this example the same effect is achieved by `A = A([1 3],:)`. The empty matrix is also useful as a placeholder in argument lists, as we will see in Section 5.5.

5.3. Matrix and Array Operations

For scalars a and b, the operators +, -, *, / and ^ produce the obvious results. As well as the usual right division operator, /, MATLAB has a left division operator, \:

MATLAB notation	Mathematical equivalent
Right division: a/b	$\dfrac{a}{b}$
Left division: a\b	$\dfrac{b}{a}$

For matrices, all these operations can be carried out in a matrix sense (according to the rules of matrix algebra) or an array sense (elementwise). Table 5.5 summarizes the syntax.

Addition and subtraction, which are identical operations in the matrix and array senses, are defined for matrices of the same dimension. The product A*B is the result of matrix multiplication, defined only when the number of columns of A and the number of rows of B are the same. The backslash and the forward slash define solutions of linear systems: A\B is a solution X of A*X = B, while A/B is a solution X of X*B = A; see Section 9.2 for more details. Examples:

```
>> A = [1 2; 3 4], B = ones(2)
A =
     1     2
     3     4
B =
     1     1
     1     1

>> A+B
```

```
ans =
        2       3
        4       5

>> A*B
ans =
        3       3
        7       7

>> A\B
ans =
       -1      -1
        1       1
```

Multiplication and division in the array, or elementwise, sense are specified by preceding the operator with a period. If A and B are matrices of the same dimensions then C = A.*B sets C(i,j) = A(i,j)*B(i,j) and C = A./B sets C(i,j) = A(i,j)/B(i,j). The assignment C = A.\B is equivalent to C = B./A. With the same A and B as in the previous example:

```
>> A.*B
ans =
        1       2
        3       4

>> B./A
ans =
    1.0000    0.5000
    0.3333    0.2500
```

Exponentiation with ^ is defined as matrix powering, but the dot form exponentiates elementwise. Thus if A is a square matrix then A^2 is the matrix product A*A, but A.^2 is A with each element squared:

```
>> A^2, A.^2
ans =
        7      10
       15      22
ans =
        1       4
        9      16
```

The dot form of exponentiation allows the power to be an array when the dimensions of the base and the power agree, or when the base is a scalar:

```
>> x = [1 2 3]; y = [2 3 4]; Z = [1 2; 3 4];

>> x.^y
ans =
        1       8      81

>> 2.^x
```

```
ans =
     2     4     8

>> 2.^Z
ans =
     2     4
     8    16
```

Matrix exponentiation is defined for all powers, not just for positive integers. If n<0 is an integer then A^n is defined as inv(A)^n. For noninteger p, A^p is evaluated using the eigensystem of A; results can be incorrect or inaccurate when A is not diagonalizable or when A has an ill-conditioned eigensystem.

The conjugate transpose of the matrix A is obtained with A'. If A is real, this is simply the transpose. The transpose without conjugation is obtained with A.'. The functional alternatives ctranspose(A) and transpose(A) are sometimes more convenient.

For the special case of column vectors x and y, x'*y is the inner or dot product, which can also be obtained using the dot function as dot(x,y). The vector or cross product of two 3-by-1 or 1-by-3 vectors (as used in mechanics) is produced by cross. Example:

```
>> x = [-1 0 1]'; y = [3 4 5]';

>> x'*y
ans =
     2

>> dot(x,y)
ans =
     2

>> cross(x,y)
ans =
    -4
     8
    -4
```

The kron function evaluates the Kronecker product of two matrices. The Kronecker product of an m-by-n A and p-by-q B has dimensions mp-by-nq and can be expressed as a block m-by-n matrix with (i, j) block $a_{ij}B$. Example:

```
>> A = [1 10; -10 100]; B = [1 2 3; 4 5 6; 7 8 9];

>> kron(A,B)
ans =
      1      2      3     10     20     30
      4      5      6     40     50     60
      7      8      9     70     80     90
    -10    -20    -30    100    200    300
    -40    -50    -60    400    500    600
    -70    -80    -90    700    800    900
```

If a scalar is added to a matrix MATLAB will expand the scalar into a matrix with all elements equal to that scalar. For example:

```
>> [4 3; 2 1] + 4
ans =
      8      7
      6      5

>> A = [1 -1] - 6
A =
     -5     -7
```

However, if an assignment makes sense without expansion then it will be interpreted in that way. Thus if the previous command is followed by A = 1 then A becomes the scalar 1, not ones(1,2).

If a matrix is multiplied or divided by a scalar, the operation is performed elementwise. For example:

```
>> [3 4 5; 4 5 6]/12
ans =
    0.2500    0.3333    0.4167
    0.3333    0.4167    0.5000
```

Most of the functions described in Section 4.3 can be given a matrix argument, in which case the functions are computed elementwise. Functions of a matrix in the linear algebra sense are signified by names ending in m (see Section 9.9): expm, funm, logm, sqrtm. For example, for A = [2 2; 0 2],

```
>> sqrt(A)
ans =
    1.4142    1.4142
         0    1.4142

>> sqrtm(A)
ans =
    1.4142    0.7071
         0    1.4142

>> ans*ans
ans =
    2.0000    2.0000
         0    2.0000
```

5.4. Matrix Manipulation

Several commands are available for manipulating matrices (commands more specifically associated with linear algebra are discussed in Chapter 9); see Table 5.6.

The reshape function changes the dimensions of a matrix: reshape(A,m,n) produces an m-by-n matrix whose elements are taken columnwise from A. For example:

Table 5.6. *Matrix manipulation functions.*

reshape	Change size
diag	Diagonal matrices and diagonals of matrix
blkdiag	Block diagonal matrix
tril	Extract lower triangular part
triu	Extract upper triangular part
fliplr	Flip matrix in left/right direction
flipud	Flip matrix in up/down direction
rot90	Rotate matrix 90 degrees

```
>> A = [1 4 9; 16 25 36], B = reshape(A,3,2)
A =
      1      4      9
     16     25     36
B =
      1     25
     16      9
      4     36
```

The function diag deals with the diagonals of a matrix and can take a vector or a matrix as argument. For a vector x, diag(x) is the diagonal matrix with main diagonal x:

```
>> diag([1 2 3])
ans =
      1      0      0
      0      2      0
      0      0      3
```

More generally, diag(x,k) puts x on the kth diagonal, where $k > 0$ specifies diagonals above the main diagonal and $k < 0$ diagonals below the main diagonal ($k = 0$ gives the main diagonal):

```
>> diag([1 2], 1)
ans =
      0      1      0
      0      0      2
      0      0      0

>> diag([3 4], -2)
ans =
      0      0      0      0
      0      0      0      0
      3      0      0      0
      0      4      0      0
```

For a matrix A, diag(A) is the column vector comprising the main diagonal of A. To produce a diagonal matrix with diagonal the same as that of A you must therefore write diag(diag(A)). Analogously to the vector case, diag(A,k) produces a column vector made up from the kth diagonal of A. Thus if

```
A =
     2       3       5
     7      11      13
    17      19      23
```

then

```
>> diag(A)
ans =
     2
    11
    23

>> diag(A,-1)
ans =
     7
    19
```

Triangular parts of a matrix can be extracted using tril and triu. The lower triangular part of A (the elements on and below the main diagonal) is specified by tril(A) and the upper triangular part of A (the elements on and above the main diagonal) is specified by triu(A). More generally, tril(A,k) gives the elements on and below the kth diagonal of A, while triu(A,k) gives the elements on and above the kth diagonal of A. With A as above:

```
>> tril(A)
ans =
     2       0       0
     7      11       0
    17      19      23

>> triu(A,1)
ans =
     0       3       5
     0       0      13
     0       0       0

>> triu(A,-1)
ans =
     2       3       5
     7      11      13
     0      19      23
```

5.5. Data Analysis

Table 5.7 lists functions for basic data analysis computations. The simplest usage is to apply these functions to vectors. For example:

```
>> x = [4 -8 -2 1 0]
x =
     4    -8    -2    1    0

>> [min(x) max(x)]
ans =
    -8    4

>> sort(x)
ans =
    -8    -2    0    1    4

>> sum(x)
ans =
    -5
```

The sort function sorts into ascending order. For a real vector x, descending order is obtained with -sort(-x). For complex vectors, sort sorts by absolute value and so descending order must be obtained by explicitly reordering the output:

```
>> x = [1+i -3-4i 2i 1];

>> y = sort(x);

>> y = y(end:-1:1)
y =
  -3.0000 - 4.0000i       0 + 2.0000i    1.0000 + 1.0000i    1.0000
```

For matrices the functions are defined columnwise. Thus max and min return a vector containing the maximum and minimum element, respectively, in each column, sum returns a vector containing the column sums, and sort sorts the elements in each column of the matrix into ascending order. The functions min and max can return a second argument that specifies in which components the minimum and maximum elements are located. For example, if

```
A =
     0    -1    2
     1    2    -4
     5    -3    -4
```

then

```
>> max(A)
ans =
     5    2    2

>> [m,i] = min(A)
m =
     0    -3    -4
i =
     1    3    2
```

As this example shows, if there are two or more minimal elements in a column then the index of the first is returned. The smallest element in the matrix can be found by applying min twice in succession:

```
>> min(min(A))
ans =
    -4
```

Functions max and min can be made to act row-wise via a third argument:

```
>> max(A,[],2)
ans =
     2
     2
     5
```

The 2 in max(A,[],2) specifies the maximum over the second dimension, that is, over the column index. The empty second argument, [], is needed because with just two arguments max and min return the elementwise maxima and minima of the two arguments:

```
>> max(A,0)
ans =
     0     0     2
     1     2     0
     5     0     0
```

Functions sort and sum can also be made to act row-wise, via a second argument. For more on sort see Section 21.3.

The diff function forms differences. Applied to a vector x of length n it produces the vector [x(2)-x(1) x(3)-x(2) ... x(n)-x(n-1)] of length n-1. Example:

```
>> x = (1:8).^2
x =
     1     4     9    16    25    36    49    64

>> y = diff(x)
y =
     3     5     7     9    11    13    15

>> z = diff(y)
z =
     2     2     2     2     2     2
```

Table 5.7. *Basic data analysis functions.*

max	Largest component
min	Smallest component
mean	Average or mean value
median	Median value
std	Standard deviation
var	Variance
sort	Sort in ascending order
sum	Sum of elements
prod	Product of elements
cumsum	Cumulative sum of elements
cumprod	Cumulative product of elements
diff	Difference of elements

Handled properly,
empty arrays relieve programmers of the
nuisance of special cases at beginnings and ends of
algorithms that construct matrices recursively from submatrices.
— WILLIAM M. KAHAN (1994)

Kirk: "You did all this in a day?"
Carol: "The matrix formed in a day.
The lifeforms grew later at a substantially accelerated rate."
— *Star Trek III: The Search For Spock* (Stardate 8130.4)

I start by looking at a 2 by 2 matrix.
Sometimes I look at a 4 by 4 matrix.
That's when things get out of control and too hard.
Usually 2 by 2 or 3 by 3 is enough, and I look at them,
and I compute with them, and I try to guess the facts.
— PAUL R. HALMOS, in *Paul Halmos: Celebrating 50 Years of Mathematics* (1991)

Chapter 6
Operators and Flow Control

6.1. Relational and Logical Operators

MATLAB's relational operators are

==	equal
~=	not equal
<	less than
>	greater than
<=	less than or equal
>=	greater than or equal

Note that a single = denotes assignment and never a test for equality in MATLAB.

Comparisons between scalars produce 1 if the relation is true and 0 if it is false. Comparisons are also defined between matrices of the same dimension and between a matrix and a scalar, the result being a matrix of 0s and 1s in both cases. For matrix–matrix comparisons corresponding pairs of elements are compared, while for matrix–scalar comparisons the scalar is compared with each matrix element. For example:

```
>> A = [1 2; 3 4]; B = 2*ones(2);

>> A == B
ans =
     0     1
     0     0

>> A > 2
ans =
     0     0
     1     1
```

To test whether matrices A and B are identical, the expression isequal(A,B) can be used:

```
>> isequal(A,B)
ans =
     0
```

The function isequal is one of many useful logical functions whose names begin with is, a selection of which is listed in Table 6.1; for a full list type doc is. The function isnan is particularly important because the test x == NaN always produces the result

Table 6.1. *Selected logical* `is*` *functions.*

`ischar`	True for char array (string)
`isempty`	True for empty array
`isequal`	True if arrays are identical
`isfinite`	True for finite array elements
`isieee`	True for machine using IEEE arithmetic
`isinf`	True for infinite array elements
`islogical`	True for logical array
`isnan`	True for NaN (Not a Number)
`isnumeric`	True for numeric array
`isreal`	True for real array
`issparse`	True for sparse array

0 (false), even if x is a NaN! (A NaN is defined to compare as unequal and unordered with everything.)

MATLAB's logical operators are

`&`	logical and
`|`	logical or
`~`	logical not
`xor`	logical exclusive or
`all`	true if all elements of vector are nonzero
`any`	true if any element of vector is nonzero

Like the relational operators, the `&`, `|` and `~` operators produce matrices of 0s and 1s when one of the arguments is a matrix. When applied to a vector, the `all` function returns 1 if all the elements of the vector are nonzero and 0 otherwise. The `any` function is defined in the same way, with "any" replacing "all". Examples:

```
>> x = [-1 1 1]; y = [1 2 -3];

>> x>0 & y>0
ans =
     0     1     0

>> x>0 | y>0
ans =
     1     1     1

>> xor(x>0,y>0)
ans =
     1     0     1

>> any(x>0)
ans =
     1

>> all(x>0)
```

Table 6.2. *Operator precedence.*

Precedence level	Operator
1 (highest)	Transpose (.'), power (.^), complex conjugate transpose ('), matrix power (^)
2	Unary plus (+), unary minus (−), logical negation (~)
3	Multiplication (.*), right division (./), left division (.\), matrix multiplication (*), matrix right division (/), matrix left division (\)
4	Addition (+), subtraction (−)
5	Colon operator (:)
6	Less than (<), less than or equal to (<=), greater than (>), greater than or equal to (>=), equal to (==), not equal to (~=)
7	Logical and (&)
8 (Lowest)	Logical or (|)

```
ans =
     0
```

Note that `xor` must be called as a function: `xor(a,b)`. The `and`, `or` and `not` operators and the relational operators can also be called in functional form as `and(a,b)`, ..., `eq(a,b)`, ... (see `help ops`).

The precedence of arithmetic, relational and logical operators is summarized in Table 6.2 (which is based on the information provided by `help precedence`). For operators of equal precedence MATLAB evaluates from left to right. Precedence can be overridden by using parentheses.

Note that in versions of MATLAB prior to MATLAB 6 the logical `and` and `or` operators had the same precedence (unlike in most programming languages). A logical expression such as

```
x | y & z
```

is evaluated in MATLAB 5.3 and earlier versions as

```
(x | y) & z
```

whereas in MATLAB 6 onwards it is evaluated as

```
x | (y & z)
```

The MathWorks recommends that parentheses are added in expressions of this form to ensure that the same results are obtained in all versions of MATLAB.

For matrices, `all` returns a row vector containing the result of `all` applied to each column. Therefore `all(all(A==B))` is another way of testing equality of the matrices A and B. The `any` function works in the corresponding way. Thus, for example, `any(any(A==B))` has the value 1 if A and B have any equal elements and 0 otherwise.

The `find` command returns the indices corresponding to the nonzero elements of a vector. For example,

```
>> x = [-3 1 0 -inf 0];
>> f = find(x)
f =
     1     2     4
```

The result of find can then be used to extract just those elements of the vector:

```
>> x(f)
ans =
    -3     1   -Inf
```

With x as above, we can use find to obtain the finite elements of x,

```
>> x(find(isfinite(x)))
ans =
    -3     1     0     0
```

and to replace negative components of x by zero:

```
>> x(find(x < 0)) = 0
x =
     0     1     0     0     0
```

When find is applied to a matrix A, the index vector corresponds to A regarded as a vector of the columns stacked one on top of the other (that is, A(:)), and this vector can be used to index into A. In the following example we use find to set to zero those elements of A that are less than the corresponding elements of B:

```
>> A = [4 2 16; 12 4 3], B = [12 3 1; 10 -1 7]
A =
     4     2    16
    12     4     3
B =
    12     3     1
    10    -1     7

>> f = find(A<B)
f =
     1
     3
     6

>> A(f) = 0
A =
     0     0    16
    12     4     0
```

An alternative usage of find for matrices is [i,j] = find(A), which returns vectors i and j containing the row and column indices of the nonzero elements.

The results of MATLAB's logical operators and logical functions are arrays of 0s and 1s that are examples of logical arrays. Logical arrays can also be created by applying the function logical to a numeric array. Logical arrays can be used for subscripting. Consider the following example.

```
>> clear
>> y = [1 2 0 -3 0]
y =
     1     2     0    -3     0

>> i1 = logical(y)
i1 =
     1     2     0    -3     0

>> i2 = (y ~= 0)
i2 =
     1     1     0     1     0

>> i3 = [1 1 0 1 0]
i3 =
     1     1     0     1     0

>> whos
  Name        Size          Bytes  Class

  i1          1x5              40   double array (logical)
  i2          1x5              40   double array (logical)
  i3          1x5              40   double array
  y           1x5              40   double array

Grand total is 20 elements using 160 bytes

>> y(i1)
ans =
     1     2    -3

>> y(i2)
ans =
     1     2    -3

>> isequal(i2,i3)
ans =
     1

>> y(i3)
??? Index into matrix is negative or zero.  See release notes on
changes to logical indices.
```

This example illustrates the rule that A(M), where M is a logical array of the same dimension as A, extracts the elements of A corresponding to the elements of M with nonzero real part. Note that even though i2 has the same elements as i3 (and compares as equal with it), only the logical array i2 can be used for subscripting.

A call to find can sometimes be avoided when its argument is a logical array. In our earlier example, x(find(isfinite(x))) can be replaced by x(isfinite(x)). We recommend using find for clarity.

6.2. Flow Control

MATLAB has four flow control structures: the `if` statement, the `for` loop, the `while` loop and the `switch` statement. The simplest form of the `if` statement is

```
if expression
    statements
end
```

where the statements are executed if the (real parts of) the elements of *expression* are all nonzero. For example, the following code swaps x and y if x is greater than y:

```
if x > y
    temp = y;
    y = x;
    x = temp;
end
```

When an `if` statement is followed on its line by further statements, a comma is needed to separate the `if` from the next statement:

```
if x > 0, x = sqrt(x); end
```

Statements to be executed only if *expression* is false can be placed after `else`, as in the example

```
e = exp(1);
if 2^e > e^2
    disp('2^e is bigger')
else
    disp('e^2 is bigger')
end
```

Finally, one or more further tests can be added with `elseif` (note that there must be no space between `else` and `if`):

```
if isnan(x)
    disp('Not a Number')
elseif isinf(x)
    disp('Plus or minus infinity')
else
    disp('A ''regular'' floating point number')
end
```

In the third `disp`, `''` prints as a single quote '.

In an `if` test of the form "if *condition*1 & *condition*2", *condition*2 is not evaluated when *condition*1 is false (a so-called "early return" `if` evaluation). This is useful when evaluating *condition*2 might otherwise give an error—perhaps because of an undefined variable or an index out of range.

The `for` loop is one of the most useful MATLAB constructs although, as discussed in Section 20.1, experienced programmers who are concerned with producing compact and fast code try to avoid `for` loops wherever possible. The syntax is

```
for variable = expression
     statements
end
```

Usually, *expression* is a vector of the form `i:s:j` (see Section 5.2). The statements are executed with *variable* equal to each element of *expression* in turn. For example, the sum of the first 25 terms of the harmonic series $1/i$ is computed by

```
>> s = 0;
>> for i = 1:25, s = s + 1/i; end, s
s =
    3.8160
```

Another way to define *expression* is using the square bracket notation:

```
>> for x = [pi/6 pi/4 pi/3], disp([x, sin(x)]), end
    0.5236    0.5000
    0.7854    0.7071
    1.0472    0.8660
```

Multiple `for` loops can of course be nested, in which case indentation helps to improve the readability. The following code forms the 5-by-5 symmetric matrix A with (i, j) element i/j for $j \geq i$:

```
n = 5; A = eye(n);
for j=2:n
    for i = 1:j-1
        A(i,j) = i/j;
        A(j,i) = i/j;
    end
end
```

The *expression* in the `for` loop can be a matrix, in which case *variable* is assigned the columns of *expression* from first to last. For example, to set x to each of the unit vectors in turn, we can write `for x=eye(n), ..., end`.

The `while` loop has the form

```
while expression
      statements
end
```

The *statements* are executed as long as *expression* is true. The following example approximates the smallest nonzero floating point number:

```
>> x = 1; while x>0, xmin = x; x = x/2; end, xmin
xmin =
   4.9407e-324
```

A `while` loop can be terminated with the `break` statement, which passes control to the first statement after the corresponding `end`. An infinite loop can be constructed using `while 1, ..., end`, which is useful when it is not convenient to put the exit test at the top of the loop. (Note that, unlike some other languages, MATLAB does not have a "repeat–until" loop.) We can rewrite the previous example less concisely as

```
x = 1;
while 1
    xmin = x;
    x = x/2;
    if x == 0, break, end
end
xmin
```

The break statement can also be used to exit a for loop. In a nested loop a break exits to the loop at the next higher level.

The continue statement causes execution of a for or while loop to pass immediately to the next iteration of the loop, skipping the remaining statements in the loop. As a trivial example,

```
for i=1:10
    if i < 5, continue, end
    disp(i)
end
```

displays the integers 5 to 10. In more complicated loops the continue statement can be useful to avoid long-bodied if statements.

The final control structure is the switch statement. It consists of "switch *expression*" followed by a list of "case *expression statements*", optionally ending with "otherwise *statements*" and followed by end. The switch expression is evaluated and the statements following the first matching case expression are executed. If none of the cases produces a match then the statements following otherwise are executed. The next example evaluates the p-norm of a vector x (i.e., norm(x,p)) for just three values of p:

```
switch p
    case 1
          y = sum(abs(x));
    case 2
          y = sqrt(x'*x);
    case inf
          y = max(abs(x));
    otherwise
          error('p must be 1, 2 or inf.')
end
```

(The error function is described in Section 14.1.) The expression following case can be a list of values enclosed in parentheses (a cell array—see Section 18.3). In this case the switch expression can match any value in the list:

```
x = input('Enter a real number: ');
switch x
     case {inf,-inf}
          disp('Plus or minus infinity')
     case 0
          disp('Zero')
     otherwise
          disp('Nonzero and finite')
end
```

C programmers should note that MATLAB's `switch` construct behaves differently from that in C: once a MATLAB `case` group expression has been matched and its statements executed control is passed to the first statement after the `switch`, with no need for `break` statements.

Kirk: "Well, Spock, here we are.
Thanks to your restored memory, a little bit of good luck,
we're walking the streets of San Francicso,
looking for a couple of humpback whales.
How do you propose to solve this minor problem?"
Spock: "Simple logic will suffice."

— *Star Trek IV: The Voyage Home* (Stardate 8390)

Things equally high on the pecking order get evaluated from left to right.
When in doubt, throw in some parentheses and be sure.
Only use good quality parentheses with nice round sides.

— ROGER EMANUEL KAUFMAN, *A FORTRAN Coloring Book* (1978)

Chapter 7
M-Files

7.1. Scripts and Functions

Although you can do many useful computations working entirely at the MATLAB command line, sooner or later you will need to write M-files. These are the equivalents of programs, functions, subroutines and procedures in other programming languages. Collecting together a sequence of commands into an M-file opens up many possibilities, including

- experimenting with an algorithm by editing a file, rather than retyping a long list of commands,

- making a permanent record of a numerical experiment,

- building up utilities that can be reused at a later date,

- exchanging M-files with colleagues.

Many useful M-files that have been written by enthusiasts can be obtained over the internet; see Appendix C.

An M-file is a text file that has a .m filename extension and contains MATLAB commands. There are two types:

Script M-files (or command files) have no input or output arguments and operate on variables in the workspace.

Function M-files contain a `function` definition line and can accept input arguments and return output arguments, and their internal variables are local to the function (unless declared `global`).

A script enables you to store a sequence of commands that are to be used repeatedly or will be needed at some future time. A simple example of a script M-file, `marks.m`, was given in Section 2.1. As another example we describe a script for playing "eigenvalue roulette" [15], which is based on counting how many eigenvalues of a random real matrix are real. If the matrix A is real and of dimension 8 then the number of real eigenvalues is 0, 2, 4, 6 or 8 (the number must be even, since nonreal eigenvalues appear in complex conjugate pairs). The short script

```
%SPIN
% Counts number of real eigenvalues of random matrix.
A = randn(8); sum(abs(imag(eig(A)))<.0001)
```

Listing 7.1. *Script* rouldist.

```
%ROULDIST        Empirical distribution of number of real eigenvalues.

k = 1000;
wheel = zeros(k,1);
for i=1:k
    A = randn(8);
    % Count number of eigenvalues with imag. part < tolerance.
    wheel(i) = sum(abs(imag(eig(A)))<.0001);
end
hist(wheel,[0 2 4 6 8]);
```

creates a random normally distributed 8×8 matrix and counts how many eigenvalues have imaginary parts with absolute value less than the (somewhat arbitrary) threshold 10^{-4}. The first two lines of this script begin with the % symbol and hence are comment lines. Whenever MATLAB encounters a % it ignores the remainder of the line. This allows you to insert text that makes the script easier for humans to understand. Assuming this script exists as a file spin.m, typing spin is equivalent to typing the two commands A = randn(8); and sum(abs(imag(eig(A)))<.0001). This "spins the roulette wheel", producing one of the five answers 0, 2, 4, 6 and 8. Each call to spin produces a different random matrix and hence may give a different answer:

```
>> spin
ans =
     2

>> spin
ans =
     4
```

To get an idea of the probability of each of the five outcomes you can run the script rouldist in Listing 7.1. It generates 1000 random matrices and plots a histogram of the distribution of the number of real eigenvalues. Figure 7.1 shows a possible result. (The exact probabilities are known and are given in [15], [16].) Note that to make rouldist more readable we have used spaces to indent the for loop and inserted a blank line before the first command.

Function M-files enable you to extend the MATLAB language by writing your own functions that accept and return arguments. They can be used in exactly the same way as existing MATLAB functions such as sin, eye, size, etc.

Listing 7.2 shows a simple function that evaluates the largest element in absolute value of a matrix. This example illustrates a number of features. The first line begins with the keyword function followed by the output argument, y, and the = symbol. On the right of = comes the function name, maxentry, followed by the input argument, A, within parentheses. (In general there can be any number of input and output arguments.) The function name must be the same as the name of the .m file in which the function is stored—in this case the file must be named maxentry.m.

The second line of a function file is called the H1 (help 1) line. It should be a comment line of a special form: a line beginning with a % character, followed without

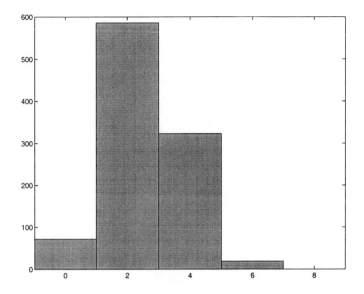

Figure 7.1. *Histogram produced by* `rouldist`.

any space by the function name in capital letters, followed by one or more spaces and then a brief description. The description should begin with a capital letter, end with a period, and omit the words "the" and "a". All the comment lines from the first comment line up to the first noncomment line (usually a blank line, for readability of the source code) are displayed when `help function_name` is typed. Therefore these lines should describe the function and its arguments. It is conventional to capitalize function and argument names in these comment lines. For the `maxentry.m` example, we have

```
>> help maxentry
MAXENTRY   Largest absolute value of matrix entries.
           MAXENTRY(A) is the maximum of the absolute values
           of the entries of A.
```

We strongly recommend documenting *all* your function files in this way, however short they may be. It is often useful to record in comment lines the date when the function was first written and to note any subsequent changes that have been made. The `help` command works in a similar manner on script files, displaying the initial sequence of comment lines.

The function `maxentry` is called just like any other MATLAB function:

```
>> maxentry(1:10)
ans =
    10

>> maxentry(magic(4))
ans =
    16
```

The function `flogist` shown in Listing 7.3 illustrates the use of multiple input and output arguments. This function evaluates the scalar logistic function $x(1 - ax)$

Listing 7.2. *Function* maxentry.

```
function y = maxentry(A)
%MAXENTRY    Largest absolute value of matrix entries.
%            MAXENTRY(A) is the maximum of the absolute values
%            of the entries of A.

y = max(max(abs(A)));
```

Listing 7.3. *Function* flogist.

```
function [f,fprime] = flogist(x,a)
%FLOGIST    Logistic function and its derivative.
%           [F,FPRIME] = FLOGIST(X,A) evaluates the logistic
%           function F(X) = X.*(1-A*X) and its derivative FPRIME
%           at the matrix argument X, where A is a scalar parameter.

f = x.*(1-a*x);
fprime = 1-2*a*x;
```

and its derivative with respect to x. The two output arguments f and fprime are enclosed in square brackets. When calling a function with multiple input or output arguments it is not necessary to request all the output arguments, but arguments must be dropped starting at the end of the list. If more than one output argument is requested the arguments must be listed within square brackets. Examples of usage are

```
>> f = flogist(2,.1)
f =
    1.6000

>> [f,fprime] = flogist(2,.1)
f =
    1.6000
fprime =
    0.6000
```

A technical point of note in function flogist is that array multiplication (.*) is used in the statement f = x.*(1-a*x). So, if a vector or matrix is supplied for x, the function is evaluated at each element simultaneously:

```
>> flogist(1:4,2)
ans =
    -1    -6    -15    -28
```

Another function using array multiplication is cheby in Listing 7.4, which is used with MATLAB's fplot to produce Figure 8.10. The kth Chebyshev polynomial,

Listing 7.4. *Function* cheby.

```
function Y = cheby(x,p)
%CHEBY     Chebyshev polynomials.
%          Y = CHEBY(X,P) evaluates the first P Chebyshev polynomials
%          at the vector X.  The K'th column of Y contains the
%          Chebyshev polynomial of degree K-1 evaluated at X.

Y = ones(length(x),p);
x = x(:);   % Ensure x is a column vector.
if p == 1, return, end

Y(:,2) = x;
for k = 3:p
  Y(:,k) = 2*x.*Y(:,k-1) - Y(:,k-2);
end
```

$T_k(x)$, can be defined by the recurrence

$$T_k(x) = 2xT_{k-1}(x) - T_{k-2}(x), \quad \text{for } k \geq 2,$$

with $T_0(x) = 1$ and $T_1(x) = x$. The function cheby accepts a vector x and an integer p and returns a matrix Y whose ith row gives the values of $T_0(x), T_1(x), \ldots, T_{p-1}(x)$ at $x = x(i)$. (This is the form of output argument required by fplot.)

Note that cheby uses the **return** command, which causes an immediate return from the M-file. It is not necessary to put a **return** statement at the end of a function or script, unlike in some other programming languages.

A more complicated function is sqrtn, shown in Listing 7.5. Given $a > 0$, it implements the Newton iteration for $\sqrt{a}$,

$$x_{k+1} = \frac{1}{2}\left(x_k + \frac{a}{x_k}\right), \qquad x_1 = a,$$

printing the progress of the iteration. Output is controlled by the fprintf command, which is described in Section 13.2. Examples of usage are

```
>> [x,iter] = sqrtn(2)
 k              x_k             rel. change
 1:  1.5000000000000000e+000   3.33e-001
 2:  1.4166666666666665e+000   5.88e-002
 3:  1.4142156862745097e+000   1.73e-003
 4:  1.4142135623746899e+000   1.50e-006
 5:  1.4142135623730949e+000   1.13e-012
 6:  1.4142135623730949e+000   0.00e+000
x =
     1.4142
iter =
     6

>> x = sqrtn(2,1e-4);
```

Listing 7.5. *Function* sqrtn.

```
function [x,iter] = sqrtn(a,tol)
%SQRTN     Square root of a scalar by Newton's method.
%          X = SQRTN(A,TOL) computes the square root of the scalar
%          A by Newton's method (also known as Heron's method).
%          A is assumed to be >= 0.
%          TOL is a convergence tolerance (default EPS).
%          [X,ITER] = SQRTN(A,TOL) returns also the number of
%          iterations ITER for convergence.

if nargin < 2, tol = eps; end

x = a;
iter = 0;
xdiff = inf;
fprintf(' k              x_k              rel. change\n')

while xdiff > tol
    iter = iter + 1;
    xold = x;
    x = (x + a/x)/2;
    xdiff = abs(x-xold)/abs(x);
    fprintf('%2.0f:  %20.16e %9.2e\n', iter, x, xdiff)
    if iter > 50
        error('Not converged after 50 iterations.')
    end
end
```

```
 k              x_k              rel. change
 1:   1.5000000000000000e+000   3.33e-001
 2:   1.4166666666666665e+000   5.88e-002
 3:   1.4142156862745097e+000   1.73e-003
 4:   1.4142135623746899e+000   1.50e-006
```

This M-file illustrates the use of optional input arguments. The function nargin returns the number of input arguments supplied when the function was called and enables default values to be assigned to arguments that have not been specified. In this case, if the call to sqrtn does not specify a value for tol, then eps is assigned to tol.

An analogous function nargout returns the number of output arguments requested. In this example there is no need to check nargout, because iter is computed by the function whether or not it is requested as an output argument. Some functions gain efficiency by inspecting nargout and computing only those output arguments that are requested (for example, eig in the next chapter). To illustrate, Listing 7.6 shows how the marks M-file on p. 22 can be rewritten as a function. Its usage is illustrated by

```
>> exmark = [12 0 5 28 87 3 56];
```

Listing 7.6. *Function* marks2.

```
function [x_sort,x_mean,x_med,x_std] = marks2(x)
%MARKS2  Statistical analysis of marks vector.
%         Given a vector of marks X,
%         [X_SORT,X_MEAN,X_MED,X_STD] = MARKS2(X) computes a
%         sorted marks list and the mean, median and standard deviation
%         of the marks.

x_sort = sort(x);
if nargout > 1, x_mean = mean(x);   end
if nargout > 2, x_med  = median(x); end
if nargout > 3, x_std  = std(x);    end
```

```
>> x_sort = marks2(exmark)
x_sort =
     0     3     5    12    28    56    87

>> [x_sort,x_mean,x_med] = marks2(exmark)
x_sort =
     0     3     5    12    28    56    87
x_mean =
   27.2857
x_med =
    12
```

7.2. Editing M-Files

To create and edit M-files you have two choices. You can use whatever editor you normally use for ASCII files (if it is a word processor you need to ensure that you save the files in standard ASCII form, not in the word processor's own format). Or you can use the built-in MATLAB Editor/Debugger, shown in Figure 7.2. On Windows systems this is invoked by typing edit at the command prompt or from the File-New or File-Open menu options. On Unix systems invocation is via the edit command only. The MATLAB editor has various features to aid in editing M-files, including automatic indentation of loops and if structures, color syntax highlighting, and bracket and quote matching. These and other features can be turned off or customized via the Tools-Options menu of the editor.

7.3. Working with M-Files and the MATLAB Path

Many MATLAB functions are M-files residing on the disk, while others are built into the MATLAB interpreter. The MATLAB search path is a list of directories that specifies where MATLAB looks for M-files. An M-file is available only if it is on the search path. Type path to see the current search path. The path can be set and added to with the path and addpath commands, or from the Path Browser that is invoked by the File-Set Path menu option or by typing pathtool.

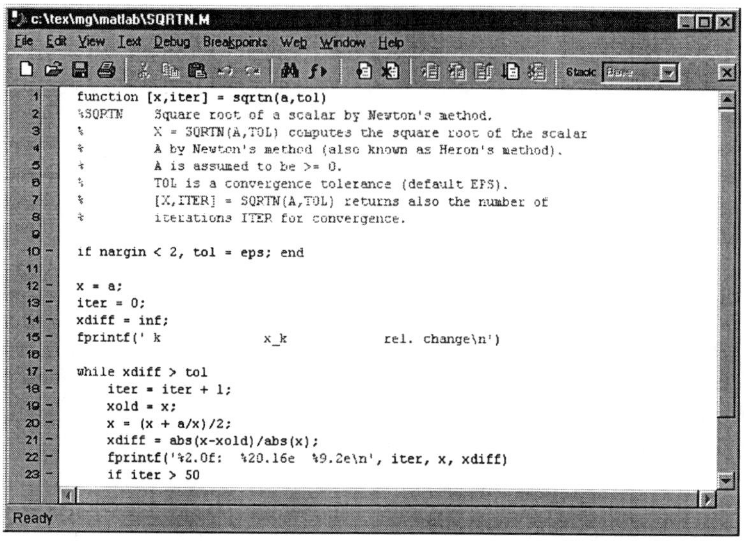

Figure 7.2. *MATLAB Editor/Debugger.*

Several commands can be used to search the path. The `what` command lists the MATLAB files in the current directory; `what dirname` lists the MATLAB files in the directory `dirname` on the path.

The command `lookfor keyword` (illustrated on p. 24) searches the path for M-files containing `keyword` in their H1 line (the first line of help text). All the comment lines displayed by the `help` command can be searched using `lookfor keyword -all`.

Some MATLAB functions use comment lines after the initial block of comment lines to provide further information, such as bibliographic references (an example is `fminsearch`). This information can be accessed using `type` but is not displayed by `help`.

Typing `which foo` displays the pathname of the function `foo` or declares it to be `built in` or `not found`. This is useful if you want to know in which directory on the path an M-file is located. If you suspect there may be more than one M-file with a given name on the path you can use `which foo -all` to display all of them.

A script (but not a function) not on the search path can be invoked by typing `run` followed by a statement in which the *full pathname* to the M-file is given.

You may list the M-file `foo.m` to the screen with `type foo` or `type foo.m`. (If there is an ASCII file called `foo` then the former command will list `foo` rather than `foo.m`.) Preceding a `type` command with `more on` will cause the listing to be displayed a page at a time (`more off` turns off paging).

Before writing an M-file it is important to check whether the name you are planning to give it is the name of an existing M-file or built-in function. This can be done in several ways: using `which` as just described, using `type` (e.g., `type lu` produces the response that `lu is a built-in function`), using `help`, or using the function `exist`. The command `exist('myname')` tests whether `myname` is a variable in the workspace, a file (with various possible extensions, including .m) on the path, or a directory. A result of 0 means no matches were found, while the numbers 1–7 indicate a match; see `help exist` for the precise meaning of these numbers.

When a function residing on the path is invoked for the first time it is compiled into memory (see the chapter "M-File Programming" in [56] for more details). MATLAB can usually detect when a function M-file has changed and then automatically recompiles it when it is invoked.

To clear function `fun` from memory, type `clear fun`. To clear all functions type `clear functions`.

7.4. Command/Function Duality

User-written functions are usually called by giving the function name followed by a list of arguments in parentheses. Yet some built-in MATLAB functions, such as `type` and `what` described in the previous section, are normally called with arguments separated from the function name by spaces. This is not an inconsistency but an illustration of command/function duality. Consider the function

```
function comfun(x,y,z)
%COMFUN    Illustrative function with three string arguments.
disp(x), disp(y), disp(z)
```

We can call it with string arguments in parentheses (functional form), or with the string arguments separated by spaces after the function name (command form):

```
>> comfun('ab','cd','ef')
ab
cd
ef

>> comfun ab cd ef
ab
cd
ef
```

The two invocations are equivalent. Other examples of command/function duality are (with the first in each pair being the most commonly used)

```
format long, format('long')
disp('Hello'), disp Hello
diary mydiary, diary('mydiary')
warning off, warning('off')
```

Note, however, that the command form should be used only for functions that take string arguments. In the example

```
>> sqrt 2
ans =
   7.07106781186548
```

MATLAB interprets 2 as a string and `sqrt` is applied to the ASCII value of 2, namely 50.

>> why
Cleve insisted on it.
>> why
Jack knew it was a good idea.
— MATLAB

Replace repetitive expressions by calls to a common function.
— BRIAN W. KERNIGHAN and P. J. PLAUGER,
The Elements of Programming Style (1978)

Much of MATLAB's power is derived from its extensive set of functions...
Some of the functions are intrinsic,
or "built-in" to the MATLAB processor itself.
Others are available in the library of external M-files distributed with MATLAB...
It is transparent to the user whether a function is intrinsic or contained in an M-file.
— 386-MATLAB User's Guide (1989)

Chapter 8
Graphics

MATLAB has powerful and versatile graphics capabilities. Figures of many types can be generated with relative ease and their "look and feel" is highly customizable. In this chapter we cover the basic use of MATLAB's most popular tools for graphing two- and three-dimensional data; Chapter 17 on Handle Graphics delves more deeply into the innards of MATLAB's graphics. Our philosophy of teaching a useful subset of MATLAB's language, without attempting to be exhaustive, is particularly relevant to this chapter. The final section hints at what we have left unsaid.

Our emphasis in this chapter is on generating graphics at the command line or in M-files, but existing figures can also be modified and annotated interactively using the Plot Editor. To use the Plot Editor see `help plotedit` and the Tools menu and toolbar of the figure window.

Note that the graphics output shown in this book is printed in black and white. Most of the output appears as color on the screen and can be printed as color on a color printer.

8.1. Two-Dimensional Graphics

8.1.1. Basic Plots

MATLAB's `plot` function can be used for simple "join-the-dots" x-y plots. Typing

```
>> x = [1.5 2.2 3.1 4.6 5.7 6.3 9.4];
>> y = [2.3 3.9 4.3 7.2 4.5 3.8 1.1];
>> plot(x,y)
```

produces the left-hand picture in Figure 8.1, where the points `x(i)`, `y(i)` are joined in sequence. MATLAB opens a figure window (unless one has already been opened as a result of a previous command) in which to draw the picture. In this example, default values are used for a number of features, including the ranges for the x- and y-axes, the spacing of the axis tick marks, and the color and type of the line used for the plot.

More generally, we could replace `plot(x,y)` with `plot(x,y,`*string*`)`, where *string* combines up to three elements that control the color, marker and line style. For example, `plot(x,y,'r*--')` specifies that a red asterisk is to be placed at each point `x(i)`, `y(i)` and that the points are to be joined by a red dashed line, whereas `plot(x,y,'y+')` specifies a yellow cross marker with no line joining the points. Table 8.1 lists the options available. The right-hand picture in Figure 8.1 was produced with `plot(x,y,'kd:')`, which gives a black dotted line with diamond marker. The three elements in *string* may appear in any order, so, for example, `plot(x,y,'ms--')`

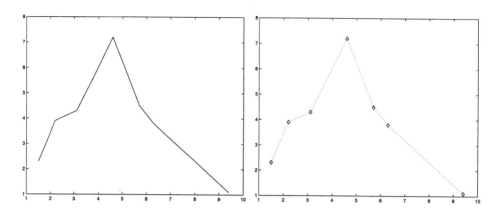

Figure 8.1. *Simple x-y plots. Left: default. Right: nondefault.*

Table 8.1. *Options for the* plot *command.*

Marker	
o	Circle
*	Asterisk
.	Point
+	Plus
x	Cross
s	Square
d	Diamond
^	Upward triangle
v	Downward triangle
>	Right triangle
<	Left triangle
p	Five-point star
h	Six-point star

Color	
r	Red
g	Green
b	Blue
c	Cyan
m	Magenta
y	Yellow
k	Black
w	White

Line style	
–	Solid line (default)
––	Dashed line
:	Dotted line
–.	Dash-dot line

and plot(x,y,'s--m') are equivalent. Note that more than one set of data can be passed to plot. For example,

```
plot(x,y,'g-',b,c,'r--')
```

superimposes plots of x(i), y(i) and b(i), c(i) with solid green and dashed red line styles, respectively.

The plot command also accepts matrix arguments. If x is an m-vector and Y is an m-by-n matrix, plot(x,Y) superimposes the plots created by x and each column of Y. Similarly, if X and Y are both m-by-n, plot(X,Y) superimposes the plots created by corresponding columns of X and Y. If nonreal numbers are supplied to plot then imaginary parts are generally ignored. The only exception to this rule arises when plot is given a single argument. If Y is nonreal, plot(Y) is equivalent to plot(real(Y),imag(Y)). In the case where Y is real, plot(Y) plots the columns of Y against their index.

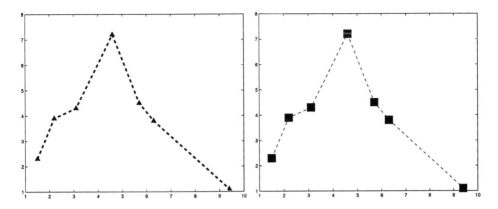

Figure 8.2. *Two nondefault x-y plots.*

You can exert further control by supplying more arguments to `plot`. The properties `LineWidth` (default 0.5 points) and `MarkerSize` (default 6 points) can be specified in points, where a point is 1/72 inch. For example, the commands

```
plot(x,y,'LineWidth',2)
plot(x,y,'p','MarkerSize',10)
```

produce a plot with a 2-point line width and 10-point marker size, respectively. For markers that have a well-defined interior, the `MarkerEdgeColor` and `MarkerFaceColor` can be set to one of the colors in Table 8.1. So, for example,

```
plot(x,y,'o','MarkerEdgeColor','m')
```

gives magenta edges to the circles. The left-hand plot in Figure 8.2 was produced with

```
plot(x,y,'m--^','LineWidth',3,'MarkerSize',5)
```

and the right-hand plot with

```
plot(x,y,'--rs','MarkerSize',20,'MarkerFaceColor','g')
```

Using `loglog` instead of `plot` causes the axes to be scaled logarithmically. This feature is useful for revealing power-law relationships as straight lines. In the example below we plot $|1+h+h^2/2-\exp(h)|$ against h for $h = 1, 10^{-1}, 10^{-2}, 10^{-3}, 10^{-4}$. This quantity behaves like a multiple of h^3 when h is small, and hence on a log-log scale the values should lie close to a straight line of slope 3. To confirm this, we also plot a dashed reference line with the predicted slope, exploiting the fact that more than one set of data can be passed to the plot commands. The output is shown in Figure 8.3.

```
h = 10.^[0:-1:-4];
taylerr = abs((1+h+h.^2/2) - exp(h));
loglog(h,taylerr,'-',h,h.^3,'--')
xlabel('h')
ylabel('abs(error)')
title('Error in quadratic Taylor series approximation to exp(h)')
box off
```

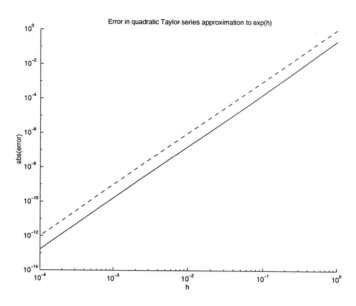

Figure 8.3. `loglog` *example.*

In this example, we used `title`, `xlabel` and `ylabel`. These functions reproduce their input string above the plot and on the x- and y-axes, respectively. We also used the command `box off`, which removes the box from the current plot, leaving just the x- and y-axes. MATLAB will, of course, complain if nonpositive data is sent to `loglog` (it displays a warning and plots only the positive data). Related functions are `semilogx` and `semilogy`, for which only the x- or y-axis, respectively, is logarithmically scaled.

If one plotting command is later followed by another then the new picture will either replace or be superimposed on the old picture, depending on the current `hold` state. Typing `hold on` causes subsequent plots to be superimposed on the current one, whereas `hold off` specifies that each new plot should start afresh. The default status corresponds to `hold off`.

The command `clf` clears the current figure window, while `close` closes it. It is possible to have several figure windows on the screen. The simplest way to create a new figure window is to type `figure`. The nth figure window (where n is displayed in the title bar) can be made current by typing `figure(n)`. The command `close all` causes all the figure windows to be closed.

Note that many aspects of a figure can be changed interactively, after the figure has been displayed, by using the items on the toolbar of the figure window or on the Tools pull-down menu. In particular, it is possible to zoom in on a particular region of the plot using mouse clicks (see `help zoom`).

8.1.2. Axes and Annotation

Various aspects of the axes of a plot can be controlled with the `axis` command. Some of the options are summarized in Table 8.2. The axes are removed from a plot with `axis off`. The aspect ratio can be set to unity, so that, for example, a circle appears circular rather than elliptical, by typing `axis equal`. The axis box can be made

Table 8.2. *Some commands for controlling the axes.*

`axis([xmin xmax ymin ymax])`	Set specified x- and y-axis limits
`axis auto`	Return to default axis limits
`axis equal`	Equalize data units on x-, y- and z-axes
`axis off`	Remove axes
`axis square`	Make axis box square (cubic)
`axis tight`	Set axis limits to range of data
`xlim([xmin xmax])`	Set specified x-axis limits
`ylim([ymin ymax])`	Set specified y-axis limits

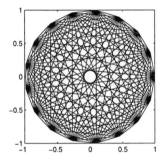 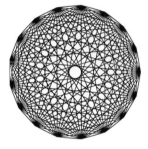

Figure 8.4. *Using* `axis off`.

square with `axis square`.

To illustrate, the left-hand plot in Figure 8.4 was produced by

```
plot(fft(eye(17))), axis equal, axis square
```

Since the plot obviously lies inside the unit circle the axes are hardly necessary. The right-hand plot in Figure 8.4 was produced with

```
plot(fft(eye(17))), axis equal, axis off
```

(The meaning of this interesting picture is described in [59].)

Setting `axis([xmin xmax ymin ymax])` causes the x-axis to run from `xmin` to `xmax` and the y-axis from `ymin` to `ymax`. To return to the default axis scaling, which MATLAB chooses automatically based on the data being plotted, type `axis auto`. If you want one of the limits to be chosen automatically by MATLAB, set it to `-inf` or `inf`; for example, `axis([-1 1 -inf 0])`. The x-axis and y-axis limits can be set individually with `xlim([xmin xmax])` and `ylim([ymin ymax])`.

Our next example plots the function $1/(x-1)^2 + 3/(x-2)^2$ over the interval $[0, 3]$:

```
x = linspace(0,3,500);
plot(x,1./(x-1).^2 + 3./(x-2).^2)
grid on
```

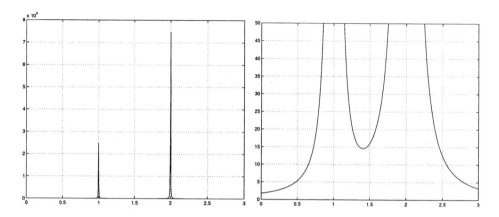

Figure 8.5. *Use of* ylim *(right) to change automatic (left) y-axis limits.*

We specified **grid on**, which introduces a light horizontal and vertical hashing that extends from the axis ticks. The result is shown in the left-hand plot of Figure 8.5. Because of the singularities at $x = 1, 2$ the plot is uninformative. However, by executing the additional command

```
ylim([0 50])
```

the right-hand plot of Figure 8.5 is produced, which focuses on the interesting part of the first plot.

In the following example we plot the epicycloid

$$\left.\begin{array}{l} x(t) = (a + b)\cos(t) - b\cos((a/b + 1)t) \\ y(t) = (a + b)\sin(t) - b\sin((a/b + 1)t) \end{array}\right\} \quad 0 \le t \le 10\pi,$$

for $a = 12$ and $b = 5$.

```
a = 12; b = 5;
t = 0:0.05:10*pi;
x = (a+b)*cos(t) - b*cos((a/b+1)*t);
y = (a+b)*sin(t) - b*sin((a/b+1)*t);

plot(x,y)
axis equal
axis([-25 25 -25 25])
grid on

title('Epicycloid: a=12, b=5')
xlabel('x(t)'), ylabel('y(t)')
```

The resulting picture appears in Figure 8.6. The **axis** limits were chosen to put some space around the epicycloid.

Next we plot the Legendre polynomials of degrees 1 to 4 (see, for example, [9]) and use the **legend** function to add a box that explains the line styles. The result is shown in Figure 8.7.

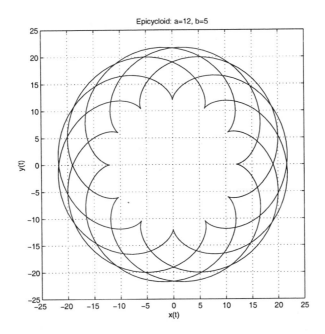

Figure 8.6. *Epicycloid example.*

```
x = -1:.01:1;
p1 = x;
p2 = (3/2)*x.^2 - 1/2;
p3 = (5/2)*x.^3 - (3/2)*x;
p4 = (35/8)*x.^4 - (15/4)*x.^2 + 3/8;

plot(x,p1,'r:',x,p2,'g--',x,p3,'b-.',x,p4,'m-')
box off

legend('\itn=1','n=2','n=3','n=4',4)
xlabel('x','FontSize',12,'FontAngle','italic')
ylabel('P_n','FontSize',12,'FontAngle','italic')
title('Legendre Polynomials','FontSize',14)
text(-.6,.7,'(n+1)P_{n+1}(x) = (2n+1)x P_n(x) - n P_{n-1}(x)',...
    'FontSize',12,'FontAngle','italic')
```

Generally, typing `legend('string1','string2',...,'stringn')` will create a legend box that puts `'stringi'` next to the color/marker/line style information for the corresponding plot. By default, the box appears in the top right-hand corner of the axis area. The location of the box can be specified by adding an extra argument as follows:

    −1   to the right of the plot
     0   automatically chosen "best" location
     1   top right-hand corner (default)
     2   top left-hand corner
     3   bottom left-hand corner
     4   bottom right-hand corner

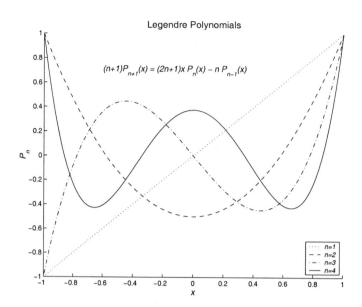

Figure 8.7. *Legendre polynomial example, using* `legend`.

In our example we chose the bottom right-hand corner. Once the plot has been drawn, the legend box can be repositioned by putting the cursor over it and dragging it using the left mouse button.

This example uses the `text` command: generally, `text(x,y,'string')` places `'string'` at the position whose coordinates are given by `x` and `y`. (A related function `gtext` allows the text location to be determined interactively via the mouse.) Note that the strings in the `ylabel` and `text` commands use the notation of the typesetting system TEX to specify Greek letters, mathematical symbols, fonts and superscripts and subscripts [23], [43], [48]. Table 8.3 lists some of the TEX notation supported, and a full list can be found in the `string` entry under `doc text_props`. Note that curly braces can be used to delimit the range of application of the font commands and of subscripts and superscripts. Thus

```
title('{\itItalic} Normal {\bfBold} \int_{-\infty}^\infty')
```

produces a title of the form "*Italic* Normal **Bold** $\int_{-\infty}^{\infty}$". (Note that, unlike in TEX, if you leave a space after a font command then that space is printed.) If you are unfamiliar with TEX or LATEX you may prefer to use `texlabel('string')`, which allows `'string'` to be given in the style of a MATLAB expression. Thus the following two commands have identical effect:

```
text(5,5,'\alpha^{3/2}+\beta^{12}-\sigma_i')
text(5,5,texlabel('alpha^(3/2)+beta^12-sigma_i'))
```

A final note about the Legendre polynomial example is that we have used the `FontSize` and `FontAngle` properties to adjust the point size and angle of the text produced by the `xlabel`, `ylabel`, `title` and `text` commands (the default value of `FontSize` is 10 and the default `FontAngle` is `normal`). However, `legend` does not accept these arguments, so we used TEX notation to make the legend italic. For plots

Table 8.3. *Some of the TeX commands supported in text strings.*

Greek letters		Selected symbols	
Lower case		$\approx$	\approx
α	\alpha	$\circ$	\circ
β	\beta	$\geq$	\geq
γ	\gamma	$\Im$	\Im
$\vdots$	$\vdots$	$\in$	\in
ω	\omega	∞	\infty
Upper case		$\int$	\int
Γ	\Gamma	$\leq$	\leq
Δ	\Delta	$\neq$	\neq
Θ	\Theta	$\otimes$	\otimes
$\vdots$	$\vdots$	∂	\partial
Ω	\Omega	$\pm$	\pm
		$\Re$	\Re
		$\sim$	\sim
		$\surd$	\surd

Fonts	
Normal	\rm
Bold	\bf
Italic	\it

that are to be incorporated into a printed document or presentation, increasing the font size can improve readability.

The `fill` function works in a similar manner to `plot`. Typing `fill(x,y,[r g b])` shades a polygon whose vertices are specified by the points `x(i)`, `y(i)`. The points are taken in order, and the last vertex is joined to the first. The color of the shading is determined by the third argument `[r g b]`. The elements `r`, `g` and `b`, which must be scalars in the range $[0,1]$, determine the level of red, green and blue, respectively, in the shading. So, `fill(x,y,[0 1 0])` uses pure green and `fill(x,y,[1 0 1])` uses magenta. Specifying equal amounts of red, green and blue gives a grey shading that can be varied between black (`[0 0 0]`) and white (`[1 1 1]`). The next example plots a cubic Bezier curve, which is defined by

$$p(u) = (1 - u)^3 \mathbf{P}_1 + 3u(1 - u)^2 \mathbf{P}_2 + 3u^2(1 - u)\mathbf{P}_3 + u^3 \mathbf{P}_4, \quad 0 \leq u \leq 1,$$

where the four control points, $\mathbf{P}_1$, $\mathbf{P}_2$, $\mathbf{P}_3$ and $\mathbf{P}_4$, have given x and y components. We use `fill` to shade the control polygon, that is, the polygon formed by the control points. The matrix P stores the control point $\mathbf{P}_j$ in its jth column, and `fill(P(1,:),P(2,:),[.8 .8 .8])` shades the control polygon with light grey. The columns of the matrix Curve are closely spaced points on the Bezier curve, and `plot(Curve(1,:),Curve(2,:),'--')` joins these with a dashed line. Figure 8.8 gives the resulting picture.

```
P = [0.1 0.3 0.7 0.8;
     0.3 0.8 0.6 0.1];
plot(P(1,:),P(2,:),'*')
axis([0 1 0 1])
hold on

u = 0:.01:1;
umat = [(1-u).^3; 3.*u.*(1-u).^2; 3.*u.^2.*(1-u); u.^3];
```

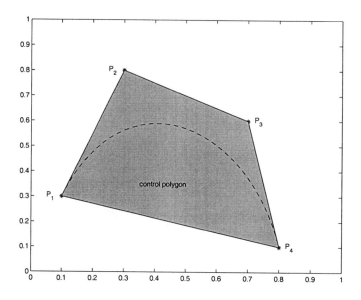

Figure 8.8. *Bezier curve and control polygon.*

```
Curve = P*umat;
fill(P(1,:),P(2,:),[.8 .8 .8])
plot(Curve(1,:),Curve(2,:),'--')

text(0.35,0.35,'control polygon')
text(0.05,0.3,'P_1')
text(0.25,0.8,'P_2')
text(0.72,0.6,'P_3')
text(0.82,0.1,'P_4')
hold off
```

8.1.3. Multiple Plots in a Figure

MATLAB's subplot allows you to place a number of plots in a grid pattern together on the same figure. Typing subplot(mnp) or, equivalently, subplot(m,n,p), splits the figure window into an m-by-n array of regions, each having its own axes. The current plotting commands will then apply to the pth of these regions, where the count moves along the first row, and then along the second row, and so on. So, for example, subplot(425) splits the figure window into a 4-by-2 matrix of regions and specifies that plotting commands apply to the fifth region, that is, the first region in the third row. If subplot(427) appears later, then the region in the (4,1) position becomes active. Several examples in which subplot is used appear below.

For plotting mathematical functions the fplot command is useful. It adaptively samples a function at enough points to produce a representative graph. The following example generates the graphs in Figure 8.9.

```
subplot(221), fplot('exp(sqrt(x)*sin(12*x))',[0 2*pi])
```

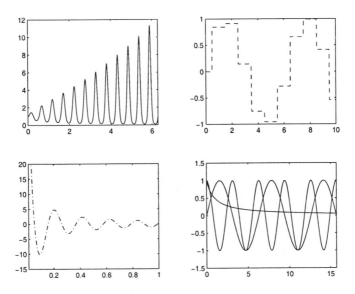

Figure 8.9. *Example with* subplot *and* fplot.

```
subplot(222), fplot('sin(round(x))',[0 10],'--')
subplot(223), fplot('cos(30*x)/x',[0.01 1 -15 20],'-.')
subplot(224), fplot('[sin(x),cos(2*x),1/(1+x)]',[0 5*pi -1.5 1.5])
```

In this example, the first call to fplot produces a graph of the function $\exp(\sqrt{x}\sin 12x)$ over the interval $0 \le x \le 2\pi$. In the second call, we override the default solid line style and specify a dashed line with '--'. The argument [0.01 1 -15 20] in the third call forces limits in both the x and y directions, $0.01 \le x \le 1$ and $-15 \le y \le 20$, and '-.' asks for a dash-dot line style. The final fplot example illustrates how more than one function can be plotted in the same call.

It is possible to supply further arguments to fplot. The general pattern is fplot('fun',lims,tol,N,'LineSpec',p1,p2,...). The argument list works as follows.

- fun is the function to be plotted.

- The x and/or y limits are given by lims.

- tol is a relative error tolerance, the default value of 2×10^{-3} corresponding to 0.2% accuracy.

- At least N+1 points will be used to produce the plot.

- LineSpec determines the line type.

- p1, p2, ... are parameters that are passed to fun, which must have input arguments x,p1,p2,....

The arguments tol, N and 'LineSpec' can be specified in any order, and an empty matrix ([]) can be passed to obtain the default for any of these arguments.

In Listing 7.4 on p. 71 is a function cheby(x,p) that returns the first p Chebyshev polynomials evaluated at x. Using this function the code

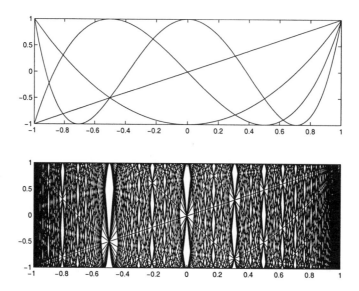

Figure 8.10. *First 5 (upper) and 35 (lower) Chebyshev polynomials, plotted using* `fplot` *and* `cheby` *in Listing 7.4.*

```
subplot(211), fplot('cheby',[-1 1],[],[],[],5)
subplot(212), fplot('cheby',[-1 1],[],[],[],35)
```

produces the pictures in Figure 8.10. Here, the first 5 and first 35 Chebyshev polynomials are plotted in the upper and lower regions, respectively.

It is possible to produce irregular grids of plots by invoking `subplot` with different grid patterns. For example, Figure 8.11 was produced as follows:

```
x = linspace(0,15,100);
subplot(2,2,1), plot(x,sin(x))
subplot(2,2,2), plot(x,round(x))
subplot(2,1,2), plot(x,sin(round(x)))
```

The third argument to `subplot` can be a vector specifying several regions, so we could replace the last line by

```
subplot(2,2,3:4), plot(x,sin(round(x)))
```

To complete this section, we list in Table 8.4 the most popular 2D plotting functions in MATLAB. Some of these functions are discussed in Section 8.3.

8.2. Three-Dimensional Graphics

The function `plot3` is the three-dimensional analogue of `plot`. The following example illustrates the simplest usage: `plot3(x,y,z)` draws a "join-the-dots" curve by taking the points `x(i)`, `y(i)`, `z(i)` in order. The result is shown in Figure 8.12.

```
t = -5:.005:5;
x = (1+t.^2).*sin(20*t);
```

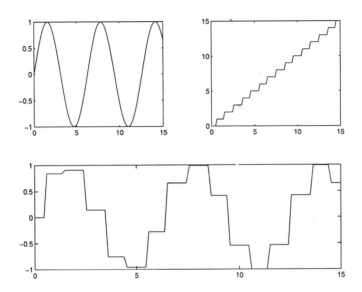

Figure 8.11. *Irregular grid of plots produced with* subplot.

Table 8.4. *2D plotting functions.*

plot	Simple x-y plot
loglog	Plot with logarithmically scaled axes
semilogx	Plot with logarithmically scaled x-axis
semilogy	Plot with logarithmically scaled y-axis
plotyy	x-y plot with y-axes on left and right
polar	Plot in polar coordinates
fplot	Automatic function plot
ezplot	Easy-to-use version of fplot
ezpolar	Easy-to-use version of polar
fill	Polygon fill
area	Filled area graph
bar	Bar graph
barh	Horizontal bar graph
hist	Histogram
pie	Pie chart
comet	Animated, comet-like, x-y plot
errorbar	Error bar plot
quiver	Quiver (velocity vector) plot
scatter	Scatter plot

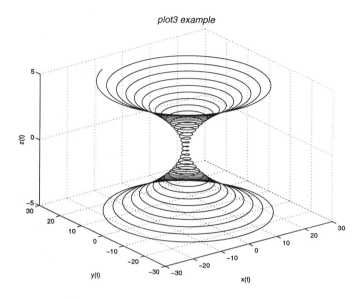

Figure 8.12. *3D plot created with* `plot3`.

```
y = (1+t.^2).*cos(20*t);
z = t;

plot3(x,y,z)
grid on
xlabel('x(t)'), ylabel('y(t)'), zlabel('z(t)')
title('\it{plot3 example}','FontSize',14)
```

This example also uses the functions `xlabel`, `ylabel` and `title`, which were discussed in the previous section, and the analogous `zlabel`. Note that we have used the TEX notation `\it` in the `title` command to produce italic text. The color, marker and line styles for `plot3` can be controlled in the same way as for `plot`. So, for example, `plot3(x,y,z,'rx--')` would use a red dashed line and place a cross at each point. Note that for 3D plots the default is `box off`; specifying `box on` adds a box that bounds the plot.

A simple contour plotting facility is provided by `ezcontour`. The call to `ezcontour` in the following example produces contours for the function $\sin(3y-x^2+1)+\cos(2y^2-2x)$ over the range $-2 \le x \le 2$ and $-1 \le y \le 1$; the result can be seen in the upper half of Figure 8.13.

```
subplot(211)
ezcontour('sin(3*y-x^2+1)+cos(2*y^2-2*x)',[-2 2 -1 1]);

x = -2:.01:2; y = -1:.01:1;
[X,Y] = meshgrid(x,y);
Z = sin(3*Y-X.^2+1)+cos(2*Y.^2-2*X);

subplot(212)
contour(x,y,Z,20)
```

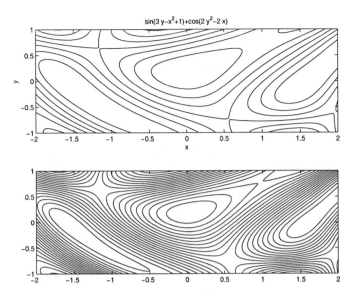

Figure 8.13. *Contour plots with* ezcontour *(upper) and* contour *(lower).*

Note that the contour levels have been chosen automatically. For the lower half of Figure 8.13 we use the more general function contour. We first assign x = -2:.01:2 and y = -1:.01:1 to obtain closely spaced points in the appropriate range. We then set [X,Y] = meshgrid(x,y), which produces matrices X and Y such that each row of X is a copy of the vector x and each column of Y is a copy of the vector y. (The function meshgrid is extremely useful for setting up data for many of MATLAB's 3D plotting tools.) The matrix Z is then generated from array operations on X and Y, with the result that Z(i,j) stores the function value corresponding to x(j), y(i). This is precisely the form required by contour. Typing contour(x,y,Z,20) tells MATLAB to regard Z as defining heights above the x-y plane with spacing given by x and y. The final input argument specifies that 20 contour levels are to be used; if this argument is omitted MATLAB automatically chooses the number of contour levels.

The next example illustrates the use of clabel to label contours, with the result shown in Figure 8.14.

```
[X,Y] = meshgrid(linspace(-3,3,100), linspace(-1.5,1.5,100));
Z = 4*X.^2 - 2.1*X.^4 + X.^6/3 + X.*Y - 4*Y.^2 + 4*Y.^4;
cvals = [linspace(-2,5,14) linspace(5,10,3)];
[C,h] = contour(X,Y,Z,cvals);
clabel(C,h,cvals([3 5 7 9 13 17]))
xlabel('x'), ylabel('y')
title('Six hump camel back function','FontSize',16)
```

Here, we are using an interesting function having a number of maxima, minima and saddle points. MATLAB's default choice of contour levels does not produce an attractive picture, so we specify the levels (chosen by trial and error) in the vector cvals. The clabel command takes as input the output from contour (C contains the contour data and h is a graphics object handle) and adds labels to the contour levels specified in its third input argument. Again the contour levels need not be

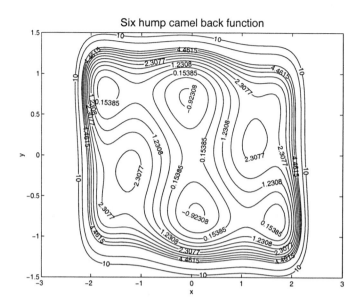

Figure 8.14. *Contour plot labelled using* `clabel`.

specified, but the default of labelling all contours produces a cluttered plot in this example. An alternative form of `clabel` is `clabel(C,h,'manual')`, which allows you to specify with the mouse the contours to be labelled: click to label a contour and press return to finish. The `h` argument of `clabel` can be omitted, in which case the labels are placed close to each contour with a plus sign marking the contour.

The function `mesh` accepts data in a similar form to `contour` and produces wire-frame surface plots. If `meshc` is used in place of `mesh`, a contour plot is appended below the surface. The example below, which produces Figure 8.15, involves the surface defined by $\sin(y^2+x) - \cos(y-x^2)$ for $0 \le x, y \le \pi$. The first subplot is produced by `mesh(Z)`. Since no x, y information is supplied to `mesh`, row and column indices are used for the axis ranges. The second subplot shows the effect of `meshc(Z)`. For the third subplot, we use `mesh(x,y,Z)`, so the tick labels on the x- and y-axes correspond to the values of `x` and `y`. We also specify the axis limits with `axis([0 pi 0 pi -5 5])`, which gives $0 \le x, y \le \pi$ and $-5 \le z \le 5$. For the final subplot, we use `mesh(Z)` again, followed by `hidden off`, which causes hidden lines to be shown.

```
x = 0:.1:pi; y = 0:.1:pi;
[X,Y] = meshgrid(x,y);
Z = sin(Y.^2+X)-cos(Y-X.^2);

subplot(221)
mesh(Z)

subplot(222)
meshc(Z)

subplot(223)
mesh(x,y,Z)
```

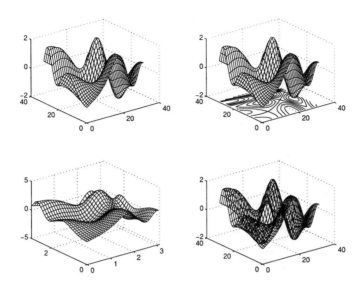

Figure 8.15. *Surface plots with* mesh *and* meshc.

```
axis([0 pi 0 pi -5 5])

subplot(224)
mesh(Z)
hidden off
```

The function surf differs from mesh in that it produces a solid filled surface plot, and surfc adds a contour plot below. In the next example we call MATLAB's membrane, which returns the first eigenfunction of an L-shaped membrane. The pictures in the first row of Figure 8.16 show the effect of surf and surfc. The (1,2) plot displays a color scale using colorbar. The color map for the current figure can be set using colormap; see doc colormap. The (2,1) plot uses the shading function with the flat option to remove the grid lines on the surface; another option is interp, which varies the color over each segment by interpolation. The (2,2) plot uses the related function waterfall, which is similar to mesh with the wireframes in the column direction removed.

```
Z = membrane; FS = 'FontSize';
subplot(221), surf(Z), title('\bf{surf}',FS,14)
subplot(222), surfc(Z), title('\bf{surfc}',FS,14), colorbar
subplot(223), surf(Z), shading flat
              title('\bf{surf} shading flat',FS,14)
subplot(224), waterfall(Z), title('\bf{waterfall}',FS,14)
```

The 3D pictures in Figures 8.12, 8.15 and 8.16 use MATLAB's default viewing angle. This can be overridden with the function view. Typing view(a,b) sets the counterclockwise rotation about the z-axis to a degrees and the vertical elevation to b degrees. The default is view(-37.5,30). The rotate 3D tool on the toolbar of the figure window enables the mouse to be used to change the angle of view by clicking and dragging within the axis area.

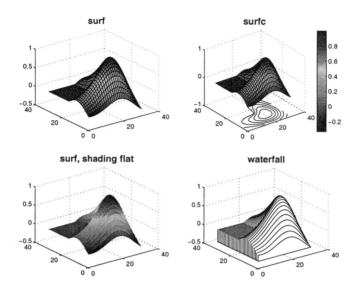

Figure 8.16. *Surface plots with* surf, surfc *and* waterfall.

It is possible to view a 2D plot as a 3D one, by using the view command to specify a viewing angle, or simply by typing view(3). Figure 8.17 shows the result of typing

```
plot(fft(eye(17))); view(3); grid
```

In the next example we generate a fractal landscape using the recursive function land shown in Listing 8.1, which uses a variant of the random midpoint displacement algorithm [64, Sec. 7.6]; see Figure 8.18. Recursion is discussed further in Section 10.5. The basic step taken by land is to update an N-by-N matrix with nonzeros only in each corner by filling in the entries in positions (1,d), (d,1), (d,d), (d,N) and (N,d), where d = (N+1)/2, in the following manner:

$$
\begin{bmatrix} a & & & & b \\ & & & & \\ & & & & \\ & & & & \\ c & & & & d \end{bmatrix}
\rightarrow
\begin{bmatrix} a & & \frac{a+b}{2} & & b \\ & & & & \\ \frac{a+c}{2} & & \frac{a+b+c+d}{4} & & \frac{b+d}{2} \\ & & & & \\ c & & \frac{c+d}{2} & & d \end{bmatrix} + \text{ noise.}
$$

The noise is introduced by adding a multiple of randn to each new nonzero element. The process is repeated recursively on the four square submatrices whose corners are defined by the nonzero elements, until the whole matrix is filled. The scaling factor for the noise is reduced by $2^{0.9}$ at each level of recursion. Note that the input argument A in land(A) must be a square matrix with dimension of the form $2^n + 1$, and only the corner elements of A have any effect on the result.

In the example below that produces Figure 8.18 we use land to set up a height matrix, B. For the surface plots, we use meshz, which works like mesh but hangs a vertical curtain around the edges of the surface. The first subplot shows the default

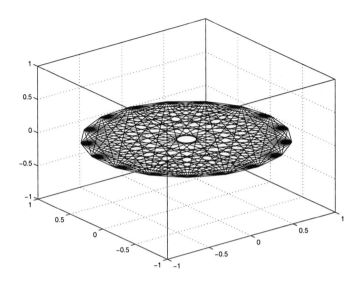

Figure 8.17. *3D view of a 2D plot.*

Listing 8.1. *Function* land.

```
function  B = land(A)
%LAND      Fractal landscape.
%          B = LAND(A) generates a random fractal landscape
%          represented by B, where A is a square matrix of
%          dimension N = 2^n + 1 whose four corner elements
%          are used as input parameters.

N = size(A,1);
d = (N+1)/2;
level = log2(N-1);
scalef = 0.05*(2^(0.9*level));

B = A;

B(d,d) = mean([A(1,1),A(1,N),A(N,1),A(N,N)]) + scalef*randn;
B(1,d) = mean([A(1,1),A(1,N)]) + scalef*randn;
B(d,1) = mean([A(1,1),A(N,1)]) + scalef*randn;
B(d,N) = mean([A(1,N),A(N,N)]) + scalef*randn;
B(N,d) = mean([A(N,1),A(N,N)]) + scalef*randn;

if N > 3
   B(1:d,1:d) = land(B(1:d,1:d));
   B(1:d,d:N) = land(B(1:d,d:N));
   B(d:N,1:d) = land(B(d:N,1:d));
   B(d:N,d:N) = land(B(d:N,d:N));
end
```

view of B. For the second subplot we impose a "sea level" by raising all heights that are below the average value. This resulting data matrix, Bisland, is also plotted with the default view. The third and fourth subplots use view([-75 40]) and view([240 65]), respectively. For these two subplots we also control the axis limits.

```
randn('state',10);
k = 2^5+1;
A = zeros(k);
A([1 k], [1 k]) = [1    1.25
                   1.1  2.0];
B = land(A);

subplot(221), meshz(B)
FS = 'FontSize'; title('Default view',FS,12)

Bisland = max(B,mean(mean(B)));
Bmin = min(min(Bisland));
Bmax = max(max(Bisland));
subplot(222), meshz(Bisland)
title('Default view',FS,12)

subplot(223), meshz(Bisland)
view([-75 40])
axis([0 k 0 k Bmin Bmax])
title('view([-75 40])',FS,12)

subplot(224), meshz(Bisland)
view([240 65])
axis([0 k 0 k Bmin Bmax])
title('view([240 65])',FS,12)
```

Table 8.5 summarizes the most popular 3D plotting functions. As the table indicates, several of the functions have "easy-to-use" alternative versions with names beginning ez. Section 8.3 discusses some of these functions.

A feature common to all graphics functions is that NaNs are interpreted as "missing data" and are not plotted. For example,

```
plot([1 2 NaN 3 4])
```

draws two disjoint lines and does not connect "2" to "3", while

```
A = peaks(80); A(28:52,28:52) = NaN; surfc(A)
```

produces the surfc plot with a hole in the middle shown in Figure 8.19. (The function peaks generates a matrix of height values corresponding to a particular function of two variables and is useful for demonstrating 3D plots.)

MATLAB contains in its demos directory several functions with names beginning cplx for visualizing functions of a complex variable (type what demos). Figure 8.20 shows the plot produced by cplxroot(3). In general, cplxroot(n) plots the Riemann surface for the function $z^{1/n}$.

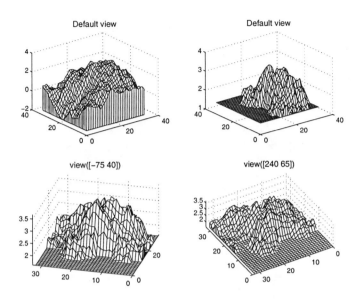

Figure 8.18. *Fractal landscape views.*

Table 8.5. *3D plotting functions.*

plot3*	Simple x-y-z plot
contour*	Contour plot
contourf*	Filled contour plot
contour3	3D contour plot
mesh*	Wireframe surface
meshc*	Wireframe surface plus contours
meshz	Wireframe surface with curtain
surf*	Solid surface
surfc*	Solid surface plus contours
waterfall	Unidirectional wireframe
bar3	3D bar graph
bar3h	3D horizontal bar graph
pie3	3D pie chart
fill3	Polygon fill
comet3	3D animated, comet-like plot
scatter3	3D scatter plot
stem3	Stem plot

* These functions **fun** have **ezfun** counterparts, too.

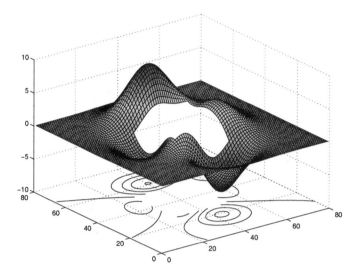

Figure 8.19. `surfc` *plot of matrix containing NaNs.*

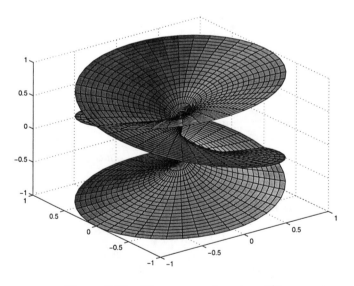

Figure 8.20. *Riemann surface for* $z^{1/3}$.

8.3. Specialized Graphs for Displaying Data

In this section we describe some additional functions from Tables 8.4 and 8.5 that are useful for displaying data (as opposed to plotting mathematical functions).

MATLAB has four functions for plotting bar graphs, covering 2D and 3D vertical or horizontal bar graphs, with options to stack or group the bars. The simplest usage of the bar plot functions is with a single m-by-n matrix input argument. For 2D bar plots elements in a row are clustered together, either in a group of n bars with the default 'grouped' argument, or in one bar apportioned among the n row entries with the 'stacked' argument.

The following code uses bar and barh to produce Figure 8.21:

```
Y = [7 6 5
     6 8 1
     4 5 9
     2 3 4
     9 7 2];

subplot(2,2,1)
bar(Y)
title('bar(...,''grouped'')')

subplot(2,2,2)
bar(0:5:20,Y)
title('bar(...,''grouped'')')

subplot(2,2,3)
bar(Y,'stacked')
title('bar(...,''stacked'')')

subplot(2,2,4)
barh(Y)
title('barh')
```

Note that in the two-argument form bar(x,Y) the vector x provides the x-axis locations for the bars.

For 3D bar graphs the default arrangement is 'detached', with the bars for the elements in each column distributed along the y-axis. The arguments 'grouped' and 'stacked' give 3D views of the corresponding 2D bar plots with the same arguments. With the same data matrix, Y, Figure 8.22 is produced by

```
subplot(2,2,1)
bar3(Y)
title('bar3(...,''detached'')')

subplot(2,2,2)
bar3(Y,'grouped')
title('bar3(...,''grouped'')')

subplot(2,2,3)
bar3(Y,'stacked')
```

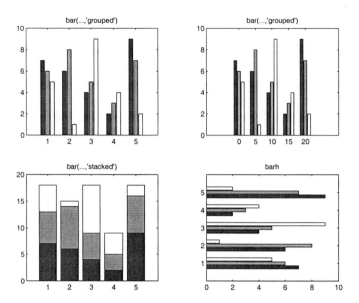

Figure 8.21. *2D bar plots.*

```
title('bar3(...,''stacked'')')

subplot(2,2,4)
bar3h(Y)
title('bar3h')
```

Note that with the default 'detached' arrangement some bars are hidden behind others. A satisfactory solution to this problem can sometimes be found by rotating the plot using view or the mouse.

Histograms are produced by the hist function, which counts the number of elements lying within intervals and, if no output arguments are specified, plots a bar graph. The first argument, y, to hist is the data vector and the second is either a scalar specifying the number of bars (or bins) or a vector defining the intervals; if only y is supplied then 10 bins are used. If y is a matrix then bins are created for each column and a grouped bar graph is produced. The following code produces Figure 8.23:

```
randn('state',1)
y = exp(randn(1000,1)/3);
subplot(2,2,1)
hist(y)
title('1000-by-1 data vector, 10 bins')

subplot(2,2,2)
hist(y,25)
title('25 bins')

subplot(2,2,3)
hist(y,min(y):.1:max(y))
```

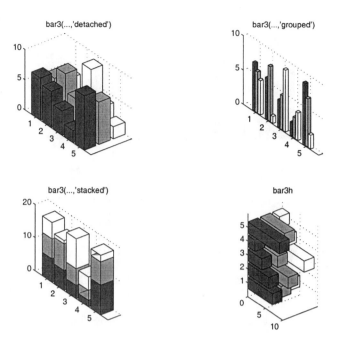

Figure 8.22. *3D bar plots.*

```
title('Bin width 0.1')

Y = exp(randn(1000,3)/3);
subplot(2,2,4)
hist(Y)
title('1000-by-3 data matrix')
```

Pie charts can be produced with `pie` and `pie3`. They take a vector argument, `x`, and corresponding to each element `x(i)` they draw a slice with area proportional to `x(i)`. A second argument `explode` can be given, which is a 0-1 vector with a 1 in positions corresponding to slices that are to be offset from the chart. By default, the slices are labelled with the percentage of the total area that they occupy; replacement labels can be specified in a cell array of strings (see Section 18.3). The following code produces Figure 8.24.

```
x = [1.5 3.4 4.2];

subplot(2,2,1)
pie(x)

subplot(2,2,2)
pie(x,[0 0 1])

subplot(2,2,3)
pie(x,{'Slice 1','Slice 2','Slice 3'})
```

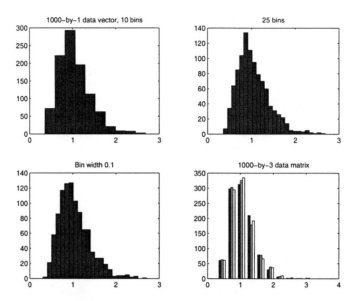

Figure 8.23. *Histograms produced with* `hist`.

```
subplot(2,2,4)
pie3(x,[0 1 0])
```

The `area` function produces a stacked area plot. With vector arguments, `area` is similar to `plot` except that the area between the y-values and 0 (or the level specified by the optional second argument) is filled; for matrix arguments the plots of the columns are stacked, showing the sum at each x-value. The following code produces Figure 8.25.

```
randn('state',1)
x = [1:12 11:-1:8 10:15]; Y = [x' x'];

subplot(2,1,1)
area(Y+randn(size(Y)))

subplot(2,1,2)
Y = Y + 5*randn(size(Y));
area(Y,min(min(Y)))
axis tight
```

8.4. Saving and Printing Figures

If your default printer has been set appropriately, simply typing `print` will send the contents of the current figure window to your printer. An alternative is to use the `print` command to save the figure as a file. For example,

```
print -deps2 myfig.eps
```

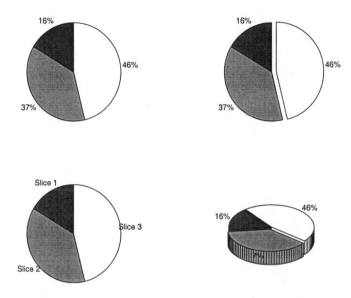

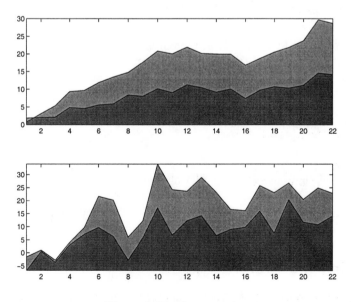

Figure 8.24. *Pie charts.*

Figure 8.25. *Area graphs.*

creates an encapsulated level 2 black and white PostScript file `myfig.eps` that can subsequently be printed on a PostScript printer or included in a document. This file can be incorporated into a LaTeX document, as in the following outline:

```
\documentclass{article}
\usepackage[dvips]{graphicx} % Assumes use of dvips dvi driver.
...
\begin{document}
...
\begin{center}
\includegraphics[width=8cm]{myfig.eps}
\end{center}
...
\end{document}
```

See [23] for more about LaTeX.

The many options of the `print` command can be seen with `help print`. The `print` command also has a functional form, illustrated by

```
print('-deps2','myfig.eps')
```

(an example of command/function duality—see Section 7.4). To illustrate the utility of the functional form, the next example generates a sequence of five figures and saves them to files `fig1.eps`, ..., `fig5.eps`:

```
x = linspace(0,2*pi,50);
for i=1:5
    plot(x,sin(i*x))
    print('-deps2',['fig' int2str(i) '.eps'])
end
```

The second argument to the `print` command is formed by string concatenation (see Section 18.1), making use of the function `int2str`, which converts its integer argument to a string. Thus when `i=1`, for example, the `print` statement is equivalent to `print('-deps2','fig1.eps')`.

The `saveas` command saves a figure to a file in a form that can be reloaded into MATLAB. For example,

```
saveas(gcf,'myfig','fig')
```

saves the current figure as a binary FIG-file, which can be reloaded into MATLAB with `open('myfig.fig')`.

It is also possible to save and print figures from the pulldown `File` menu in the figure window.

8.5. On Things Not Treated

We have restricted our treatment in this chapter to high-level graphics functions that deal with common 2D and 3D visualization tasks. MATLAB's graphics capabilities extend far beyond what is described here. On the one hand, MATLAB provides access to lighting, transparency control, solid model building, texture mapping, and the construction of graphical user interfaces. On the other hand, it is possible to control

Figure 8.26. *From the* 1964 *Gatlinburg Conference on Numerical Algebra. From left to right: J. H. Wilkinson, W. J. Givens, G. E. Forsythe, A. S. Householder, P. Henrici and F. L. Bauer. (Source of photograph: Oak Ridge National Laboratory.)*

low-level details such as the tick labels and the position and size of the axes, and to produce animation; how to do this is described in Chapter 17 on Handle Graphics. A good place to learn more about MATLAB graphics is [57]. You can also learn by exploring the demonstrations in the `matlab\demos` directory. Try `help demos`, but note that not all files in this directory are documented in the help information.

Another area of MATLAB that we have not discussed is image handling and manipulation. If you type `what demos`, you will find that the `demos` directory contains a selection of MAT-files, most of which contain image data. These can be loaded and displayed as in the following example, which produces the image shown in Figure 8.26:

```
>> load gatlin, image(X); colormap(map), axis off
```

This picture was taken at a meeting in Gatlinburg, Tennessee, in 1964, and shows six major figures in the development of numerical linear algebra and scientific computing (you can find some of their names in Table 5.3).

Before coding graphs in MATLAB you should think carefully about the design, aiming for a result that is uncluttered and conveys clearly the intended message. Good references on graphical design are [8, Chaps. 10, 11], [76], [77], [78].

"What is the use of a book," thought Alice,
"without pictures or conversation?"
— LEWIS CARROLL, *Alice's Adventures in Wonderland* (1865)

The close *command closes the current figure window.*
If there is no open figure window MATLAB opens one and then closes it.
— CLEVE B. MOLER

A picture is worth a thousand words.
— ANONYMOUS

Given their low data-density and
failure to order numbers along a visual dimension,
pie charts should never be used.
— EDWARD R. TUFTE, *The Visual Display of Quantitative Information* (1983)

It's kind of scandalous that the world's calculus books,
up until recent years, have never had a good picture[3] of a cardioid. . .
Nobody ever knew what a cardioid looked like, when I took calculus,
because the illustrations were done by graphic artists
who were trying to imitate drawings by previous artists,
without seeing the real thing.
— DONALD E. KNUTH, *Digital Typography* (1999)

_____

[3] ezpolar('1+cos(t)')

Chapter 9
Linear Algebra

MATLAB was originally designed for linear algebra computations, so it not surprising that it has a rich set of functions for solving linear equation and eigenvalue problems. Many of the linear algebra functions are based on routines from the LAPACK [3] Fortran library.

Most of the linear algebra functions work for both real and complex matrices. We write A^* for the conjugate transpose of A. Recall that a square matrix A is Hermitian if $A^* = A$ and unitary if $A^*A = I$, where I is the identity matrix. To avoid clutter, we use the appropriate adjectives for complex matrices. Thus, when the matrix is real, "Hermitian" can be read as "symmetric" and "unitary" can be read as "orthogonal". For background on numerical linear algebra see [13], [21], [73] or [75].

9.1. Norms and Condition Numbers

A norm is a scalar measure of the size of a vector or matrix. The p-norm of an n-vector x is defined by

$$\|x\|_p = \left(\sum_{i=1}^{n} |x_i|^p \right)^{1/p}, \qquad 1 \le p < \infty.$$

For $p = \infty$ the norm is defined by

$$\|x\|_\infty = \max_{1 \le i \le n} |x_i|.$$

The norm function can compute any p-norm and is invoked as norm(x,p), with default p = 2. As a special case, for p = -inf the quantity $\min_i |x_i|$ is computed. Example:

```
>> x = 1:4;
>> [norm(x,1) norm(x,2) norm(x,inf) norm(x,-inf)]
ans =
   10.0000    5.4772    4.0000    1.0000
```

The p-norm of a matrix is defined by

$$\|A\|_p = \max_{x \neq 0} \frac{\|Ax\|_p}{\|x\|_p}.$$

The 1- and ∞-norms of an m-by-n matrix A can be characterized as

$$\|A\|_1 = \max_{1 \le j \le n} \sum_{i=1}^{m} |a_{ij}|, \qquad \text{"max column sum"},$$

$$\|A\|_\infty = \max_{1 \le i \le m} \sum_{j=1}^{n} |a_{ij}|, \qquad \text{"max row sum"}.$$

The 2-norm of A can be expressed as the largest singular value of A, `max(svd(A))` (singular values and the `svd` function are described in Section 9.6). For matrices the `norm` function is invoked as `norm(A,p)` and supports $p = 1, 2, \text{inf}$ and $p = \text{'fro'}$, the Frobenius norm

$$\|A\|_F = \left(\sum_{i=1}^m \sum_{j=1}^n |a_{ij}|^2 \right)^{1/2}.$$

(This is a an example of a function with an argument that can vary in type: `p` can be a `double` or a string.) Example:

```
>> A = [1 2 3; 4 5 6; 7 8 9]
A =
     1     2     3
     4     5     6
     7     8     9
>> [norm(A,1) norm(A,2) norm(A,inf) norm(A,'fro')]
ans =
    18.0000   16.8481   24.0000   16.8819
```

For cases in which computation of the 2-norm of a matrix is too expensive the function `normest` can be used to obtain an estimate. The call `normest(A,tol)` uses the power method on A^*A to estimate $\|A\|_2$ to within a relative error `tol`; the default is `tol = 1e-6`.

For a nonsingular square matrix A, $\kappa(A) = \|A\| \|A^{-1}\| \geq 1$ is the condition number with respect to inversion. It measures the sensitivity of the solution of a linear system $Ax = b$ to perturbations in A and b. The matrix A is said to be well conditioned or ill conditioned according as $\kappa(A)$ is small or large. A large condition number implies that A is close to a singular matrix. The condition number is computed by the `cond` function as `cond(A,p)`. The p-norm choices $p = 1, 2, \text{inf}, \text{'fro'}$ are supported, with default $p = 2$. For $p = 2$, rectangular matrices are allowed, in which case the condition number is defined by $\kappa_2(A) = \|A\|_2 \|A^+\|_2$, where A^+ is the pseudo-inverse (see Section 9.3).

Computing the exact condition number is expensive, so MATLAB provides two functions for estimating the 1-norm condition number of a square matrix A, `rcond` and `condest`. Both functions produce estimates usually of the correct order of magnitude at about one third the cost of explicitly computing A^{-1}. Function `rcond` uses the LAPACK condition estimator to estimate the reciprocal of $\kappa_1(A)$, producing a result between 0 and 1, with 0 signalling exact singularity. Function `condest` estimates $\kappa_1(A)$ and also returns an approximate null vector, which is required in some applications. The command `[c,v] = condest(A)` produces a scalar `c` and vector `v` so that $c \leq \kappa_1(A)$ and `norm(A*v,1) = norm(A,1)*norm(v,1)/c`. Example:

```
>> A = gallery('grcar',8);

>> [cond(A,1) 1/rcond(A) condest(A)]
ans =
    7.7778    5.3704    7.7778

>> [cond(A,1) 1/rcond(A) condest(A)]
ans =
    7.7778    5.3704    7.2222
```

As this example illustrates, condest does not necessarily return the same result on each invocation, as it makes use of rand.

9.2. Linear Equations

The fundamental tool for solving a linear system of equations is the backslash operator, \. It handles three types of linear system $Ax = b$, where the matrix A and the vector b are given. The three possible shapes for A lead to square, overdetermined and underdetermined systems, as described below. More generally, the \ operator can be used to solve $AX = B$, where B is a matrix with p columns; in this case MATLAB solves $AX(:, j) = B(:, j)$ for $j = 1:p$.

9.2.1. Square System

If A is an n-by-n nonsingular matrix then A\b is the solution x to $Ax = b$, computed by LU factorization with partial pivoting. During the solution process MATLAB computes rcond(A), and it prints a warning message if the result is smaller than about eps:

```
>> x = hilb(15)\ones(15,1);

Warning: Matrix is close to singular or badly scaled.
         Results may be inaccurate. RCOND = 9.178404e-019.
```

These warning messages can be turned off using warning off; see Section 14.1.

MATLAB recognizes two special forms of square systems and takes advantage of them to reduce the computation.

- Triangular matrix, or permutation of a triangular matrix. The system is solved by substitution.

- Hermitian positive definite matrix. (The Hermitian matrix A is positive definite if $x^* A x > 0$ for all nonzero vectors x, or, equivalently, if all the eigenvalues are real and positive.) Cholesky factorization is used instead of LU factorization. How does MATLAB know the matrix is definite? When \ is called with a Hermitian matrix that has positive diagonal elements MATLAB attempts to Cholesky factorize the matrix. If the Cholesky factorization succeeds it is used to solve the system; otherwise an LU factorization is carried out.

9.2.2. Overdetermined System

If A has dimension m-by-n with $m > n$ then $Ax = b$ is an overdetermined system: there are more equations than unknowns. In general, there is no x satisfying the system. MATLAB's A\b gives a least squares solution to the system, that is, it minimizes norm(A*x-b) (the 2-norm of the residual) over all vectors x. If A has full rank n there is a unique least squares solution. If A has rank k less than n then A\b is a basic solution—one with at most k nonzero elements (k is determined, and x computed, using the QR factorization with column pivoting). In the latter case MATLAB displays a warning message.

A least squares solution to $Ax = b$ can also be computed as x_min = pinv(A)*b, where the function pinv computes the pseudo-inverse; see Section 9.3. In the case where A is rank-deficient x_min is the unique solution of minimal 2-norm.

A vector that minimizes the 2-norm of $Ax - b$ over all nonnegative vectors x, for real A and b, is computed by lsqnonneg. The simplest usage is x = lsqnonneg(A,b), and several other input and output arguments can be specified, including a starting vector for the iterative algorithm that is used. Example:

```
>> A = gallery('lauchli',3,0.25), b = [1 2 4 8]';
A =
      1.0000      1.0000      1.0000
      0.2500           0           0
           0      0.2500           0
           0           0      0.2500

>> x = A\b;                    % Least squares solution.

>> xn = lsqnonneg(A,b);   % Nonnegative least squares solution.
Optimization terminated successfully.

>> [x xn], [norm(A*x-b) norm(A*xn-b)]
ans =
     -9.9592           0
     -1.9592           0
     14.0408      2.8235
ans =
      7.8571      8.7481
```

9.2.3. Underdetermined System

If A has dimension m-by-n with $m < n$ then $Ax = b$ is an underdetermined system: there are fewer equations than unknowns. The system has either no solution or infinitely many. In the latter case A\b produces a basic solution, one with at most k nonzero elements, where k is the rank of A. This solution is generally not the solution of minimal 2-norm, which can be computed as pinv(A)*b. If the system has no solution (that is, it is inconsistent) then A\b is a least squares solution. Here is an example that illustrates the difference between the \ and pinv solutions:

```
>> A = [1 1 1; 1 1 -1], b = [3; 1]
A =
      1      1      1
      1      1     -1
b =
      3
      1

>> x = A\b; y = pinv(A)*b;
>> [x y]
ans =
      2.0000      1.0000
           0      1.0000
      1.0000      1.0000
```

```
>> [norm(x) norm(y)]
ans =
     2.2361     1.7321
```

9.3. Inverse, Pseudo-Inverse and Determinant

The inverse of an n-by-n matrix A is a matrix X satisfying $AX = XA = I$, where I is the identity matrix (eye(n)). A matrix without an inverse is called singular. A singular matrix can be characterized in several ways: in particular, its determinant is zero and it has a nonzero null vector, that is, there exists a nonzero vector v such that $Av = 0$.

The matrix inverse is computed by the function inv. For example:

```
>> A = pascal(3), X = inv(A)
A =
     1     1     1
     1     2     3
     1     3     6
X =
     3    -3     1
    -3     5    -2
     1    -2     1

>> norm(A*X-eye(3))
ans =
     0
```

The inverse is formed using LU factorization with partial pivoting and the recipro-cal condition estimate rcond is computed. A warning message is produced if exact singularity is detected or if rcond is very small.

Note that it is rarely necessary to compute the inverse of a matrix. For example, solving a square linear system $Ax = b$ by A\b is 2–3 times faster than by inv(A)*b and often produces a smaller residual. It is usually possible to reformulate computations involving a matrix inverse in terms of linear system solving, so that explicit inversion is avoided.

The determinant of a square matrix is computed by the function det. It is calcu-lated from the LU factors. Although the computation is affected by rounding errors in general, det(A) returns an integer when A has integer entries:

```
>> A = vander(1:5)
A =
       1     1     1     1     1
      16     8     4     2     1
      81    27     9     3     1
     256    64    16     4     1
     625   125    25     5     1

>> det(A)
ans =
     288
```

It is not recommended to test for nearness to singularity using det. Instead, cond, rcond or condest should be used.

The (Moore–Penrose) pseudo-inverse generalizes the notion of inverse to rectangular and rank-deficient matrices A and is written A^+. It is computed with pinv(A). The pseudo-inverse A^+ of A can be characterized as the unique matrix $X = A^+$ satisfying the four conditions $AXA = A$, $XAX = X$, $(XA)^* = XA$ and $(AX)^* = AX$. It can also be written explicitly in terms of the singular value decomposition (SVD): if the SVD of A is given by (9.1) on p. 115 then $A^+ = V \Sigma^+ U^*$, where Σ^+ is n-by-m diagonal with (i,i) entry $1/\sigma_i$ if $\sigma_i > 0$ and otherwise 0. To illustrate,

```
>> pinv(ones(3))
ans =
     0.1111     0.1111     0.1111
     0.1111     0.1111     0.1111
     0.1111     0.1111     0.1111
```

and if

```
A =
     0     0     0     0
     0     1     0     0
     0     0     2     0
```

then

```
>> pinv(A)
ans =
        0          0          0
        0     1.0000          0
        0          0     0.5000
        0          0          0
```

9.4. LU and Cholesky Factorizations

An LU factorization of a square matrix A is a factorization $A = LU$ where L is unit lower triangular (that is, lower triangular with 1s on the diagonal) and U is upper triangular. Not every matrix can be factorized in this way, but when row interchanges are incorporated the factorization always exists. The lu function computes an LU factorization with partial pivoting $PA = LU$, where P is a permutation matrix. The call [L,U,P] = lu(A) returns the triangular factors and the permutation matrix. With just two output arguments, [L,U] = lu(A) returns L $= P^T L$, so L is a triangular matrix with its rows permuted. Example:

```
>> format short g
>> A = gallery('fiedler',3), [L,U] = lu(A)
A =
     0     1     2
     1     0     1
     2     1     0
L =
              0              1              0
```

```
              0.5            -0.5             1
                1               0             0
U =
       2      1      0
       0      1      2
       0      0      2
```

Note that the LU factorization is mathematically defined for rectangular matrices, but lu accepts only square matrices as input.

Using x = A\b to solve a linear system $Ax = b$ with a square A is equivalent to LU factorizing the matrix and then solving with the factors:

```
[L,U] = lu(A); x = U\(L\b);
```

As noted in Section 9.2.1, MATLAB takes advantage of the fact that L is a permuted triangular matrix when forming L\b. An advantage of this two-step approach is that if further linear systems involving A are to be solved then the LU factors can be reused, with a saving in computation.

Any Hermitian positive definite matrix has a Cholesky factorization $A = R^*R$, where R is upper triangular with real, positive diagonal elements. The Cholesky factor is computed by R = chol(A). For example:

```
>> A = pascal(4)
A =
       1      1      1      1
       1      2      3      4
       1      3      6     10
       1      4     10     20

>> R = chol(A)
R =
       1      1      1      1
       0      1      2      3
       0      0      1      3
       0      0      0      1
```

Note that chol looks only at the elements in the upper triangle of A (including the diagonal)—it factorizes the Hermitian matrix agreeing with the upper triangle of A. An error is produced if A is not positive definite. The chol function can be used to test whether a matrix is positive definite (indeed, this is as good a test as any) using the call [R,p] = chol(A), where the integer p will be zero if the factorization succeeds and positive otherwise; see help chol for more details about p.

Function cholupdate modifies the Cholesky factorization when the original matrix is subjected to a rank 1 perturbation (either an update, $+xx^*$, or a downdate, $-xx^*$).

9.5. QR Factorization

A QR factorization of an m-by-n matrix A is a factorization $A = QR$, where Q is m-by-m unitary and R is m-by-n upper triangular. This factorization is very useful for the solution of least squares problems and for constructing an orthonormal basis for the columns of A. The command [Q,R] = qr(A) computes the factorization, while when $m > n$ [Q,R] = qr(A,0) produces an "economy size" version in which Q has only n columns and R is n-by-n. Here is an example, with an already constructed A:

```
>> format short e, A
A =
         1       0       1
         1      -1       1
         2       0       0

>> [Q,R] = qr(A)
Q =
  -4.0825e-001   1.8257e-001  -8.9443e-001
  -4.0825e-001  -9.1287e-001  -6.1745e-017
  -8.1650e-001   3.6515e-001   4.4721e-001
R =
  -2.4495e+000   4.0825e-001  -8.1650e-001
             0   9.1287e-001  -7.3030e-001
             0             0  -8.9443e-001
```

A QR factorization with column pivoting has the form $AP = QR$, where P is a permutation matrix. The permutation strategy that is used produces a factor R whose diagonal elements are nonincreasing: $|r_{11}| \geq |r_{22}| \geq \cdots \geq |r_{nn}|$. Column pivoting is particularly appropriate when A is suspected of being rank-deficient, as it helps to reveal near rank-deficiency. Roughly speaking, if A is near a matrix of rank $r < n$ then the last $n - r$ diagonal elements of R will be of order eps*norm(A). A third output argument forces function qr to use column pivoting and return the permutation matrix: [Q,R,P] = qr(A). Continuing the previous example, we make A nearly singular and see how column pivoting reveals the near singularity in the last diagonal element of R:

```
>> A(2,2) = eps
A =
   1.0000e+000              0   1.0000e+000
   1.0000e+000   2.2204e-016   1.0000e+000
   2.0000e+000              0             0

>> [Q,R,P] = qr(A); R, P
R =
  -2.4495e+000  -8.1650e-001  -9.0649e-017
             0  -1.1547e+000  -1.2820e-016
             0             0   1.5701e-016
P =
         1       0       0
         0       0       1
         0       1       0
```

Functions qrdelete, qrinsert and qrupdate modify the QR factorization when a column of the original matrix is deleted or inserted and when a rank 1 perturbation is added.

9.6. Singular Value Decomposition

The singular value decomposition of an m-by-n matrix A has the form

$$A = U\Sigma V^*, \tag{9.1}$$

where U is an m-by-m unitary matrix, V is an n-by-n unitary matrix and Σ is a real m-by-n diagonal matrix with (i, i) entry σ_i. The singular values σ_i satisfy $\sigma_1 \geq \sigma_2 \geq \cdots \geq \sigma_{\min(m,n)} \geq 0$. The SVD is an extremely useful tool [21]. For example, the rank of A is the number of nonzero singular values and the smallest singular value is the 2-norm distance to the nearest rank-deficient matrix. The complete SVD is computed using [U,S,V] = svd(A); if only one output argument is specified then a vector of singular values is returned. When $m > n$ the command [U,S,V] = svd(A,0) produces an "economy size" SVD in which U is m-by-n with orthonormal columns and S is n-by-n. Example:

```
>> A = reshape(1:9,3,3); format short e
>> svd(A)'
ans =
   1.6848e+001   1.0684e+000   5.5431e-016
```

Here, the matrix is singular. The smallest computed singular value is at the level of the unit roundoff rather than zero because of rounding errors.

Functions rank, null and orth compute, respectively, the rank, an orthonormal basis for the null space and an orthonormal basis for the range of their matrix argument. All three base their computation on the SVD, using a tolerance proportional to eps to decide when a computed singular value can be regarded as zero. For example, using the previous matrix:

```
>> format
>> rank(A)
ans =
     2

>> null(A)
ans =
    0.4082
   -0.8165
    0.4082

>> orth(A)
ans =
   -0.4797    0.7767
   -0.5724    0.0757
   -0.6651   -0.6253
```

Another function connected with rank computations is rref, which computes the reduced row echelon form. Since the computation of this form is very sensitive to rounding errors, this function is mainly of pedagogical interest.

The generalized singular value decomposition of an m-by-p matrix A and an n-by-p matrix B can be written

$$A = UCX^*, \quad B = VSX^*, \quad C^*C + S^*S = I,$$

where U and V are unitary and C and S are real diagonal matrices with nonnegative diagonal elements. The numbers $C(i,i)/S(i,i)$ are the generalized singular values. This decomposition is computed by [U,V,X,C,S] = gsvd(A,B). See help gsvd for more details about the dimensions of the factors.

9.7. Eigenvalue Problems

Algebraic eigenvalue problems are straightforward to define, but their efficient and reliable numerical solution is a complicated subject. MATLAB's eig function simplifies the solution process by recognizing and taking advantage of the number of input matrices, as well as their structure and the output requested. It automatically chooses among 16 different algorithms or algorithmic variants, corresponding to

- standard (eig(A)) or generalized (eig(A,B)) problem,

- real or complex matrices A and B,

- symmetric/Hermitian A and B with B positive definite, or not,

- eigenvectors requested or not.

9.7.1. Eigenvalues

The scalar λ and nonzero vector x are an eigenvalue and corresponding eigenvector of the n-by-n matrix A if $Ax = \lambda x$. The eigenvalues are the n roots of the degree n characteristic polynomial $\det(\lambda I - A)$. The $n+1$ coefficients of this polynomial are computed by p = poly(A):

$$\det(\lambda I - A) = p_1 \lambda^n + p_2 \lambda^{n-1} + \cdots + p_n \lambda + p_{n+1}.$$

The eigenvalues of A are computed with the eig function: e = eig(A) assigns the eigenvalues to the vector e. More generally, [V,D] = eig(A) computes an n-by-n diagonal matrix D and an n-by-n matrix V such that A*V = V*D. Thus D contains eigenvalues on the diagonal and the columns of V are eigenvectors. Not every matrix has n linearly independent eigenvectors, so the matrix V returned by eig may be singular (or, because of roundoff, nonsingular but very ill conditioned). The matrix in the following example has two eigenvalues 1 and only one eigenvector:

```
>> [V,D] = eig([2 -1; 1  0])
V =
    0.7071    0.7071
    0.7071    0.7071
D =
    1    0
    0    1
```

The scaling of eigenvectors is arbitrary (if x is an eigenvector then so is any nonzero multiple of x). As the last example illustrates, MATLAB normalizes so that each column of V has unit 2-norm. Note that eigenvalues and eigenvectors can be complex, even for a real (non-Hermitian) matrix.

A Hermitian matrix has real eigenvalues and its eigenvectors can be taken to be mutually orthogonal. For Hermitian matrices MATLAB returns eigenvalues sorted in increasing order and the matrix of eigenvectors is unitary to working precision:

```
>> [V,D] = eig([2 -1; -1  1])
V =
    -0.5257    -0.8507
    -0.8507     0.5257
D =
     0.3820          0
          0     2.6180

>> norm(V'*V-eye(2))
ans =
  2.2204e-016
```

In the following example eig is applied to the (non-Hermitian) Frank matrix:

```
>> F = gallery('frank',5)
F =
     5     4     3     2     1
     4     4     3     2     1
     0     3     3     2     1
     0     0     2     2     1
     0     0     0     1     1

>> e = eig(F)'
e =
    10.0629    3.5566    1.0000    0.0994    0.2812
```

This matrix has some special properties, one of which we can see by looking at the reciprocals of the eigenvalues:

```
>> 1./e
ans =
     0.0994    0.2812    1.0000   10.0629    3.5566
```

Thus if λ is an eigenvalue then so is $1/\lambda$. The reason is that the characteristic polynomial is anti-palindromic:

```
>> poly(F)
ans =
     1.0000   -15.0000   55.0000   -55.0000   15.0000   -1.0000
```

Thus $\det(F - \lambda I) = -\lambda^5 \det(F - \lambda^{-1}I)$.

Function condeig computes condition numbers for the eigenvalues: a large condition number indicates an eigenvalue that is sensitive to perturbations in the matrix. The following example displays eigenvalues in the first row and condition numbers in the second:

```
>> A = gallery('frank',6);
>> [V,D,s] = condeig(A);
>> [diag(D)'; s']
ans =
    12.9736    5.3832    1.8355    0.5448    0.0771    0.1858
     1.3059    1.3561    2.0412   15.3255   43.5212   56.6954
```

For this matrix the small eigenvalues are slightly ill conditioned.

9.7.2. More about Eigenvalue Computations

The function eig works in several stages. First, when A is nonsymmetric, it balances the matrix, that is, it carries out a similarity transformation $A \leftarrow Y^{-1}AY$, where Y is a permutation of a diagonal matrix chosen to give A rows and columns of approximately equal norm. The motivation for balancing is that it can lead to a more accurate computed eigensystem. However, balancing can worsen rather than improve the accuracy (see doc eig for an example), so it may be necessary to turn balancing off with eig(A,'nobalance').

After balancing, eig reduces A to Hessenberg form, then uses the QR algorithm to reach Schur form, after which eigenvectors are computed by substitution if required. The Hessenberg factorization takes the form $A = QHQ^*$, where H is upper Hessenberg ($h_{ij} = 0$ for $i > j + 1$) and Q is unitary. If A is Hermitian then H is Hermitian and tridiagonal. The Hessenberg factorization is computed by H = hess(A) or [Q,H] = hess(A). The real Schur decomposition of a real A has the form $A = QTQ^T$, where T is upper quasi-triangular, that is, block triangular with 1-by-1 and 2-by-2 diagonal blocks, and Q is orthogonal. The (complex) Schur decomposition has the form $A = QTQ^*$, where T is upper triangular and Q is unitary. If A is real then T = schur(A) and [Q,T] = schur(A) produce the real Schur decomposition. If A is complex then schur produces the complex Schur form. The complex Schur form can be obtained for a real matrix with schur(A,'complex') (it differs from the real form only when A has one or more nonreal eigenvalues).

If A is real and symmetric (complex Hermitian), [V,D] = eig(A) reduces initially to symmetric (Hermitian) tridiagonal form then iterates to produce a diagonal Schur form, resulting in an orthogonal (unitary) V and a real, diagonal D.

9.7.3. Generalized Eigenvalues

The generalized eigenvalue problem is defined in terms of two n-by-n matrices A and B: λ is an eigenvalue and $x \neq 0$ an eigenvector if $Ax = \lambda Bx$. The generalized eigenvalues are computed by e = eig(A,B), while [V,D] = eig(A,B) computes an n-by-n diagonal matrix D and an n-by-n matrix V of eigenvectors such that A*V = B*V*D. The theory of the generalized eigenproblem is more complicated than that of the standard eigenproblem, with the possibility of zero, finitely many or infinitely many eigenvalues and of eigenvalues that are infinitely large. When B is singular eig may return computed eigenvalues containing NaNs. To illustrate the computation of generalized eigenvalues:

```
>> A = gallery('triw',3), B = magic(3)
A =
        1      -1      -1
        0       1      -1
        0       0       1
B =
        8       1       6
        3       5       7
        4       9       2

>> [V,D] = eig(A,B); V, eivals = diag(D)'
V =
     -1.0000    -1.0000     0.3526
```

```
          0.4844     -0.4574     0.3867
          0.2199     -0.2516    -1.0000
eivals =
          0.2751      0.0292    -0.3459
```

When A is Hermitian and B is Hermitian positive definite (the Hermitian definite generalized eigenproblem) the eigenvalues are real and A and B are simultaneously diagonalizable. In this case eig returns real computed eigenvalues sorted in increasing order, with the eigenvectors normalized (up to roundoff) so that V'*B*V = eye(n); moreover, V'*A*V is diagonal. The method that eig uses (Cholesky factorization of B, followed by reduction to a standard eigenproblem and solution by the QR algorithm) can be numerically unstable when B is ill conditioned. You can force eig to ignore the structure and solve the problem in the same way as for general A and B by invoking it as eig(A,B,'qz'); the QZ algorithm (see below) is then used, which has guaranteed numerical stability but does not guarantee real computed eigenvalues. Example:

```
>> A = gallery('fiedler',3), B = gallery('moler',3)
A =
     0     1     2
     1     0     1
     2     1     0
B =
     1    -1    -1
    -1     2     0
    -1     0     3

>> format short g
>> [V,D] = eig(A,B); V, eivals = diag(D)'
V =
        0.55335        0.23393         2.3747
        0.15552       -0.57301         1.2835
       -0.36921        0.19163        0.90938
eivals =
       -0.75993       -0.30839         17.068

>> V'*A*V
ans =
       -0.75993 -2.1748e-016 -2.6845e-015
   -2.1982e-016      -0.30839  1.8584e-015
   -2.6665e-015  1.7522e-015         17.068

>> V'*B*V
ans =
              1 -8.4568e-018 -2.9295e-016
    2.1549e-018            1 -7.7954e-017
   -2.4248e-016 -7.7927e-017            1
```

The generalized Schur decomposition of a pair of matrices A and B has the form

$$QAZ = T, \quad QBZ = S,$$

where Q and Z are unitary and T and S are upper triangular. The generalized eigenvalues are the ratios T(i,i)/S(i,i) of the diagonal elements of T and S. The generalized real Schur decomposition of real A and B has the same form with Q and Z orthogonal and T and S upper quasi-triangular. These decompositions are computed by the qz function with the command [T,S,Q,Z,V] = qz(A,B), where the final output argument V is a matrix of generalized eigenvectors; the function is named after the QZ algorithm that it implements. By default the (possibly) complex form with upper triangular T and S is produced. For real matrices, qz(A,B,'real') produces the real form and qz(A,B,'complex') the default complex form.

Function polyeig solves the polynomial eigenvalue problem $(\lambda^p A_p + \lambda^{p-1} A_{p-1} + \cdots + \lambda A_1 + A_0)x = 0$, where the A_i are given square coefficient matrices. The generalized eigenproblem is obtained for $p = 1$, with $A_0 = I$ then giving the standard eigenproblem. The quadratic eigenproblem $(\lambda^2 A + \lambda B + C)x = 0$ corresponds to $p = 2$. If A_p is n-by-n and nonsingular then there are pn eigenvalues. MATLAB's syntax is e = polyeig(A0,A1,..,Ap) or [X,e] = polyeig(A0,A1,..,Ap), with e a pn-vector of eigenvalues and X an n-by-pn matrix whose columns are the corresponding eigenvectors. Example:

```
>> A = eye(2); B = [20 -10; -10 20]; C = [15 -5; -5 15];

>> [X,e] = polyeig(C,B,A)
X =
    -0.7071    -0.7071     0.7071     0.7071
     0.7071     0.7071     0.7071     0.7071
e =
   -29.3178
    -0.6822
    -1.1270
    -8.8730
```

9.8. Iterative Linear Equation and Eigenproblem Solvers

In this section we describe functions that are based on iterative methods and primarily intended for large, possibly sparse problems, for which solution by one of the methods described earlier in the chapter could be prohibitively expensive. Sparse matrices are discussed further in Chapter 15.

Several functions implement iterative methods for solving square linear systems $Ax = b$; see Table 9.1. All apply to general A except minres and symmlq, which require A to be Hermitian, and pcg, which requires A to be Hermitian positive definite. All the methods employ matrix–vector products Ax and possibly A^*x and do not require explicit access to the elements of A. The functions have identical calling sequences, apart from gmres (see below). The simplest usage is x = solver(A,b) (where solver is one of the functions in Table 9.1). Alternatively, x = solver(A,b,tol) specifies a convergence tolerance tol, which defaults to 1e-6. Convergence is declared when an iterate x satisfies norm(b-A*x) <= tol*norm(b). The argument A can be a full or sparse matrix, or the name of an operator afun such that afun(x) returns A*x and, in the case of bicg and qmr, such that afun(x,'transp') returns A'*x. This operator can be a function handle, a string expression or an inline object (see Section 10.1).

These iterative methods usually need preconditioning if they are to be efficient. All accept further arguments M_1 and M_2 or $M = M_1 M_2$ and effectively solve the preconditioned system

$$M_1^{-1}AM_2^{-1} \cdot M_2 x = M_1^{-1}b \quad \text{or} \quad M^{-1}Ax = M^{-1}b.$$

The aim is to choose M_1 and M_2 so that $M_1^{-1}AM_2^{-1}$ or $M^{-1}A$ is in some sense close to the identity matrix. Choosing a good preconditioner is a difficult task and usually requires knowledge of the application from which the linear system came. The functions luinc and cholinc compute incomplete factorizations that provide one way of constructing preconditioners; see doc luinc, doc cholinc and doc bicg. For background on iterative linear equation solvers and preconditioning see [7], [22], [38].

To illustrate the usage of the iterative solvers we give an example involving pcg, which implements the preconditioned conjugate gradient method. For A we take a symmetric positive definite finite element matrix called the Wathen matrix, which has a fixed sparsity pattern and random entries.

```
>> A = gallery('wathen',12,12); n = length(A)
n =
    481
>> b = ones(n,1);

>> x = pcg(A,b);
pcg stopped at iteration 20 without converging to the desired
tolerance 1e-006 because the maximum number of iterations was
reached.
The iterate returned (number 20) has relative residual 0.063

>> x = pcg(A,b,1e-6,100);
pcg converged at iteration 86 to a solution with relative residual
8.8e-007
```

The bare minimum of arguments to pcg is the matrix and the right-hand side. The conjugate gradient method did not converge to the default tolerance (10^{-6}) within the default of 20 iterations, so we tried again with the same tolerance and a new limit of 100 iterations; convergence was then achieved. For this matrix it can be shown that M = diag(diag(A)) is a good preconditioner. Supplying this preconditioner as a fifth argument leads to a useful reduction in the number of iterations:

```
>> [x,flag,relres,iter] = pcg(A,b,1e-6,100,diag(diag(A)));
>> flag, relres, iter
flag =
     0
relres =
   9.0568e-007
iter =
    28
```

Notice that when more than one output argument is requested the messages are suppressed. A zero value of flag denotes convergence with relative residual relres = norm(b-A*x)/norm(b) after iter iterations.

All the other functions in Table 9.1 have the same calling sequence as pcg with the exception of gmres, which has an extra argument restart in the third position that specifies at which iteration to restart the method.

Table 9.1. *Iterative linear equation solvers.*

Function	Matrix type	Method
bicg	General	BiConjugate gradient method
bicgstab	General	BiConjugate gradient stabilized method
cgs	General	Conjugate gradient squared method
gmres	General	Generalized minimum residual method
minres	Hermitian	Minimum residual method
lsqr	General	Conjugate gradients on normal equations
pcg	Hermitian pos. def.	Preconditioned conjugate gradient method
qmr	General	Quasi-minimal residual method
symmlq	Hermitian	Symmetric LQ method

Function eigs computes a few selected eigenvalues and eigenvectors for the standard eigenvalue problem or for the symmetric definite generalized eigenvalue problem $Ax = \lambda Bx$ with B real and symmetric positive definite. This is in contrast to eig, which always computes the full eigensystem. Like the iterative linear equation solvers, eigs needs just the ability to form matrix–vector products, so A can be given either as an explicit matrix or as a function that performs matrix–vector products. In its simplest form, eigs can be called in the same way as eig, with [V,D] = eigs(A), when it computes the six eigenvalues of largest magnitude and the corresponding eigenvectors. See doc eigs and doc arpack for more details and examples of usage. This function is an interface to the ARPACK package [49]. As an example, we form a sparse symmetric matrix and compute its five algebraically largest eigenvalues using eigs. For comparison, we also apply eig, which requires that the matrix first be converted to a full matrix and always computes all the eigenvalues:

```
>> A = delsq(numgrid('N',40));
>> n = length(A)
n =
        1444

>> nnz(A)/n^2 % Percentage of nonzeros
ans =
    0.0034

>> tic, e_all = eig(full(A))'; toc
elapsed_time =
    28.9400
>> e_all(n:-1:n-4)
ans =
    7.9870    7.9676    7.9676    7.9482    7.9354

>> options.disp = 0; % Turn off intermediate output.
>> tic, e_big = eigs(A,5,'LA',options)'; toc % LA = largest algebraic
elapsed_time =
    3.2400
>> e_big
```

```
e_big =
    7.9870     7.9676     7.9676     7.9482     7.9354
```

The `tic` and `toc` functions provide an easy way of timing (in seconds) the code that they surround. Clearly, `eigs` is much faster than `eig` in this example, and it also uses much less storage.

A corresponding function `svds` computes a few singular values and singular vectors of an m-by-n matrix A. It does so by applying `eigs` to the Hermitian matrix

$$\begin{bmatrix} 0_m & A \\ A^* & 0_n \end{bmatrix}.$$

9.9. Functions of a Matrix

As mentioned in Section 5.3, some of the elementary functions defined for arrays have counterparts defined in the matrix sense, implemented in functions whose names end in `m`. The three main examples are `expm`, `logm` and `sqrtm`. The exponential of a square matrix A can be defined by

$$e^A = I + A + \frac{A^2}{2!} + \frac{A^3}{3!} + \cdots$$

It is computed by `expm`. The logarithm of a matrix is an inverse to the exponential. A nonsingular matrix has infinitely many logarithms. Function `logm` computes the principal logarithm, which, for a matrix with no nonpositive real eigenvalues, is the logarithm whose eigenvalues have imaginary parts lying strictly between $-\pi$ and π.

A square root of a square matrix A is a matrix X for which $X^2 = A$. Every nonsingular matrix has at least two square roots. Function `sqrtm` computes the principal square root, which, for a matrix with no nonpositive real eigenvalues, is the square root with eigenvalues having positive real part.

Other matrix functions can be computed as `funm(A,'fun')`, where `fun` is a function that evaluates the required function in the array sense. Note, however, that `funm` uses an algorithm that can be unstable; see `help funm` for how to detect instability.

We give some examples. The matrix

```
A =
    17     8     1     0
     8    18     8     1
     1     8    18     8
     0     1     8    17
```

has a tridiagonal square root:

```
>> sqrtm(A)
ans =
    4.0000    1.0000   -0.0000    0.0000
    1.0000    4.0000    1.0000   -0.0000
   -0.0000    1.0000    4.0000    1.0000
    0.0000   -0.0000    1.0000    4.0000
```

The Jordan block

```
>> A = gallery('jordbloc',4,1)
A =
     1     1     0     0
     0     1     1     0
     0     0     1     1
     0     0     0     1
```

has exponential

```
>> X = expm(A)
X =
     2.7183     2.7183     1.3591     0.4530
          0     2.7183     2.7183     1.3591
          0          0     2.7183     2.7183
          0          0          0     2.7183
```

and we can recover the original matrix using logm:

```
>> real(logm(X))
ans =
     1.0000     1.0000     0.0000     0.0000
    -0.0000     1.0000     1.0000    -0.0000
    -0.0000     0.0000     1.0000     1.0000
     0.0000     0.0000    -0.0000     1.0000
```

Note that we have used **real** to suppress tiny imaginary parts which are introduced by rounding errors in this example.

> Nichols: "Transparent aluminum?"
> Scott: "That's the ticket, laddie."
> Nichols: "It'd take years just to figure out the dynamics of this matrix."
> McCoy: "Yes, but you would be rich beyond the dreams of avarice!"
>
> — *Star Trek IV: The Voyage Home* (Stardate 8390)

> We share a philosophy about linear algebra:
> we think basis-free,
> we write basis-free,
> but when the chips are down we close the office door and
> compute with matrices like fury.
>
> — IRVING KAPLANSKY, *Reminiscences [of Paul Halmos]* (1991)

> The matrix of that equation system is negative definite—which is a
> positive definite system that has been multiplied through by -1.
> For all practical geometries the common finite difference
> Laplacian operator gives rise to these,
> the best of all possible matrices.
> Just about any standard solution method will succeed,
> and many theorems are available for your pleasure.
>
> — FORMAN S. ACTON, *Numerical Methods That Work* (1970)

Chapter 10
More on Functions

10.1. Passing a Function as an Argument

Common to many problems tackled with MATLAB is the need to pass a function as an argument to another function. This can be done in several ways, depending on how the function being called has been written. We illustrate using `ezplot`, which plots a function $f(x)$ over a default range of $[-2\pi, 2\pi]$. First, the function can be passed via a function handle. A function handle is a MATLAB datatype that contains all the information necessary to evaluate a function. A function handle can be created by putting the @ character before the function name. Thus if `fun` is a function M-file of the form required by `ezplot` then we can write

```
ezplot(@fun)
```

As well as being an M-file, `fun` can be the name of a built-in function:

```
ezplot(@sin)
```

The name of a function can also be passed as a string:

```
ezplot('exp')
```

Function handles are new to MATLAB 6 and are preferred to the use of strings, as they are more efficient and more versatile. However, you may occasionally come across a function that accepts a function argument in the form of a string but will not accept a function handle. You can convert between function handles and strings using `func2str` and `str2func`. For help on function handles type `help function_handle`.

There are two further ways to pass a function to `ezplot`: as a string expression,

```
ezplot('x^2-1'), ezplot('1/(1+x^2)')
```

or as an inline object,

```
ezplot(inline('exp(x)-1'))
```

An inline object is essentially a "one line" function defined by a string and it can be assigned to a variable and then evaluated:

```
>> f = inline('exp(x)-1'), f(2)
f =
     Inline function:
     f(x) = exp(x)-1
ans =
    6.3891
```

MATLAB automatically determines and orders the arguments to an inline function. If its choice is not suitable then the arguments can be explicitly defined and ordered via extra arguments to inline:

```
>> f = inline('log(a*x)/(1+y^2)')
f =
     Inline function:
     f(a,x,y) = log(a*x)/(1+y^2)

>> f = inline('log(a*x)/(1+y^2)','x','y','a')
f =
     Inline function:
     f(x,y,a) = log(a*x)/(1+y^2)
```

The key to writing a function that accepts another function as an argument is to use feval to evaluate the passed function. The syntax is feval(fun,x1,x2,...,xn), where fun is the function and x1, x2, ..., xn are its arguments. Consider the function fd_deriv in Listing 10.1. This function evaluates the finite difference approximation

$$f'(x) \approx \frac{f(x+h) - f(x)}{h}$$

to the function passed as its first argument. When we type

```
>> fd_deriv(@sqrt,0.1)
ans =
     1.5811
```

the first feval call in fd_deriv is equivalent to sqrt(x+h). We can use our Newton square root function sqrtn (Listing 7.5) instead of the built-in square root:

```
>> fd_deriv(@sqrtn,0.1)
  k                x_k                   rel. change
  1:  5.5000000745058064e-001   8.18e-001
% Remaining output from sqrtn omitted.
ans =
     1.5811
```

We can pass an inline object to fd_deriv, but a string expression does not work:

```
>> f = inline('exp(-x)/(1+x^2)');
>> fd_deriv(f,pi)
ans =
    -0.0063

>> fd_deriv('exp(-x)/(1+x^2)',pi)
??? Cannot find function 'exp(-x)/(1+x^2)'.
Error in ==> FD_DERIV.M
On line 8  ==> y = (feval(f,x+h) - feval(f,x))/h;
```

To convert fd_deriv into a function that accepts a string expression we simply need to insert

```
f = fcnchk(f);
```

Listing 10.1. *Function* fd_deriv.

```
function y = fd_deriv(f,x,h)
%FD_DERIV   Finite difference approximation to derivative.
%           FD_DERIV(F,X,H) is a finite difference approximation
%           to the derivative of function F at X with difference
%           parameter H.  H defaults to SQRT(EPS).

if nargin < 3, h = sqrt(eps); end
y = (feval(f,x+h) - feval(f,x))/h;
```

at the top of the function (this is how ezplot does it).

It is sometimes necessary to "vectorize" an inline object or string expression, that is, to convert multiplication, exponentiation and division to array operations, so that vector and matrix arguments can be used. This can be done with the vectorize function:

```
>> f = inline('log(a*x)/(1+y^2)');
>> f = vectorize(f)
f =
     Inline function:
     f(a,x,y) = log(a.*x)./(1+y.^2)
```

If fcnchk is given a final argument 'vectorized', as in fcnchk(f,'vectorized'), then it vectorizes the string f.

10.2. Subfunctions

A function M-file may contain other functions, called subfunctions, which appear in any order after the main (or primary) function. Subfunctions are visible only to the main function and to any other subfunctions. They typically carry out a task that needs to be separated from the main function but that is unlikely to be needed in other M-files, or they may override existing functions of the same names (since subfunctions take precedence). The use of subfunctions helps to avoid proliferation of M-files.

For an example of a subfunction see poly1err[4] in Listing 10.2, which approximates the maximum error in the linear interpolating polynomial to subfunction f on $[0,1]$ based on n sample points on the interval:

```
>> poly1err(5)
ans =
     0.0587

>> poly1err(50)
ans =
     0.0600
```

Alternative ways to code poly1err are to define f as an inline object rather than a subfunction, or to make f an input argument.

---

[4]This function is readily vectorized; see Section 20.1.

Listing 10.2. *Function* `poly1err`.

```
function max_err = poly1err(n)
%POLY1ERR    Error in linear interpolating polynomial.
%            POLY1ERR(N) is an approximation based on N sample points
%            to the maximum difference between subfunction F and its
%            linear interpolating polynomial at 0 and 1.

max_err = 0;
f0 = f(0); f1 = f(1);
for x = linspace(0,1,n)
    p = x*f1 + (x-1)*f0;
    err = abs(f(x)-p);
    max_err = max(max_err,err);
end

% Subfunction.
function y = f(x)
%F       Function to be interpolated, F(X).
y = sin(x);
```

Help for a subfunction is displayed by specifying the main function name followed by "/" and the subfunction name. Thus help for subfunction `f` of `poly1err` is listed by

```
>> help poly1err/f
```

```
F       Function to be interpolated, F(X).
```

A subfunction can be passed to another function as a function handle. Thus, for example, in the main body of `poly1err` we can write `ezplot(@f)` in order to plot the subfunction `f`.

For less trivial examples of subfunctions see Listings 12.2–12.6.

10.3. Variable Numbers of Arguments

In certain situations a function must accept or return a variable, possibly unlimited, number of input or output arguments. This can be achieved using the `varargin` and `varargout` functions. Suppose we wish to write a function `companb` to form the mn-by-mn block companion matrix corresponding to the n-by-n matrices A_1, A_2, ..., A_m:

$$C = \begin{bmatrix} -A_1 & -A_2 & \cdots & \cdots & -A_m \\ I & 0 & & & 0 \\ & I & \ddots & & \vdots \\ & & \ddots & 0 & \vdots \\ & & & I & 0 \end{bmatrix}.$$

We could use a standard function definition such as

```
function C = companb(A_1,A_2,A_3,A_4,A_5)
```

but m is then limited to 5 and handling the different values of m between 1 and 5 is tedious. The solution is to use varargin, as shown in Listing 10.3. When varargin is specified as the input argument list, the input arguments supplied are copied into a cell array called varargin. Cell arrays, described in Section 18.3, are a special kind of array in which each element can hold a different type and size of data. The elements of a cell array are accessed using curly braces. Consider the call

```
>> X = ones(2); C = companb(X, 2*X, 3*X)
C =
    -1    -1    -2    -2    -3    -3
    -1    -1    -2    -2    -3    -3
     1     0     0     0     0     0
     0     1     0     0     0     0
     0     0     1     0     0     0
     0     0     0     1     0     0
```

If we insert the line

```
varargin
```

at the beginning of companb then the above call produces

```
varargin =
    [2x2 double]    [2x2 double]    [2x2 double]
```

Thus varargin is a 1-by-3 cell array whose elements are the 2-by-2 matrices passed as arguments to companb, and varargin{j} is the jth input matrix, A_j.

It is not necessary for varargin to be the only input argument but it must be the last one, appearing after any named input arguments.

An example using the analogous statement varargout for output arguments is shown in Listing 10.4. Here we use nargout to determine how many output arguments have been requested and then create a varargout cell array containing the required output. To illustrate:

```
>> m1 = moments(1:4)
m1 =
    2.5000

>> [m1,m2,m3] = moments(1:4)
m1 =
    2.5000
m2 =
    7.5000
m3 =
    25
```

10.4. Global Variables

Variables within a function are local to that function's workspace. Occasionally it is convenient to create variables that exist in more than one workspace including, possibly, the main workspace. This can be done using the global statement. As an example, suppose we wish to study plots of the function $f(x) = 1/(a + (x - b)^2)$ on $[0, 1]$ for various a and b. We can define a function

Listing 10.3. *Function* companb.

```
function C = companb(varargin)
%COMPANB     Block companion matrix.
%            C = COMPANB(A_1,A_2,...,A_m) is the block companion matrix
%            corresponding to the n-by-n matrices A_1,A_2,...,A_m.

m = nargin;
n = length(varargin{1});

C = diag(ones(n*(m-1),1),-n);
for j = 1:m
    Aj = varargin{j};
    C(1:n,(j-1)*n+1:j*n) = -Aj;
end
```

Listing 10.4. *Function* moments.

```
function varargout = moments(x)
%MOMENTS  Moments of a vector.
%         [m1,m2,...,m_k] = MOMENTS(X) returns the first, second, ...,
%         k'th moments of the vector X, where the j'th moment
%         is SUM(X.^j)/LENGTH(X).

for j=1:nargout, varargout(j) = {sum(x.^j)/length(x)}; end
```

```
function f = myfun(x)
global A B
f = 1/(A + (x-B)^2);
```

At the command line we type

```
>> global A B
>> A = 0.01; B = 0.5;
>> fplot(@myfun,[0 1])
```

The values of A and B set at the command line are available within myfun. New values for A and B can be assigned and fplot called again without editing myfun.m. Note that it is possible to avoid the use of global in this example by passing the parameters a and b through the argument list of fplot, as in the example on p. 87. For a good use of global look at the timing functions tic and toc (type them).

Within a function, the global declaration should appear before the first occurrence of the relevant variables, ideally at the top of the file. By convention the names of global variables are comprised of capital letters, and ideally the names are long in order to reduce the chance of clashes with other variables.

10.5. Recursive Functions

Functions can be recursive, that is, they can call themselves, as we have seen with function gasket in Listing 1.7 and function land in Listing 8.1. Recursion is a powerful tool, but not all computations that are described recursively are best programmed this way.

The function koch in Listing 10.5 uses recursion to draw a Koch curve [64, Sec. 2.4]. The basic construction in koch is to replace a line by four shorter lines. The upper left-hand picture in Figure 10.1 shows the four lines that result from applying this construction to a horizontal line. The upper right-hand picture then shows what happens when each of these four lines is processed. The lower left- and right-hand pictures show the next two levels of recursion.

We see that koch has three input arguments. The first two, pl and pr, give the (x, y) coordinates of the current line and the third, level, indicates the level of recursion required. If level $= 0$ then a line is drawn; otherwise koch calls itself four times with level one less and with endpoints that define the four shorter lines.

Figure 10.1 was produced by the following code:

```
pl = [0;0]; % Left endpoint
pr = [1;0]; % Right endpoint

for k = 1:4
    subplot(2,2,k)
    koch(pl,pr,k)
    axis('equal')
    title(['Koch curve: level = ' num2str(k)],'FontSize',16)
end
hold off
```

Listing 10.5. *Function* koch.

```
function koch(pl,pr,level)
%KOCH    Recursively generated Koch curve.
%        KOCH(PL, PR, LEVEL) recursively generates a Koch curve,
%        where PL and PR are the current left and right endpoints and
%        LEVEL is the level of recursion.

if level == 0
  plot([pl(1),pr(1)],[pl(2),pr(2)]); % Join pl and pr.
  hold on
else
  A = (sqrt(3)/6)*[0 1; -1 0];        % Rotate/scale matrix.

  pmidl = (2*pl + pr)/3;
  koch(pl,pmidl,level-1)             % Left branch.

  ptop = (pl + pr)/2 + A*(pl-pr);
  koch(pmidl,ptop,level-1)           % Left mid branch.

  pmidr = (pl + 2*pr)/3;
  koch(ptop,pmidr,level-1)           % Right mid branch.

  koch(pmidr,pr,level-1)             % Right branch.

end
```

To produce Figure 10.2 we called koch with pairs of endpoints equally spaced around the unit circle, so that each edge of the snowflake is a copy of the same Koch curve. The relevant code is

```
level = 4; edges = 7;

for k = 1:edges
    pl = [cos(2*k*pi/edges); sin(2*k*pi/edges)];
    pr = [cos(2*(k+1)*pi/edges); sin(2*(k+1)*pi/edges)];
    koch(pl,pr,level)
end
axis('equal')
title('Koch snowflake','FontSize',16,'FontAngle','italic')
hold off
```

For another example of recursion, look at the functions quad and quadl described in Section 12.1.

10.6. Exemplary Functions in MATLAB

Perhaps the best way to learn how to write functions is by studying well-written examples. An excellent source of examples is MATLAB itself, since all functions that

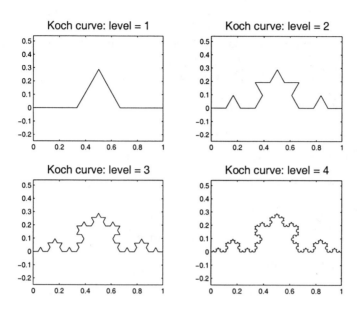

Figure 10.1. *Koch curves created with function* koch.

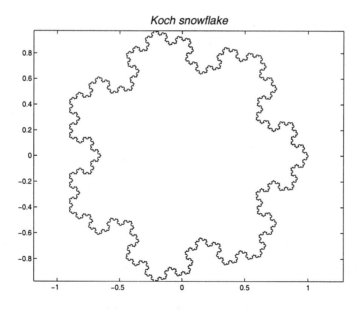

Figure 10.2. *Koch snowflake created with function* koch.

are not built into the interpreter are M-files that can be examined. We list below some M-files that illustrate particular aspects of MATLAB programming. The source can be viewed with `type function_name`, by loading the file into the Editor/Debugger with `edit function_name` (the editor searches the path for the function, so the pathname need not be given), or by loading the file into your favorite editor (in which case you will need to know the path, which we indicate).

- datafun/cov: use of `varargin`.

- datafun/var: argument checking.

- elmat/hadamard: matrix building.

- elmat/why: `switch` construct, subfunctions.

- funfun/fminbnd: argument checking, loop constructs.

- funfun/quad, funfun/quadl: recursive functions.

- matfun/gsvd: subfunctions.

- sparfun/pcg: sophisticated argument handling and error checking.

Use recursive procedures for recursively-defined data structures.
— BRIAN W. KERNIGHAN and P. J. PLAUGER,
The Elements of Programming Style (1978)

Great fleas have little fleas upon their backs to bite 'em,
And little fleas have lesser fleas and so ad infinitum.
And the great fleas themselves, in turn, have greater fleas to go on;
While these again have greater still, and greater still, and so on.
— AUGUSTUS DEMORGAN

Chapter 11
Numerical Methods: Part I

This chapter describes MATLAB's functions for solving problems involving polynomials, nonlinear equations, optimization and the fast Fourier transform. In many cases a function fun must be passed as an argument. As described in Section 10.1, fun can be a function handle, a string expression or an inline object. The MATLAB functions described in this chapter place various demands on the function that is to be passed, but most require it to return a vector of values when given a vector of inputs.

For mathematical background on the methods described in this and the next chapter suitable textbooks are [5], [6], [11], [18], [35], [61], [70], [81].

11.1. Polynomials and Data Fitting

MATLAB represents a polynomial

$$p(x) = p_1 x^n + p_2 x^{n-1} + \cdots + p_n x + p_{n+1}$$

by a row vector p = [p(1) p(2) ... p(n+1)] of the coefficients. (Note that compared with the representation $\sum_{i=0}^{n} p_i x^i$ used in many textbooks, MATLAB's vector is reversed and its subscripts are increased by 1.)

Here are three problems related to polynomials:

Evaluation: Given the coefficients evaluate the polynomial at one or more points.

Root finding: Given the coefficients find the roots (the points at which the polynomial evaluates to zero).

Data fitting: Given a set of data $\{x_i, y_i\}_{i=1}^{m}$, find a polynomial that "fits" the data.

The standard technique for evaluating $p(x)$ is Horner's method, which corresponds to the nested representation

$$p(x) = \Big(\ldots \Big((p_1 x + p_2) x + p_3 \Big) x + \cdots + p_n \Big) x + p_{n+1}.$$

Function polyval carries out Horner's method: y = polyval(p,x). In this command x can be a matrix, in which case the polynomial is evaluated at each element of the matrix (that is, in the array sense). Evaluation of the polynomial p in the matrix (as opposed to array) sense is defined for a square matrix argument X by

$$p(X) = p_1 X^n + p_2 X^{n-1} + \cdots + p_n X + p_{n+1} I.$$

The command Y = polyvalm(p,X) carries out this evaluation.

The roots (or zeros) of p are obtained with z = roots(p). Of course, some of the roots may be complex even if p is a real polynomial. The function poly carries out the converse operation: given a set of roots it constructs a polynomial. Thus if z is an n-vector then p = poly(z) gives the coefficients of the polynomial

$$p_1 x^n + p_2 x^{n-1} + \cdots + p_n x + p_{n+1} = (x - z_1)(x - z_2) \ldots (x - z_n).$$

(The normalization $p_1 = 1$ is always used.) The function poly also accepts a matrix argument: as explained in Section 9.7, for a square matrix A, p = poly(A) returns the coefficients of the characteristic polynomial $\det(xI - A)$.

Function polyder computes the coefficients of the derivative of a polynomial, but it does not evaluate the polynomial.

As an example, consider the quadratic $p(x) = x^2 - x - 1$. First, we find the roots:

```
>> p = [1 -1 -1]; z = roots(p)
z =
    1.6180
   -0.6180
```

The next command verifies that these are roots, up to roundoff:

```
>> polyval(p,z)
ans =
  1.0e-015 *
   -0.1110
    0.2220
```

Next, we observe that a certain 2-by-2 matrix has p as its characteristic polynomial:

```
>> A = [0 1; 1 1]; cp = poly(A)
cp =
    1.0000   -1.0000   -1.0000
```

The Cayley–Hamilton theorem says that every matrix satisfies its own characteristic polynomial. This is confirmed, modulo roundoff, for our matrix:

```
>> polyvalm(cp, A)
ans =
  1.0e-015 *
    0.1110         0
         0    0.1110
```

Polynomials can be multiplied and divided using conv and deconv, respectively. When a polynomial g is divided by a polynomial h there is a quotient q and a remainder r: $g(x) = h(x)q(x) + r(x)$, where the degree of r is less than that of h. The syntax for deconv is [q,r] = deconv(g,h). In the following example we divide $x^3 - 6x^2 + 12x - 8$ by $x - 2$, obtaining quotient $x^2 - 4x + 4$ and zero remainder. Then we reproduce the original polynomial using conv.

```
>> g = [1 -6 12 -8]; h = [1 -2];

>> [q,r] = deconv(g,h)
q =
```

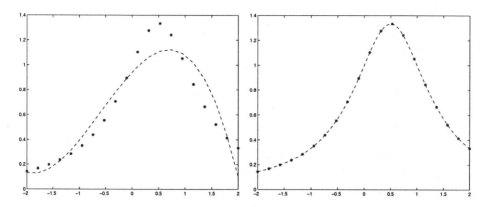

Figure 11.1. *Left: least squares polynomial fit of degree 3. Right: cubic spline. Data is from* $1/(x + (1 - x)^2)$.

```
        1     -4      4
r =
        0      0      0      0

>> conv(h,q)
ans =
        1     -6     12     -8
```

The data fitting problem can be addressed with `polyfit`. Suppose the data $\{x_i, y_i\}_{i=1}^m$ has distinct x_i values, and we wish to find a polynomial p of degree at most n such that $p(x_i) \approx y_i$, $i = 1{:}m$. The `polyfit` function computes the least squares polynomial fit, that is, it determines p so that $\sum_{i=1}^m (p(x_i) - y_i)^2$ is minimized. The syntax is p = `polyfit(x,y,n)`. Specifying the degree n so that $n \geq m$ produces an interpolating polynomial, that is, $p(x_i) = y_i$, $i = 1{:}m$, so the polynomial fits the data exactly. However, high-degree polynomials can be extremely oscillatory, so small values of n are generally preferred. The following example computes and plots a least squares polynomial fit of degree 3. The data comprises the function $1/(x+(1-x)^2)$ evaluated at 20 equally spaced points on the interval $[-2, 2]$, generated by `linspace`. The resulting plot is on the left-hand side of Figure 11.1.

```
x = linspace(-2,2,20);
y = 1./(x+(1-x).^2);
p = polyfit(x,y,3);
plot(x,y,'*',x,polyval(p,x),'--')
```

The `spline` function can be used if exact data interpolation is required. It fits a cubic spline, $sp(x)$, to the data: $sp(x)$ is a cubic polynomial between successive x points and $sp(x_i) = y_i$, $i = 1{:}m$. Given data vectors x and y, the command yy = `spline(x,y,xx)` returns in the vector yy the value of the spline at the points given by xx. In the next example we use this approach to fit a spline to the data used for the polynomial example above. The resulting curve is on the right-hand side of Figure 11.1.

```
x = linspace(-2,2,20);
```

```
y = 1./(x+(1-x).^2);
xx = linspace(-2,2,60);
yy = spline(x,y,xx);
plot(x,y,'*',xx,yy,'--')
```

It is also possible to work with the coefficients of the spline curve. The command pp = spline(x,y) stores the coefficients in a structure (see Section 18.3) that is interpreted by the ppval function, so plot(x,y,'*',xx,ppval(pp,xx),'--') would then produce the same plot as in the example above. Low-level manipulation of splines is possible with the functions mkpp and unmkpp.

MATLAB has functions for interpolation in one, two and more dimensions. Function interp1 accepts x(i),y(i) data pairs and a further vector xi. It fits an interpolant to the data and then returns the values of the interpolant at the points in xi:

```
yi = interp1(x,y,xi)
```

The vector x must have monotonically increasing elements. Four types of interpolant are supported, as specified by a fourth input parameter, which is one of

'nearest'	nearest neighbor interpolation
'linear'	linear interpolation (default)
'spline'	cubic spline interpolation
'cubic'	cubic interpolation

Linear interpolation puts a line between adjacent data pairs, while nearest neighbor interpolation reproduces the y-value of the nearest x point. The following example illustrates interp1.

```
x = [0 pi/4 3*pi/8 3*pi/4 pi]; y = sin(x);
xi = linspace(0,pi,40)';
ys = interp1(x,y,xi,'spline');
yn = interp1(x,y,xi,'nearest');
yl = interp1(x,y,xi,'linear');
xx = linspace(0,pi,50);
plot(xx,sin(xx),'-',x,y,'.','MarkerSize',20), hold on
set(gca,'XTick',x), set(gca,'XTickLabel','0|pi/4|3pi/8|3pi/4|pi')
set(gca,'XGrid','on')
h = plot(xi,ys,'x', xi,yn,'o', xi,yl,'+');
axis([-0.25 3.5 -0.1 1.1])
legend(h,'spline','nearest','linear'), hold off
```

This code samples 5 points from a sine curve on $[0, \pi]$, computes interpolants using three of the methods (cubic is omitted, as the results are the same to visual accuracy as for spline), and evaluates the interpolants at 40 points on the interval. In Figure 11.2 the solid circles plot the x(i),y(i) data pairs and the symbols plot the interpolants. The graphics commands are discussed in Chapters 8 and 17.

MATLAB has two functions for two-dimensional interpolation: griddata and interp2. The syntax for griddata is

```
ZI = griddata(x,y,z,XI,YI)
```

Here, the vectors x, y and z are the data and ZI is a matrix of interpolated values corresponding to the matrices XI and YI, which are usually produced using meshgrid. A sixth string argument specifies the method:

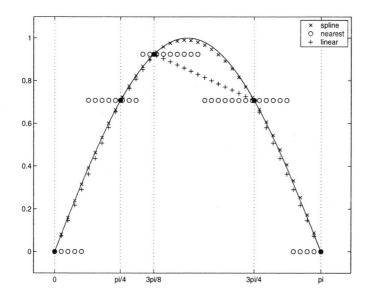

Figure 11.2. *Interpolating a sine curve using* `interp1`.

`'linear'`	Triangle-based linear interpolation (default)
`'cubic'`	Triangle-based cubic interpolation
`'nearest'`	Nearest neighbor interpolation

Function `interp2` has a similar argument list, but it requires x and y to be monotonic matrices in the form produced by `meshgrid`. Here is an example in which we use `griddata` to interpolate values on a surface.

```
x = rand(100,1)*4-2; y = rand(100,1)*4-2;
z = x.*exp(-x.^2-y.^2);
hi = -2:.1:2;
[XI,YI] = meshgrid(hi);
ZI = griddata(x,y,z,XI,YI);
mesh(XI,YI,ZI), hold
plot3(x,y,z,'o'), hold off
```

The result is shown in Figure 11.3, which plots the original data points as circles and the interpolated surface as a mesh.

Other interpolation functions include `interp3` and `interpn` for three- and n-dimensional interpolation, respectively.

11.2. Nonlinear Equations and Optimization

MATLAB has routines for finding a zero of a function of one variable (`fzero`) and for minimizing a function of one variable (`fminbnd`) or of n variables (`fminsearch`). In all cases the function must be real-valued and have real arguments. Unfortunately, there is no provision for directly solving a system of n nonlinear equations in n unknowns.[5]

---

[5]However, an attempt at solving such a system could be made by minimizing the sum of squares of the residual. The Optimization Toolbox contains a nonlinear equation solver.

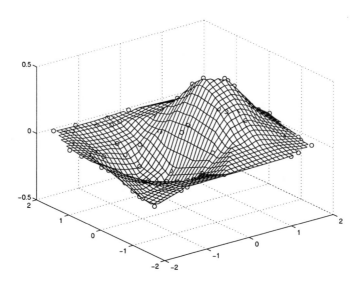

Figure 11.3. *Interpolation with* griddata.

The simplest invocation of fzero is x = fzero(fun,x0), with x0 a scalar, which attempts to find a zero of fun near x0. For example,

```
>> fzero('cos(x)-x',0)
Zero found in the interval: [-0.9051, 0.9051].
ans =
    0.7391
```

More precisely, fzero looks for a point where fun changes sign, and will not find zeros of even multiplicity. An initial search is carried out starting from x0 to find an interval on which fun changes sign. The function fun must return a real scalar when passed a real scalar argument. Failure of fzero is signalled by the return of a NaN.

If instead of being a scalar x0 is a 2-vector such that fun(x0(1)) and fun(x0(2)) have opposite sign, then fzero works on the interval defined by x0. Providing a starting interval in this way can be important when the function has a singularity. Consider the example

```
>> [x, fval] = fzero('x-tan(x)',1)
Zero found in the interval: [0.36, 1.64].
x =
    1.5708
fval =
    1.2093e+015
```

The second output argument is the function value at x, the purported zero. Clearly, in this example x is not a zero but an approximation to the point $\pi/2$ at which the function has a singularity; see Figure 11.4. To force fzero to keep away from singularities we can give it a starting interval that encloses a zero but not a singularity:

```
>> [x, fval] = fzero('x-tan(x)',[-1 1])
Zero found in the interval: [-1, 1].
```

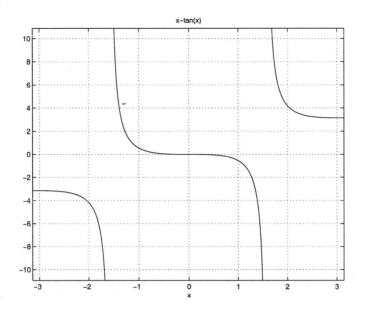

Figure 11.4. *Plot produced by* `ezplot('x-tan(x)',[-pi,pi])`, `grid`.

```
x =
     0
fval =
     0
```

The convergence tolerance and the display of output in `fzero` are controlled by a third argument, the structure `options`, which is best defined using the `optimset` function. (A structure is one of MATLAB's data types; see Section 18.3.) Only two of the fields of the `options` structure are used: `Display` specifies the level of reporting, with values `off` for no output, `iter` for output at each iteration, and `final` for just the final output; and `TolX` is a convergence tolerance. Example uses are

```
fzero(fun,x0,optimset('Display','iter'))
fzero(fun,x0,optimset('TolX',1e-4))
```

The default corresponds to `optimset('display','final','TolX',eps)`. (Note that the field names passed to `optimset` can be any combination of upper and lower case.) Arguments p1, p2, ... in addition to x can be passed to `fun` using the syntax

```
x = fzero(fun,x0,options,p1,p2,...)
```

If p1, p2, ... are being passed and the default `options` structure is required, the empty matrix [] can be specified in the `options` position. Functions `fminbnd` and `fminsearch` described below allow extra arguments to be passed in the same way.

The algorithm used by `fzero`, a combination of the bisection method, the secant method, and inverse quadratic interpolation, is described in [18, Chap. 7].

The command `x = fminbnd(fun,x1,x2)` attempts to find a local minimizer x of the function of one variable specified by `fun` over the interval [x1, x2]. A point x is a local minimizer of f if it minimizes f in an interval around x. In general, a function can have many local minimizers. MATLAB does not provide a function for the difficult problem of computing a global minimizer (one that minimizes $f(x)$ over all x). Example:

```
>> [x,fval] = fminbnd('sin(x)-cos(x)',-pi,pi)
Optimization terminated successfully:
 the current x satisfies the termination criteria using
 OPTIONS.TolX of 1.000000e-004
x =
   -0.7854
fval =
   -1.4142
```

As for `fzero`, options can be specified using a structure `options` set via the `optimset` function. In addition to the fields used by `fzero`, `fminbnd` uses `MaxFunEvals` (the maximum number of function evaluations allowed) and `MaxIter` (the maximum number of iterations allowed). The defaults correspond to

```
optimset('Display','final','MaxFunEvals',500,'MaxIter',500,...
        'TolX',1e-4)
```

The algorithm used by `fminbnd`, a combination of golden section search and parabolic interpolation, is described in [18, Chap. 8].

If you wish to maximize a function f rather than minimize it you can minimize $-f$, since $\max_x f(x) = -\min_x(-f(x))$.

Function `fminsearch` searches for a local minimum of a real function of n real variables. The syntax is similar to `fminbnd` except that a starting vector rather than an interval is supplied: `x = fminsearch(fun,x0,options)`. The fields in `options` are those supported by `fminbnd` plus `TolFun`, a termination tolerance on the function value. Both `TolX` and `TolFun` default to `1e-4`. To illustrate the use of `fminsearch` we consider the quadratic function

$$F(x) = x_1^2 + x_2^2 - x_1 x_2,$$

which has a minimum at $x = [0\ 0]^T$. Given the function

```
function f = fquad(x)
f = x(1)^2 + x(2)^2 - x(1)*x(2);
```

we can type

```
>> [x,fval] = fminsearch(@fquad,ones(2,1))
Optimization terminated successfully:
 the current x satisfies the termination criteria using
 OPTIONS.TolX of 1.000000e-04
 and F(X) satisfies the convergence criteria using
 OPTIONS.TolFun of 1.000000e-04
x =
   1.0e-04 *
   -0.4582
   -0.4717
fval =
   2.1635e-09
```

Alternatively, we can define F in the argument list:

```
[x,fval] = fminsearch('x(1)^2+x(2)^2-x(1)*x(2)',ones(2,1))
```

Function `fminsearch` is based on the Nelder–Mead simplex algorithm [67, Sec. 10.4], a direct search method that uses function values but not derivatives. The method can be very slow to converge, or may fail to converge to a local minimum. However, it has the advantage of being insensitive to discontinuities in the function. More sophisticated minimization functions can be found in the Optimization Toolbox.

11.3. The Fast Fourier Transform

The discrete Fourier transform of an n-vector x is the vector $y = F_n x$ where F_n is an n-by-n unitary matrix made up of roots of unity and illustrated by

$$F_4 = \begin{bmatrix} 1 & 1 & 1 & 1 \\ 1 & \omega & \omega^2 & \omega^3 \\ 1 & \omega^2 & \omega^4 & \omega^6 \\ 1 & \omega^3 & \omega^6 & \omega^9 \end{bmatrix}, \qquad \omega = e^{-2\pi i/4}.$$

The fast Fourier transform (FFT) is a more efficient way of forming y than the obvious matrix–vector multiplication. The `fft` function implements the FFT and is called as `y = fft(x)`. The efficiency of `fft` depends on the value of n; prime values are bad, highly composite numbers are better, and powers of 2 are best. A second argument can be given to `fft`: `y = fft(x,n)` causes x to be truncated or padded with zeros to make x of length n before the FFT algorithm is applied. The inverse FFT, $x = F_n^* y$, is carried out by the `ifft` function: `x = ifft(y)`. Example:

```
>> y = fft([1 1 -1 -1]')
y =
          0
    2.0000 - 2.0000i
          0
    2.0000 + 2.0000i

>> x = ifft(y)
x =
        1
        1
       -1
       -1
```

MATLAB also implements higher dimensional discrete Fourier transforms and their inverses: see functions `fft2`, `fftn`, `ifft2` and `ifftn`.

Life as we know it would be very different without the FFT.
— CHARLES F. VAN LOAN, *Computational Frameworks for the Fast Fourier Transform* (1992)

Do you ever want to kick the computer?
Does it iterate endlessly on your newest algorithm
that should have converged in three iterations?
And does it finally come to a crashing halt
with the insulting message that you divided by zero?
These minor trauma are, in fact,
the ways the computer manages to kick you and,
unfortunately, you almost always deserve it!
For it is a sad fact that most of us
can more easily compute than think—
which might have given rise to that famous definition,
"Research is when you don't know what you're doing."
— FORMAN S. ACTON, *Numerical Methods That Work* (1970)

Chapter 12
Numerical Methods: Part II

We now move on to MATLAB's capabilities for evaluating integrals and solving ordinary and partial differential equations.

Most of the functions discussed in this chapter support mixed absolute/relative error tests, with tolerances AbsTol and RelTol, respectively. This means that they test whether an estimate err of some measure of the error in the vector x is small enough by testing whether, for all i,

```
err(i) <= max(AbsTol,RelTol*abs(x(i)))
```

If AbsTol is zero this is a pure relative error test and if RelTol is zero it is a pure absolute error test. Since we cannot expect to obtain an answer with more correct significant digits than the 16 or so to which MATLAB works, RelTol should be no smaller than about eps; and since x = 0 is a possibility we should also take AbsTol > 0. A rough way of interpreting the mixed error test above is that err(i) is acceptably small if x(i) has as many correct digits as specified by RelTol or is smaller than AbsTol in absolute value. AbsTol can be a vector of absolute tolerances, in which case the test is

```
err(i) <= max(AbsTol(i),RelTol*abs(x(i)))
```

12.1. Quadrature

Quadrature is a synonym for numerical integration, the approximation of definite integrals $\int_a^b f(x)\,dx$. MATLAB has two main functions for quadrature, quad and quadl. Both require a and b to be finite and the integrand to have no singularities on $[a, b]$. For infinite integrals and integrals with singularities a variety of approaches can be used in order to produce an integral that can be handled by quad and quadl; these include change of variable, integration by parts, and analytic treatment of the integral over part of the range. See numerical analysis textbooks for details, for example, [5, Sec. 5.6], [11, Sec. 7.4.3], and [70, Sec. 5.4].

The basic usage is q = quad(fun,a,b,tol) (similarly, for quadl), where fun specifies the function to be integrated. The function fun must accept a vector argument and return a vector of function values. The argument tol is an absolute error tolerance, which defaults to a small multiple of eps times an estimate of the integral. Given the function

```
function f = fxlog(x)
f = x.*log(x);
```

we type

```
>> quad(@fxlog,2,4)
ans =
    6.7041
```

to obtain an approximation to $\int_2^4 x \log x \, dx$. Note the use of array multiplication (.*) in fxlog to make the function work for vectors.

The number of (scalar) function evaluations is returned in a second output argument:

```
[q,count] = quad(fun,a,b)
```

The quad routine is based on Simpson's rule, which is a Newton–Cotes 3-point rule (exact for polynomials of degree up to 3), whereas quadl employs a more accurate 4-point Gauss–Lobatto rule together with a 7-point Kronrod extension [19] (exact for polynomials of degrees up to 5 and 9, respectively). Both routines use adaptive quadrature. They break the range of integration into subintervals and apply the basic integration rule over each subinterval. They choose the subintervals according to the local behavior of the integrand, placing the smallest ones where the integrand is changing most rapidly. Warning messages are produced if the subintervals become very small or if an excessive number of function evaluations is used, either of which could indicate that the integrand has a singularity.

To illustrate how quad and quadl work, we consider the integral

$$\int_0^1 \left(\frac{1}{(x - 0.3)^2 + 0.01} + \frac{1}{(x - 0.9)^2 + 0.04} - 6 \right) dx = 29.858 \ldots .$$

The integrand is the function humps provided with MATLAB, which has a large peak at 0.3 and a smaller one at 0.9. We applied quad to this integral, using a tolerance of 1e-4. Figure 12.1 plots the integrand and shows with tick marks on the x-axis where the integrand was evaluated; circles mark the corresponding values of the integrand. The figure shows that the subintervals are smallest where the integrand is most rapidly varying.

For another example we take the Fresnel integrals

$$x(t) = \int_0^t \cos(u^2) \, du, \qquad y(t) = \int_0^t \sin(u^2) \, du.$$

Plotting $x(t)$ against $y(t)$ produces a spiral [24, Sec. 2.6]. The following code plots the spiral by sampling at 2001 equally spaced points t on the interval $[-4\pi, 4\pi]$; the result is shown in Figure 12.2. For efficiency we exploit symmetry and avoid repeatedly integrating from 0 to t by integrating over each subinterval and then evaluating the cumulative sums using cumsum:

```
n = 1000;
x = zeros(1,n); y = x;
t = linspace(0,4*pi,n+1);
for i=1:n
    x(i) = quadl(inline('cos(x.^2)'),t(i),t(i+1),1e-3);
    y(i) = quadl(inline('sin(x.^2)'),t(i),t(i+1),1e-3);
end
x = cumsum(x); y = cumsum(y);
plot([-x(end:-1:1) 0 x], [-y(end:-1:1) 0 y])
axis equal
```

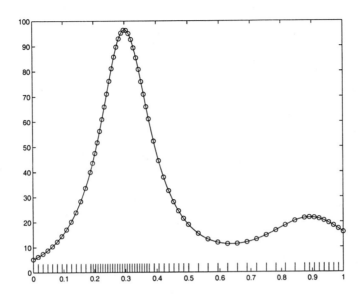

Figure 12.1. *Integration of* humps *function by* quad.

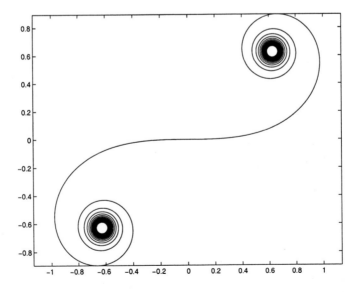

Figure 12.2. *Fresnel spiral.*

Another quadrature function is `trapz`, which applies the repeated trapezium rule. It differs from `quad` and `quadl` in that its input comprises vectors of x_i and $f(x_i)$ values rather than a function representing the integrand f; therefore it is not adaptive. Example:

```
>> x = linspace(0,2*pi,10);
>> f = sin(x).^2./sqrt(1+cos(x).^2);
>> trapz(x,f)
ans =
    2.8478
```

In this example the error in the computed integral is of the order 10^{-7}, which is much smaller than the standard error expression for the repeated trapezium rule would suggest. The reason is that we are integrating a periodic function over a whole number of periods and the repeated trapezium rule is known to be highly accurate in this situation [5, Sec. 5.4], [70, p. 182]. In general, provided that a function is available to evaluate the integrand at arbitrary points, `quad` and `quadl` are preferable to `trapz`.

Double integrals can be evaluated with `dblquad`. To illustrate, suppose we wish to approximate the integral

$$\int_4^6 \int_0^1 \left(y^2 e^x + x \cos y \right) dx\, dy.$$

Using the function

```
function out = fxy(x,y)
    out = y^2*exp(x)+x*cos(y);
```

we type

```
>> dblquad(@fxy,0,1,4,6)
ans =
   87.2983
```

The function passed to `dblquad` must accept a vector `x` and a scalar `y` and return a vector as output. Additional arguments to `dblquad` can be used to specify the tolerance and the integrator (the default is `quad`).

12.2. Ordinary Differential Equations

MATLAB has a range of functions for solving initial value ordinary differential equations (ODEs). These mathematical problems have the form

$$\frac{d}{dt} y(t) = f(t, y(t)), \quad y(t_0) = y_0,$$

where t is a real scalar, $y(t)$ is an unknown m-vector, and the given function f of t and y is also an m-vector. To be concrete, we regard t as representing time. The function f defines the ODE and the initial condition $y(t_0) = y_0$ then defines an initial value problem. The simplest way to solve such a problem is to write a function that evaluates f and then call one of MATLAB's ODE solvers. The minimum information that the solver must be given is the function name, the range of t values over which the solution is required and the initial condition y_0. However, MATLAB's ODE solvers allow for extra (optional) input and output arguments that make it possible to specify more about the mathematical problem and how it is to be solved. Each of MATLAB's ODE solvers is designed to be efficient in specific circumstances, but all are essentially interchangeable. In the next subsection we develop examples that illustrate the use of ode45. This function implements an adaptive Runge–Kutta algorithm and is typically the most efficient solver for the classes of ODEs that concern MATLAB users. The full range of ODE solving functions is discussed in Section 12.2.3 and listed in Table 12.1 on p. 160. The functions follow a naming convention: all names begin ode and are followed by digits denoting the orders of the underlying integration formulae, with a final "s", "t" or "tb" denoting a function intended for stiff problems.

Note that the ODE solvers in MATLAB 6 use a different syntax than was used in MATLAB 5. For an explanation of the old syntax, see help odefile.

12.2.1. Examples with ode45

In order to solve the scalar $(m = 1)$ ODE

$$\frac{d}{dt}y(t) = -y(t) - 5e^{-t}\sin 5t, \quad y(0) = 1,$$

for $0 \le t \le 3$ with ode45, we create in the file myf.m the function

```
function yprime = myf(t,y)
%MYF    ODE example function.
%       YPRIME = MYF(T,Y) evaluates derivative.

yprime = -y - 5*exp(-t)*sin(5*t);
```

and then type

```
tspan = [0 3]; yzero = 1;
[t,y] = ode45(@myf,tspan,yzero);
plot(t,y,'*--')
xlabel t, ylabel y(t)
```

This produces the plot in Figure 12.3. (Note that here we have exploited command/function duality in setting the x- and y-axis labels—see Section 7.4.) The input arguments to ode45 are the function myf, the 2-vector tspan that specifies the time interval, and the initial condition yzero. Two output arguments t and y are returned. The t values are ordered in the range $[0, 3]$ and y(i) approximates the solution at time t(i). So t(1) = 0 and t(end) = 3, with the points t(2:end-1) chosen automatically by ode45 in much the same way that the adaptive quadrature routines choose their subintervals—the points are more closely spaced in regions where the solution is rapidly varying.

The solution to the scalar ODE above is $y(t) = e^{-t}\cos 5t$, so we may check the maximum error in the ode45 approximation:

```
>> max(abs(y - exp(-t).*cos(5*t)))
ans =
   2.8991e-04
```

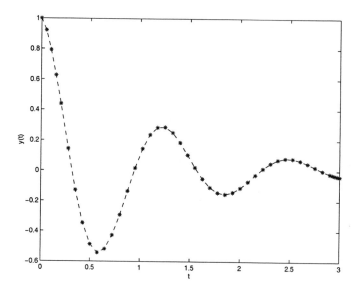

Figure 12.3. *Scalar ODE example.*

If more than two time values are specified, then `ode45` returns the solution at these times only, suppressing any solution values that may have been computed for intervening times.

```
>> tspan2 = 0:4;
>> [t2,y2] = ode45(@myf,tspan2,yzero);
>> disp([t2 y2])
         0    1.0000
    1.0000    0.1043
    2.0000   -0.1136
    3.0000   -0.0378
    4.0000    0.0075
```

Requesting the solution at specific times in this way has little effect on the computational cost of the integration. A decreasing list of times is allowed, so that integration is backward in time:

```
>> tspan3 = [0 -0.5 -1];
>> [t3,y3] = ode45(@myf,tspan3,yzero);
>> disp([t3 y3])
         0    1.0000
   -0.5000   -1.3209
   -1.0000    0.7711
```

Higher order ODEs can be solved if they are first rewritten as a larger system of first-order ODEs [69, Chap. 1]. For example, the simple pendulum equation [74, Sec. 6.7] has the form

$$\frac{d^2}{dt^2}\theta(t) + \sin\theta(t) = 0.$$

Defining $y_1(t) = \theta(t)$ and $y_2(t) = d\theta(t)/dt$, we may rewrite this equation as the two first-order equations

$$\frac{d}{dt}y_1(t) = y_2(t),$$

$$\frac{d}{dt}y_2(t) = -\sin y_1(t).$$

This information can be encoded for use by ode45 in the function pend as follows.

```
function yprime = pend(t,y)
%PEND    Simple pendulum.
%        YPRIME = PEND(T,Y).

yprime = [y(2); -sin(y(1))];
```

The following commands compute solutions over $0 \le t \le 10$ for three different initial conditions. Since we are solving a system of $m = 2$ equations, in the output [t,y] from ode45 the ith row of the matrix y approximates $(y_1(t), y_2(t))$ at time $t = $ t(i).

```
tspan = [0 10];
yazero = [1; 1]; ybzero = [-5; 2]; yczero = [5; -2];
[ta,ya] = ode45(@pend,tspan,yazero);
[tb,yb] = ode45(@pend,tspan,ybzero);
[tc,yc] = ode45(@pend,tspan,yczero);
```

To produce phase plane plots, that is, plots of $y_1(t)$ against $y_2(t)$, we simply plot the first column of the numerical solution against the second. In this context, it is often informative to superimpose a "vector field" using quiver (see Table 8.4 on p. 89). The commands below generate phase plane plots of the solutions ya, yb and yc computed above, and make use of quiver. The arrows produced by quiver point in the direction of the vector $[y_2, -\sin y_1]$ and have length proportional to the 2-norm of this vector. The resulting picture is shown in Figure 12.4.

```
[y1,y2] = meshgrid(-5:.5:5,-3:.5:3);
Dy1Dt = y2; Dy2Dt = -sin(y1);
quiver(y1,y2,Dy1Dt,Dy2Dt)
hold on
plot(ya(:,1),ya(:,2),yb(:,1),yb(:,2),yc(:,1),yc(:,2))
axis equal, axis([-5 5 -3 3])
xlabel y_1(t), ylabel y_2(t), hold off
```

The pendulum ODE preserves energy: any solution keeps $y_2(t)^2/2 - \cos y_1(t)$ constant for all t. We can check that this is approximately true for yc as follows.

```
>> Ec = .5*yc(:,2).^2 - cos(yc(:,1));
>> max(abs(Ec(1)-Ec))
ans =
    0.0263
```

The general form of a call to ode45 is[6]

---

[6]In this argument list, and in those in the rest of the chapter, we assume that functions passed as arguments are specified by their handles (see Section 10.1), which is usually the case for the differential equation solvers.

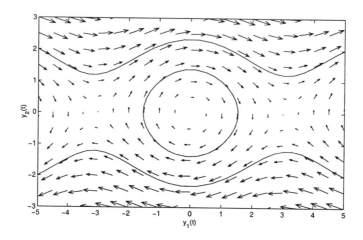

Figure 12.4. *Pendulum phase plane solutions.*

```
[t,y] = ode45(@fun,tspan,yzero,options,p1,p2,...);
```

The optional trailing arguments p1, p2, ... represent problem parameters that, if provided, are passed on to the function fun. The optional argument options is a structure that controls many features of the solver and can be set via the odeset function. In our next example we create a structure options by the assignment

```
options = odeset('AbsTol',1e-7,'RelTol',1e-4);
```

Passing this structure as an input argument to ode45 causes the absolute and relative error tolerances to be set to 10^{-7} and 10^{-4}, respectively. (The default values are 10^{-6} and 10^{-3}; see help odeset for the precise meaning of the tolerances.) These tolerances apply on a local, step-by-step, basis and it is not generally the case that the overall error is kept within these limits. However, under reasonable assumptions about the ODE, it can be shown that decreasing the tolerances by some factor, say 100, will decrease the overall error by a similar factor, so the error is usually roughly proportional to the tolerances. See [69, Chap. 7] for further details about error control in ODE solvers.

Our example below solves the Rössler system [74, Secs. 10.6, 12.3],

$$\frac{d}{dt}y_1(t) = -y_2(t) - y_3(t),$$

$$\frac{d}{dt}y_2(t) = y_1(t) + ay_2(t),$$

$$\frac{d}{dt}y_3(t) = b + y_3(t)\left(y_1(t) - c\right),$$

where a, b and c are parameters. These parameters can be included in the function that defines the ODE as follows:

```
function yprime = rossler(t,y,a,b,c)
%ROSSLER    Rossler system, parameterized.
%           YPRIME  = ROSSLER(T,Y,A,B,C).

yprime = [-y(2)-y(3); y(1)+a*y(2); b+y(3)*(y(1)-c)];
```

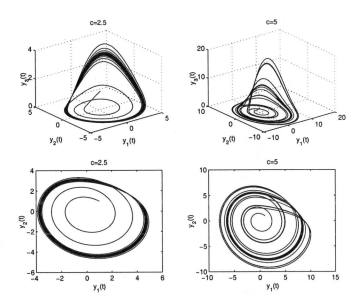

Figure 12.5. *Rössler system phase space solutions.*

Here, the third, fourth and fifth input arguments are parameter values. These are supplied to ode45, which passes them on to rossler unchanged. The following script file solves the Rössler system over $0 \leq t \leq 100$ with initial condition $y(0) = [1; 1; 1]$ for $(a, b, c) = (0.2, 0.2, 2.5)$ and $(a, b, c) = (0.2, 0.2, 5)$. Figure 12.5 shows the results. The 221 subplot gives the 3D phase space solution for $c = 2.5$ and the 223 subplot gives the 2D projection onto the y_1-y_2 plane. The 222 and 224 subplots give the corresponding pictures for $c = 5$.

```
tspan = [0,100]; yzero = [1;1;1];
options = odeset('AbsTol',1e-7,'RelTol',1e-4);

a = 0.2; b = 0.2; c = 2.5;
[t,y] = ode45(@rossler,tspan,yzero,options,a,b,c);
subplot(221), plot3(y(:,1),y(:,2),y(:,3)), title('c=2.5'), grid
xlabel y_1(t), ylabel y_2(t), zlabel y_3(t)
subplot(223), plot(y(:,1),y(:,2)), title('c=2.5')
xlabel y_1(t), ylabel y_2(t)

c = 5;
[t,y] = ode45(@rossler,tspan,yzero,options,a,b,c);
subplot(222), plot3(y(:,1),y(:,2),y(:,3)), title('c=5'), grid
xlabel y_1(t), ylabel y_2(t), zlabel y_3(t)
subplot(224), plot(y(:,1),y(:,2)), title('c=5')
xlabel y_1(t), ylabel y_2(t)
```

12.2.2. Case Study: Pursuit Problem with Event Location

Next we consider a pursuit problem [12, Chap. 5]. Suppose that a rabbit follows a predefined path $(r_1(t), r_2(t))$ in the plane, and that a fox chases the rabbit in such a way that (a) at each moment the tangent of the fox's path points towards the rabbit and (b) the speed of the fox is some constant k times the speed of the rabbit. Then the path $(y_1(t), y_2(t))$ of the fox is determined by the ODE

$$\frac{d}{dt}y_1(t) = s(t)\,(r_1(t) - y_1(t)),$$
$$\frac{d}{dt}y_2(t) = s(t)\,(r_2(t) - y_2(t)),$$

where

$$s(t) = \frac{k\sqrt{\left(\frac{d}{dt}r_1(t)\right)^2 + \left(\frac{d}{dt}r_2(t)\right)^2}}{\sqrt{(r_1(t) - y_1(t))^2 + (r_2(t) - y_2(t))^2}}.$$

Note that this ODE system becomes ill-defined if the fox approaches the rabbit. We let the rabbit follow an outward spiral,

$$\begin{bmatrix} r_1(t) \\ r_2(t) \end{bmatrix} = \sqrt{1+t}\begin{bmatrix} \cos t \\ \sin t \end{bmatrix},$$

and start the fox at $y_1(0) = 3, y_2(0) = 0$. The function fox1 implements the ODE, with k set to 0.75:

```
function yprime = fox1(t,y)
%FOX1   Fox-rabbit pursuit simulation.
%       YPRIME = FOX1(T,Y).

k = 0.75;
r = sqrt(1+t)*[cos(t); sin(t)];
r_p =(0.5/sqrt(1+t))*[cos(t)-2*(1+t)*sin(t);sin(t)+2*(1+t)*cos(t)];
dist = norm(r-y);
if dist > 1e-4
    factor = k*norm(r_p)/dist;
    yprime = factor*(r-y);
else
    error('ODE model ill-defined.')
end
```

The error function (see Section 14.1) has been used so that execution terminates with an error message if the denominator of $s(t)$ in the ODE becomes too small. The script below calls fox1 to produce Figure 12.6. Initial conditions are denoted by circles and the dashed and solid lines show the phase plane paths of the rabbit and fox, respectively.

```
tspan = [0 10]; yzero = [3;0];
[tfox,yfox] = ode45(@fox1,tspan,yzero);
plot(yfox(:,1),yfox(:,2)), hold on
plot(sqrt(1+tfox).*cos(tfox),sqrt(1+tfox).*sin(tfox),'--')
plot([3 1],[0 0],'o');
axis equal, axis([-3.5 3.5 -2.5 3.1])
legend('Fox','Rabbit',0), hold off
```

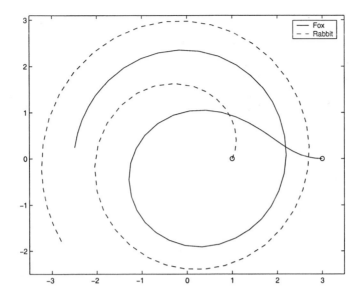

Figure 12.6. *Pursuit example.*

The implementation above is unsatisfactory for $k > 1$, that is, when the fox is faster than the rabbit. In this case, if the rabbit is caught within the specified time interval then no solution is displayed. It would be more natural to ask ode45 to return with the computed solution if the fox and rabbit become close. This can be done using the event location facility. The following script file uses the functions fox2 and events, which are given in Listing 12.1, to produce Figure 12.7. We have allowed k to be a parameter, and set k = 1.1 in the script file. The initial condition and the rabbit's path are as for Figure 12.6.

```
k = 1.1;
tspan = [0;10]; yzero = [3;0];
options = odeset('RelTol',1e-6,'AbsTol',1e-6,'Events',@events);
[tfox,yfox,te,ye,ie] = ode45(@fox2,tspan,yzero,options,k);
plot(yfox(:,1),yfox(:,2)), hold on
plot(sqrt(1+tfox).*cos(tfox),sqrt(1+tfox).*sin(tfox),'--')
plot([3 1],[0 0],'o'), plot(yfox(end,1),yfox(end,2),'*')
axis equal, axis([-3.5 3.5 -2.5 3.1])
legend('Fox','Rabbit',0), hold off
```

Here, we use odeset to set the event location property to the handle of the function events in Listing 12.1. This function has the three output arguments value, isterminal, and direction. It is the responsibility of ode45 to use events to check whether any component passes through zero by monitoring the quantity returned in value. In our example value is a scalar, corresponding to the distance between the rabbit and fox, minus a threshold of 10^{-4}. Hence, ode45 checks if the fox has approached within distance 10^{-4} of the rabbit. We set direction = -1, which signifies that value must be decreasing through zero in order for the event to be considered. The alternative choice direction = 1 tells MATLAB to consider only crossings where value is increasing, and direction = 0 allows for any type of

Listing 12.1. *Functions* fox2 *and* events.

```
function yprime = fox2(t,y,k)
%FOX2    Fox-rabbit pursuit simulation with relative speed parameter.
%        YPRIME = FOX2(T,Y,K).

r = sqrt(1+t)*[cos(t); sin(t)];
r_p = (0.5/sqrt(1+t)) * [cos(t)-2*(1+t)*sin(t); sin(t)+2*(1+t)*cos(t)];
dist = max(norm(r-y),1e-6);
factor = k*norm(r_p)/dist;
yprime = factor*(r-y);
```

```
function [value,isterminal,direction] = events(t,y,k)
%EVENTS     Events function for FOX2.
%           Locate when fox is close to rabbit.

r = sqrt(1+t)*[cos(t); sin(t)];
value = norm(r-y) - 1e-4;      % Fox close to rabbit.
isterminal = 1;                % Stop integration.
direction = -1;                % Value must be decreasing through zero.
```

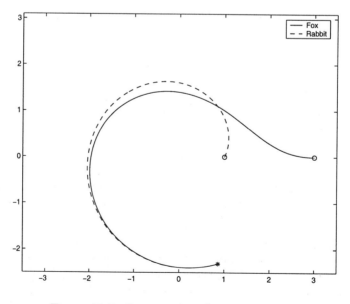

Figure 12.7. *Pursuit example, with capture.*

zero. Since we set `isterminal = 1`, integration will cease when a suitable zero crossing is detected. With the other option, `isterminal = 0`, the event is recorded and the integration continues. Note that the function `events` must accept the additional parameter k passed to `ode45`, even though it does not need it in this example.

The output arguments from `ode45` are `[tfox,yfox,te,ye,ie]`. Here, `tfox` and `yfox` are the usual solution approximations, so `yfox(i)` approximates $y(t)$ at time $t =$ `tfox(i)`. The arguments `te` and `ye` record those t and y values at which the event(s) were recorded and, for vector valued events, `ie` specifies which component of the event occurred each time. (If no events are detected then `te`, `ye` and `ie` are returned as empty matrices.) In our example, we have

```
>> te, ye
te =
     5.0710
ye =
     0.8646    -2.3073
```

showing that the rabbit was captured after 5.07 time units at the point $(0.86, -2.31)$.

12.2.3. Stiff Problems and the Choice of Solver

The Robertson ODE system

$$\frac{d}{dt}y_1(t) = -0.04y_1(t) + 10^4 y_2(t)y_3(t),$$

$$\frac{d}{dt}y_2(t) = 0.04y_1(t) - 10^4 y_2(t)y_3(t) - 3 \times 10^7 y_2(t)^2,$$

$$\frac{d}{dt}y_3(t) = 3 \times 10^7 y_2(t)^2$$

models a reaction between three chemicals [25, p. 3], [69, p. 418]. We set the system up as the function `chem`:

```
function yprime = chem(t,y)
%CHEM     Robertson's chemical reaction model.
%         YPRIME = CHEM(T,Y).

yprime = [-0.04*y(1) + 1e4*y(2)*y(3);
          0.04*y(1) - 1e4*y(2)*y(3) - 3e7*y(2)^2;
          3e7*y(2)^2];
```

The script file below solves this ODE for $0 \le t \le 3$ with initial condition $[1;0;0]$, first using `ode45` and then using another solver, `ode15s`, which is based on implicit linear multistep methods. (Implicit means that a nonlinear equation must be solved at each step.) The results for $y_2(t)$ are plotted in Figure 12.8.

```
tspan = [0 3]; yzero = [1;0;0];
[ta,ya] = ode45(@chem,tspan,yzero);
subplot(121), plot(ta,ya(:,2),'-*')
ax = axis; ax(1) = -0.2; axis(ax) % Make initial transient clearer.
xlabel('t'), ylabel('y_2(t)'), title('ode45','FontSize',14)
[tb,yb] = ode15s(@chem,tspan,yzero);
subplot(122), plot(tb,yb(:,2),'-*'), axis(ax)
xlabel('t'), ylabel('y_2(t)'), title('ode15s','FontSize',14)
```

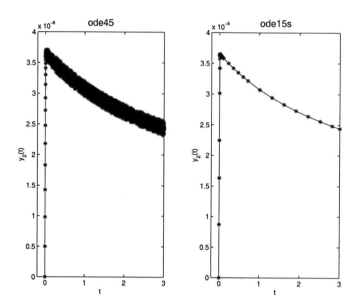

Figure 12.8. *Chemical reaction solutions. Left:* ode45. *Right:* ode15s.

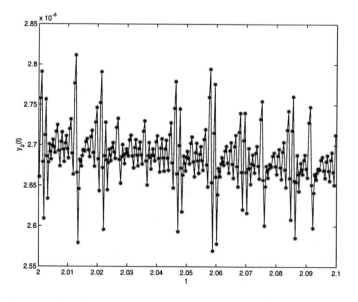

Figure 12.9. *Zoom of chemical reaction solution from* ode45.

We see from Figure 12.8 that the solutions agree to within a small absolute tolerance (note the scale factor 10^{-5} for the y-axis labels). However, the left-hand solution from ode45 has been returned at many more time values than the right-hand solution from ode15s and seems to be less smooth. To emphasize these points, Figure 12.9 plots ode45's $y_2(t)$ for $2.0 \leq t \leq 2.1$. We see that the t values are densely packed and spurious oscillations are present at the level of the default absolute error tolerance, 10^{-6}. The Robertson problem is a classic example of a *stiff* ODE; see [25] or [69, Chap. 8] for full discussions about stiffness and its effects. Stiff ODEs arise in a number of application areas, including the modelling of chemical reactions and electrical circuits. Semi-discretized time-dependent partial differential equations are also a common source of stiffness (we give an example below). Many solvers behave inefficiently on stiff ODEs—they take an unnecessarily large number of intermediate steps in order to complete the integration and hence make an unnecessarily large number of calls to the ODE function (in this case, chem). We can obtain statistics on the computational cost of the integration by setting

```
options = odeset('Stats','on');
```

and providing options as an input argument:

```
[ta,ya] = ode45(@chem,tspan,yzero,options);
```

On completion of the run of ode45, the following statistics are then printed:

```
2051 successful steps
448 failed attempts
14995 function evaluations
0 partial derivatives
0 LU decompositions
0 solutions of linear systems
```

Using the same options argument with ode15s gives

```
33 successful steps
5 failed attempts
73 function evaluations
2 partial derivatives
13 LU decompositions
63 solutions of linear systems
```

The behavior of ode45 typifies what happens when an adaptive algorithm designed for nonstiff ODEs operates in the presence of stiffness. The solver does not break down or compute an inaccurate solution, but it does behave nonsmoothly and extremely inefficiently in comparison with solvers that are customized for stiff problems. This is one reason why MATLAB provides a suite of ODE solvers.

Note that in the computation above, we have

```
>> disp([length(ta), length(tb)])
      8205              34
```

showing that ode45 returned output at almost 250 times as many points as ode15s. However, the statistics show that ode45 took 2051 steps, only about 62 times as many as ode15s. The explanation is that by default ode45 uses interpolation to

Table 12.1. *MATLAB's ODE solvers.*

Solver	Problem type	Type of algorithm
ode45	Nonstiff	Explicit Runge–Kutta pair, orders 4 and 5
ode23	Nonstiff	Explicit Runge–Kutta pair, orders 2 and 3
ode113	Nonstiff	Explicit linear multistep, orders 1 to 13
ode15s	Stiff	Implicit linear multistep, orders 1 to 5
ode23s	Stiff	Modified Rosenbrock pair (one-step), orders 2 and 3
ode23t	Mildly stiff	Trapezoidal rule (implicit), orders 2 and 3
ode23tb	Stiff	Implicit Runge–Kutta type algorithm, orders 2 and 3

return four solution values at equally spaced points over each "natural" step. The default interpolation level can be overridden via the `Refine` property with `odeset`.

A full list of MATLAB's ODE solvers is given in Table 12.1. The authors of these solvers, Shampine and Reichelt, discuss some of the theoretical and practical issues that arose during their development in [72]. The functions are designed to be interchangeable in basic use. So, for example, the illustrations in the previous subsection continue to work if `ode45` is replaced by any of the other solvers. The functions mainly differ in (a) their efficiency on different problem types and (b) their capacity for accepting information about the problem in connection with Jacobians and mass matrices. With regard to efficiency, Shampine and Reichelt write in [72]:

> The experiments reported here and others we have made suggest that except in special circumstances, `ode45` should be the code tried first. If there is reason to believe the problem to be stiff, or if the problem turns out to be unexpectedly difficult for `ode45`, the `ode15s` code should be tried.

The stiff solvers in Table 12.1 use information about the Jacobian matrix, $\partial f_i / \partial y_j$, at various points along the solution. By default, they automatically generate approximate Jacobians using finite differences. However, the reliability and efficiency of the solvers is generally improved if a function that evaluates the Jacobian is supplied. Further options are also available for providing information about whether the Jacobian is sparse, constant or written in vectorized form. To illustrate how Jacobian information can be encoded, we look at the system of ODEs

$$\frac{d}{dt}y(t) = Ay(t) + y(t).*(1 - y(t)) + v,$$

where A is N-by-N and v is N-by-1 with

$$A = r_1 \begin{bmatrix} 0 & 1 & & & \\ -1 & 0 & 1 & & \\ & \ddots & \ddots & \ddots & \\ & & \ddots & \ddots & 1 \\ & & & -1 & 0 \end{bmatrix} + r_2 \begin{bmatrix} -2 & 1 & & & \\ 1 & -2 & 1 & & \\ & \ddots & \ddots & \ddots & \\ & & \ddots & \ddots & 1 \\ & & & 1 & -2 \end{bmatrix},$$

$v = [r_2 - r_1, 0, \ldots, 0, r_2 + r_1]^T$, $r_1 = -a/(2\Delta x)$ and $r_2 = b/\Delta x^2$. Here, a, b and Δx are parameters with values $a = 1$, $b = 5 \times 10^{-2}$ and $\Delta x = 1/(N+1)$. This ODE system

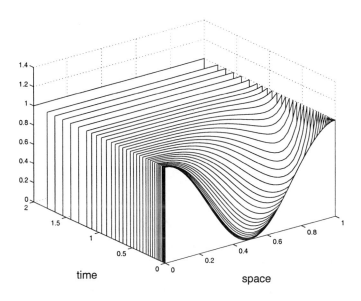

Figure 12.10. *Stiff ODE example, with Jacobian information supplied.*

arises when the method of lines based on central differences is used to semi-discretize the partial differential equation (PDE)

$$\frac{\partial}{\partial t}u(x,t) + a\frac{\partial}{\partial x}u(x,t) = b\frac{\partial^2}{\partial x^2}u(x,t) + u(x,t)(1 - u(x,t)), \quad 0 \le x \le 1,$$

with Dirichlet boundary conditions $u(0,t) = u(1,t) = 1$. This PDE is of reaction-convection-diffusion type (and could be solved directly with pdepe, described in Section 12.4). The ODE solution component $y_j(t)$ approximates $u(j\Delta x, t)$. We suppose that the PDE comes with the initial data $u(x,0) = (1 + \cos 2\pi x)/2$, for which it can be shown that $u(x,t)$ tends to the steady state $u(x,t) \equiv 1$ as $t \to \infty$. The corresponding ODE initial condition is $(y_0)_j = (1 + \cos(2\pi j/(N+1)))/2$. The Jacobian for this ODE has the form $A + I - 2\,\mathrm{diag}(y(t))$, where I denotes the identity.

Listing 12.2 shows a function rcd that implements and solves this system using ode15s. It illustrates how a complete problem specification and solution can be encapsulated in a single function, by making use of subfunctions and function handles. We have set $N = 38$ and $0 \le t \le 2$. We specify via the Jacobian property of odeset the subfunction jacobian that evaluates the Jacobian, and the sparsity pattern of the Jacobian, encoded as a sparse matrix of 0s and 1s, is assigned to the Jpattern property. See Chapter 15 for details about sparse matrices and the function spdiags. The jth column of the output matrix y contains the approximation to $y_j(t)$, and we have created U by appending an extra column ones(size(t)) at each end of y to account for the PDE boundary conditions. The plot produced by rcd is shown in Figure 12.10.

The ODE solvers can be applied to problems of the form

$$M(t, y(t))\frac{d}{dt}y(t) = f(t, y(t)), \quad y(t_0) = y_0,$$

where the *mass matrix*, $M(t, y(t))$, is square and nonsingular. (The ode23s solver applies only when M is independent of t and $y(t)$.) Mass matrices arise naturally when

Listing 12.2. *Function* rcd.

```
function rcd
%RCD Stiff ODE from method of lines on reaction-convection-diffusion problem.

N = 38; a = 1; b = 5e-2;
tspan = [0;2]; space = [1:N]/(N+1);

y0 = 0.5*(1+cos(2*pi*space));
y0 = y0(:);
options = odeset('Jacobian',@jacobian,'Jpattern',jpattern(N));
options = odeset(options,'RelTol',1e-3,'AbsTol',1e-3);

[t,y] = ode15s(@f,tspan,y0,options,N,a,b);
e = ones(size(t)); U = [e y e];
waterfall([0:1/(N+1):1],t,U)
xlabel('space','FontSize',16), ylabel('time','FontSize',16)

% -------------------------------------------------------------------------
% Subfunctions.
% -------------------------------------------------------------------------
function dydt = f(t,y,N,a,b)
%F          Differential equation.

r1 = -a*(N+1)/2;
r2 = b*(N+1)^2;
up = [y(2:N);0]; down = [0;y(1:N-1)];
e1 = [1;zeros(N-1,1)]; eN = [zeros(N-1,1);1];

dydt = r1*(up-down) + r2*(-2*y+up+down) + (r2-r1)*e1 + (r2+r1)*eN + y.*(1-y);

% -------------------------------------------------------------------------
function dfdy = jacobian(t,y,N,a,b)
%JACOBIAN  Jacobian matrix.

r1 = -a*(N+1)/2;
r2 = b*(N+1)^2;
u = (r2-r1)*ones(N,1);
v = (-2*r2+1)*ones(N,1) - 2*y;
w = (r2+r1)*ones(N,1);

dfdy = spdiags([u v w],[-1 0 1],N,N);

% -------------------------------------------------------------------------
function S = jpattern(N)
%JPATTERN  Sparsity pattern of Jacobian matrix.

e = ones(N,1);
S = spdiags([e e e],[-1 0 1],N,N);
```

semi-discretization is performed with a finite element method. A mass matrix can be specified in a similar manner to a Jacobian, via odeset. The ode15s and ode23t functions can solve certain problems where M is singular but does not depend on $y(t)$—more precisely, they can be used if the resulting differential-algebraic equation is of index 1 and y_0 is close to being consistent.

The ODE solvers offer other features that you may find useful. Type help odeset to see the full range of properties that can be controlled through the options structure. The function odeget extracts the current value of the options structure. The MATLAB ODE solvers are well documented and are supported by a rich variety of example files, some of which we list below. In each case, help filename gives an informative description of the file, type filename lists the contents of the file, and typing filename runs a demonstration.

rigidode: nonstiff ODE.

brussode, vdpode: stiff ODEs.

ballode: event location problem.

orbitode: problem involving event location and the use of an output function (odephas2) to process the solution as the integration proceeds.

fem1ode, fem2ode, batonode: ODEs with mass matrices.

hb1dae, amp1dae: differential-algebraic equations.

Type odedemo to run the example ODEs from a Graphical User Interface that offers a choice of solvers and plots the solutions.

12.3. Boundary Value Problems with bvp4c

The function bvp4c uses a collocation method to solve systems of ODEs in two-point boundary value form. These systems may be written

$$\frac{d}{dx}y(x) = f(x, y(x)), \quad g(y(a), y(b)) = 0.$$

Here, as for the initial value problem in the previous section, $y(x)$ is an unknown m-vector and f is a given function of x and y that also produces an m-vector. The solution is required over the range $a \leq x \leq b$ and the given function g specifies the boundary conditions. Note that the independent variable was labeled t in the previous section and is now labeled x. This is consistent with MATLAB's documentation and reflects the fact that two-point boundary value problems (BVPs) usually arise over an interval of space rather than time. Generally, BVPs are more computationally challenging than initial value problems. In particular, it is common for more than one solution to exist. For this reason, bvp4c requires an initial guess to be supplied for the solution. The initial guess and the final solution are stored in structures (see Section 18.3). We introduce bvp4c through a simple example before giving more details.

A scalar BVP describing the cross-sectional shape of a water droplet on a flat surface is given by [66]

$$\frac{d^2}{dx^2}h(x) + (1 - h(x))\left(1 + \left(\frac{d}{dx}h(x)\right)^2\right)^{3/2} = 0, \quad h(-1) = 0, \ h(1) = 0.$$

Here, $h(x)$ measures the height of the droplet at point x. We set $y_1(x) = h(x)$ and $y_2(x) = dh(x)/dx$ and rewrite the equation as a system of two first-order equations:

$$\frac{d}{dx}y_1(x) = y_2(x),$$
$$\frac{d}{dx}y_2(x) = (y_1(x) - 1)\left(1 + y_2(x)^2\right)^{3/2}.$$

This system is represented by the function

```
function yprime = drop(x,y)
%DROP      ODE/BVP water droplet example.
%          YPRIME = DROP(X,Y) evaluates derivative.

yprime = [y(2); (y(1)-1)*((1+y(2)^2)^(3/2))];
```

The boundary conditions are specified via a residual function. This function returns zero when evaluated at the boundary values. Our boundary conditions $y_1(-1) = y_1(1) = 0$ can be encoded in the following function:

```
function res = dropbc(ya,yb)
%DROPBC    ODE/BVP water droplet boundary conditions.
%          RES = DROPBC(YA,YB) evaluates residual.

res = [ya(1); yb(1)];
```

As an initial guess for the solution, we use $y_1(x) = \sqrt{1 - x^2}$ and $y_2(x) = -x/(0.1 + \sqrt{1 - x^2})$. This information is set up by the function $\texttt{dropinit}$:

```
function yinit = dropinit(x)
%DROPINIT  ODE/BVP water droplet initial guess.
%          YINIT = DROPINIT(X) evaluates initial guess at X.

yinit = [sqrt(1-x.^2); -x./(0.1+sqrt(1+x.^2))];
```

The following code solves the BVP and produces Figure 12.11.

```
solinit = bvpinit(linspace(-1,1,20),@dropinit);
sol = bvp4c(@drop,@dropbc,solinit);
fill(sol.x,sol.y(1,:),[0.7 0.7 0.7])
axis([-1 1 0 1])
xlabel('x','FontSize',16)
ylabel('h','Rotation',0,'FontSize',16)
```

Here, the call to $\texttt{bvpinit}$ sets up the structure $\texttt{solinit}$, which contains the data produced by evaluating $\texttt{dropinit}$ at 20 equally spaced values between -1 and 1. We then call $\texttt{bvp4c}$, which returns the solution in the structure $\texttt{sol}$. The $\texttt{fill}$ command fills the curve that the solution makes in the x-y_1 plane.

In general, $\texttt{bvp4c}$ can be called in the form

```
sol = bvp4c(@odefun,@bcfun,solinit,options,p1,p2,...);
```

Here, $\texttt{odefun}$ evaluates the differential equations and $\texttt{bcfun}$ gives the residual for the boundary conditions. The function $\textbf{odefun}$ has the general form

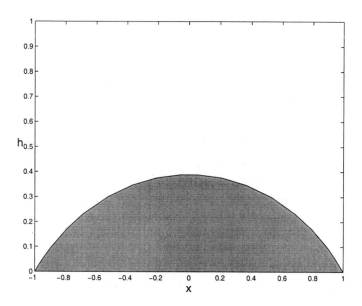

Figure 12.11. *Water droplet BVP solved by* bvp4c.

```
yprime = odefun(x,y,p1,p2,...)
```

and bcfun has the general form

```
res = bcfun(ya,yb,p1,p2,...)
```

The arguments p1,p2,... are optional; they represent problem parameters that may be required by the two functions. Both functions must return column vectors. The initial guess structure solinit has two required fields: solinit.x contains the x values at which the initial guess is supplied, ordered from left to right with solinit.x(1) and solinit.x(end) giving a and b, respectively. Correspondingly, solinit.y(:,i) gives the initial guess for the solution at the point solinit.x(i). The helper function bvpinit can be used to create the initial guess structure, as in the example above. The remaining arguments for bvp4c are optional. The options structure allows various properties of the collocation algorithm to be altered from their default values, including the error tolerances and the maximum number of meshpoints allowed. The function bvpset can be used to create the required structure; we do not give details here. The remaining optional input arguments p1, p2, ... to bvp4c are parameters to be passed to odefun and bcfun.

The output argument sol is a structure that contains the numerical solution. The field sol.x gives the array of x values at which the solution has been computed. (These points are chosen automatically by bvp4c.) The approximate solution at sol.x(i) is given by sol.y(:,i). Similarly, an approximate solution to the first derivative of the solution at sol.x(i) is given by sol.yp(:,i).

Note that the structures solinit and sol above can be given any names, but the field names x, y and yp must be used.

Our next example shows how a parameter can be passed through bvp4c and emphasizes that nonlinear BVPs can have nonunique solutions. The equation

$$\frac{d^2}{dx^2}\theta(x) + \lambda \sin \theta(x) \cos \theta(x) = 0, \quad \theta(-1) = 0, \; \theta(1) = 0,$$

arises in liquid crystal theory [50]. Here, $\theta(x)$ quantifies the average local molecular orientation and the constant parameter $\lambda > 0$ is a measure of an applied magnetic field. If λ is small then the only solution to this problem is the trivial one, $\theta(x) \equiv 0$. However, for $\lambda > \pi^2/4$ a solution with $\theta(x) > 0$ for $-1 < x < 1$ exists, and $-\theta(x)$ is then also a solution. (Physically, a distorted state of the material may arise if the magnetic field is sufficiently strong.) For the positive solution the midpoint value, $\theta(0)$, increases monotonically with λ and approaches $\pi/2$ as λ tends to infinity. Writing $y_1(x) = \theta(x)$ and $y_2(x) = d\theta(x)/dx$ the ODE becomes

$$\frac{d}{dx}y_1(x) = y_2(x),$$

$$\frac{d}{dx}y_2(x) = -\lambda \sin y_1(x) \cos y_1(x).$$

The function `lcrun` in Listing 12.3 solves the BVP for parameter values $\lambda = 2.4$, 2.5, 3 and 10, producing Figure 12.12. In this example, as for the initial value problem in Listing 12.2 on p. 162, we have written a function `lcrun` that has no input or output arguments and created `lc`, `lcbc` and `lcinit` as subfunctions of `lcrun`. This allows us to solve the BVP with a single M-file. The subfunction `lc` evaluates the ODE right-hand side. The boundary conditions, which are the same as those in the previous example, are coded in `lcbc`. Note that `lambda` must be passed to `lcbc` even though it is not used. As an initial guess, we use $y_1(x) = \sin((x+1)\pi/2)$ and $y_2(x) = \pi \cos((x+1)\pi/2)/2$, which is set up by `lcinit`. In the calls to `bvp4c` we use the empty matrix `[]` as a placeholder for the `options` argument. From Figure 12.12 we see that `bvp4c` has found the nontrivial positive solution for the three `lambda` values beyond $\pi^2/4 \approx 2.467$.

Our final example involves the equation

$$\frac{d^2}{dx^2}y(x) + \mu y(x) = 0,$$

with boundary conditions

$$y(0) = 0, \quad \left(\frac{d}{dx}y(x)\right)_{x=0} = 1, \quad \left(y(x) + \frac{d}{dx}y(x)\right)_{x=1} = 0.$$

This equation models the displacement of a skipping rope that is fixed at $x = 0$, has elastic support at $x = 1$, and rotates with uniform angular velocity about its equilibrium position along the x-axis [31, Sec. 5.2]. This BVP is an *eigenvalue problem*—we must find a value of the parameter μ for which a solution exists. (We can regard the two conditions at $x = 0$ as defining an initial value problem; we must then find a value of μ for which the solution matches the boundary condition at $x = 1$.) We can use `bvp4c` to solve this eigenvalue problem if we supply a guess for the unknown parameter μ as well as a guess for the corresponding solution $y(x)$. This is done in the function `skiprun` in Listing 12.4. As a first-order system, the differential equation may be written

$$\frac{d}{dx}y_1(x) = y_2(x),$$

$$\frac{d}{dx}y_2(x) = -\mu y_1(x).$$

Listing 12.3. *Function* lcrun.

```
function lcrun
%LCRUN   Liquid crystal BVP.
%        Solves the liquid crystal BVP for four different lambda values.

lambda = [2.4, 2.5, 3, 10];

solinit = bvpinit(linspace(-1,1,20),@lcinit);
sola = bvp4c(@lc,@lcbc,solinit,[],lambda(1));
solb = bvp4c(@lc,@lcbc,solinit,[],lambda(2));
solc = bvp4c(@lc,@lcbc,solinit,[],lambda(3));
sold = bvp4c(@lc,@lcbc,solinit,[],lambda(4));
plot(sola.x,sola.y(1,:),'-','LineWidth',4), hold on
plot(solb.x,solb.y(1,:),'--','LineWidth',2)
plot(solc.x,solc.y(1,:),'--','LineWidth',4)
plot(sold.x,sold.y(1,:),'--','LineWidth',6), hold off
legend([repmat('\lambda = ',4,1) num2str(lambda')])
xlabel('x','FontSize',16)
ylabel('\theta','Rotation',0,'FontSize',16)

% --------------------------------------------------------------------
% Subfunctions.
% --------------------------------------------------------------------
function yprime = lc(x,y,lambda)
%LC      ODE/BVP liquid crystal system.
%        YPRIME = LC(X,Y,LAMBDA) evaluates derivative.

yprime = [y(2); -lambda*sin(y(1))*cos(y(1))];

% --------------------------------------------------------------------
function res = lcbc(ya,yb,lambda)
%LCBC    ODE/BVP liquid crystal boundary conditions.
%        RES = LCBC(YA,YB,LAMBDA) evaluates residual.

res = [ya(1); yb(1)];

% --------------------------------------------------------------------
function yinit = lcinit(x)
%LCINIT  ODE/BVP liquid crystal initial guess.
%        YINIT = LCINIT(X) evaluates initial guess at X.

yinit = [sin(0.5*(x+1)*pi); 0.5*pi*cos(0.5*(x+1)*pi)];
```

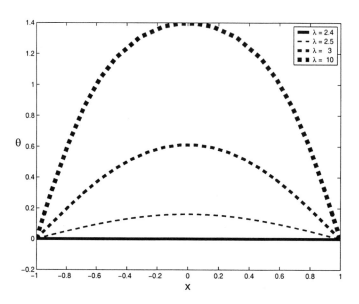

Figure 12.12. *Liquid crystal BVP solved by* bvp4c.

This system is encoded in the subfunction `skip` and the boundary conditions in `skipbc`. Our initial guess for the solution is $y_1(x) = \sin(x)$, $y_2(x) = \cos(x)$, specified in `skipinit`. Note that the input argument 5 is added in the call to bvpinit. This is our guess for μ, and it is stored in the `parameters` field of the structure `solinit` and hence passed to bvp4c. Figure 12.13 shows the solution computed by bvp4c. The computed value for μ is returned in the `parameters` field of the structure `sol`. We have

```
>> sol = skiprun
sol =
              x: [0 0.1111 0.2222 0.3333 0.4444 0.5556 0.6667 ...
                 0.7778 0.8889 1]
              y: [2x10 double]
             yp: [2x10 double]
     parameters: 4.1159
```

It is known that this BVP has eigenvalues given by $\mu = \gamma^2$, where γ is a solution of $\tan(\gamma) + \gamma = 0$. Using `fzero` to locate a γ value near 2, we can check the accuracy of the computed μ as follows:

```
>> gam = fzero('tan(x)+x',2); mu = gam^2;
Zero found in the interval: [1.9434, 2.0566].

>> error = abs(sol.parameters - mu)
error =
   2.5541e-05
```

The tutorial [71] gives a range of examples that illustrate the versatility of bvp4c. The examples deal with a number of issues, including

Listing 12.4. *Function* skiprun.

```
function sol = skiprun
%SKIPRUN  Skipping rope BVP/eigenvalue example.

solinit = bvpinit(linspace(0,1,10),@skipinit,5);
sol = bvp4c(@skip,@skipbc,solinit);
plot(sol.x,sol.y(1,:),'-', sol.x,sol.yp(1,:),'--', 'LineWidth',4)
xlabel('x','FontSize',12)
legend('y_1','y_2',0)

% -------------------------------------------------------------------
% Subfunctions.
% -------------------------------------------------------------------
function yprime = skip(x,y,mu)
%SKIP     ODE/BVP skipping rope example.
%         YPRIME = SKIP(X,Y,MU) evaluates derivative.

yprime = [y(2); -mu*y(1)];

% -------------------------------------------------------------------
function res = skipbc(ya,yb,mu)
%SKIPBC   ODE/BVP skipping rope boundary conditions.
%         RES = SKIPBC(YA,YB,MU) evaluates residual.

res = [ya(1); ya(2)-1; yb(1)+yb(2)];

% -------------------------------------------------------------------
function yinit = skipinit(x)
%SKIPINIT ODE/BVP skipping rope initial guess.
%         YINIT = SKIPINIT(X) evaluates initial guess at X.

yinit = [sin(x); cos(x)];
```

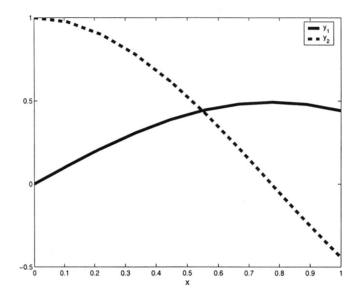

Figure 12.13. *Skipping rope eigenvalue BVP solved by* bvp4c.

- changing the error tolerances,

- evaluating the solution at any point in the range $[a, b]$,

- choosing appropriate initial guesses by continuation,

- dealing with singularities,

- solving problems with periodic boundary conditions,

- solving problems over an infinite interval,

- solving multipoint BVPs (where non-endpoint conditions are specified for the solution).

Further information can also be obtained from the help for the functions bvp4c, bvpget, bvpinit, bvpval, bvpset, and the example files

twobvp: solves a BVP that has exactly two solutions;

mat4bvp: finds the fourth eigenvalue of Mathieu's equation;

shockbvp: solves a difficult BVP with a shock layer.

12.4. Partial Differential Equations with pdepe

MATLAB's pdepe solves a class of parabolic/elliptic partial differential equation (PDE) systems. These systems involve a vector-valued unknown function u that depends on a scalar space variable, x, and a scalar time variable, t. The general class to which pdepe applies has the form

$$c\left(x, t, u, \frac{\partial u}{\partial x}\right)\frac{\partial u}{\partial t} = x^{-m}\frac{\partial}{\partial x}\left(x^{m}f\left(x, t, u, \frac{\partial u}{\partial x}\right)\right) + s\left(x, t, u, \frac{\partial u}{\partial x}\right),$$

where $a \leq x \leq b$ and $t_0 \leq t \leq t_f$. The integer m can be 0, 1 or 2, corresponding to slab, cylindrical and spherical symmetry, respectively. The function c is a diagonal matrix and the flux and source functions f and s are vector valued. Initial and boundary conditions must be supplied in the following form. For $a \leq x \leq b$ and $t = t_0$ the solution must satisfy $u(x, t_0) = u_0(x)$ for a specified function u_0. For $x = a$ and $t_0 \leq t \leq t_f$ the solution must satisfy

$$p_a(x, t, u) + q_a(x, t)f\left(x, t, u, \frac{\partial u}{\partial x}\right) = 0,$$

for specified functions p_a and q_a. Similarly, for $x = b$ and $t_0 \leq t \leq t_f$,

$$p_b(x, t, u) + q_b(x, t)f\left(x, t, u, \frac{\partial u}{\partial x}\right) = 0$$

must hold for specified functions p_b and q_b. Certain other restrictions are placed on the class of problems that can be solved by pdepe; see doc pdepe for details.

A call to pdepe has the general form

```
sol = pdepe(m,@pdefun,@pdeic,@pdebc,xmesh,tspan,options,p1,p2,...);
```

which is similar to the syntax for bvp4c. The input argument m can take the values 0, 1 or 2, as described above. The function pdefun has the form

```
function [c,f,s] = pdefun(x,t,u,DuDx,p1,p2,...)
```

It accepts the space and time variables together with vectors u and DuDx that approximate the solution u and the partial derivative $\partial u/\partial x$, and returns vectors containing the diagonal of the matrix c and the flux and source functions f and s. Initial conditions are encoded in the function pdeic, which takes the form

```
function u0 = pdeic(x,p1,p2,...)
```

The function pdebc of the form

```
function [pa,qa,pb,qb] = pdebc(xa,ua,xb,ub,t,p1,p2,...)
```

evaluates p_a, q_a, p_b and q_b for the boundary conditions at xa $= a$ and xb $= b$. The vector xmesh in the argument list of pdepe is a set of points in $[a, b]$ with xmesh(1) $= a$ and xmesh(end) $= b$, ordered so that xmesh(i) < xmesh(i+1). This defines the x values at which the numerical solution is computed. The algorithm uses a second-order spatial discretization method based on the xmesh values. Hence the choice of xmesh has a strong influence on the accuracy and cost of the numerical solution. Closely spaced xmesh points should be used in regions where the solution is likely to vary rapidly with respect to x. The vector tspan specifies the time points in $[t_0, t_f]$ where the solution is to be returned, with tspan(1) $= t_0$, tspan(end) $= t_f$ and tspan(i) < tspan(i+1). The time integration in pdepe is performed by ode15s and the actual timestep values are chosen dynamically—the tspan points simply determine where the solution is returned and have little impact on the cost or accuracy. The default properties of $\texttt{ode15s}$ can be overridden via the optional input argument $\texttt{options}$, which can be created with the $\texttt{odeset}$ function (see Section 12.2.1). Altering the defaults is not usually necessary so we do not discuss this further. The remaining input arguments $\texttt{p1,p2,}\ldots$ are optional problem parameters that are passed to the functions $\texttt{pdefun, pdeic}$ and $\texttt{pdebc}$. These functions should have $\texttt{p1,p2,}\ldots$ as input arguments only if they are present in the call to $\texttt{pdepe}$.

The output argument $\texttt{sol}$ is a three-dimensional array such that $\texttt{sol(j,k,i)}$ is the approximation to the ith component of u at the point $t = \texttt{tspan(j)}$, $x = \texttt{xmesh(k)}$. A postprocessing function $\texttt{pdeval}$ is available for computing u and $\partial u/\partial x$ at points that are not in $\texttt{xmesh}$.

To illustrate the use of $\texttt{pdepe}$, we begin with the Black–Scholes PDE, famous for modelling derivative prices in financial mathematics. In transformed and dimensionless form [84, Sec. 5.4], using parameter values from [63, Chap. 13], we have

$$\frac{\partial u}{\partial t} = \frac{\partial^2 u}{\partial x^2} + (k-1)\frac{\partial u}{\partial x} - ku, \quad a \leq x \leq b, \quad t_0 \leq t \leq t_f,$$

where $k = r/(\sigma^2/2)$, $r = 0.065$, $\sigma = 0.8$, $a = \log(2/5)$, $b = \log(7/5)$, $t_0 = 0$, $t_f = 5$, with initial condition

$$u(x,0) = \max(\exp(x) - 1, 0)$$

and boundary conditions

$$u(a,t) = 0, \quad u(b,t) = \frac{7 - 5\exp(-kt)}{5}.$$

This is of the general form allowed by $\texttt{pdepe}$ with $m = 0$ and

$$c(x,t,u) = 1, \quad f\left(x,t,u,\frac{\partial u}{\partial x}\right) = \frac{\partial u}{\partial x}, \quad s\left(x,t,u,\frac{\partial u}{\partial x}\right) = (k-1)\frac{\partial u}{\partial x} - ku.$$

At $x = a$ the boundary conditions have $p(x,t,u) = u$ and $q(x,t,u) = 0$, and at $x = b$ they have $p(x,t,u) = u - (7 - 5\exp(-kt))/5$ and $q(x,t,u) = 0$. The function $\texttt{bs}$ in Listing 12.5 implements the problem. Here, we have used $\texttt{linspace}$ to generate 40 equally spaced x-values between a and b for the spatial mesh and 20 equally spaced t-values between t_0 and t_f for the output times. The call to $\texttt{pdepe}$ includes the input argument $\texttt{[]}$ as a placeholder for $\texttt{options}$. The subfunction $\texttt{bspde}$ defines the PDE in terms of $\texttt{c}$, $\texttt{f}$ and $\texttt{s}$ and $\texttt{bsic}$ specifies the initial condition. Similarly, in the subfunction $\texttt{bsbc}$ the boundary conditions at $x = a$ and $x = b$ are returned in $\texttt{pa, qa,}$ $\texttt{pb}$ and $\texttt{qb}$. Note that the parameter $\texttt{k}$ must be passed to each of these subfunctions. We use the 3D plotting function $\texttt{mesh}$ to display the solution. Figure 12.14 shows the resulting picture.

Next, we look at a system of two reaction-diffusion equations of a type that arises in mathematical biology [33, Chap. 11]:

$$\frac{\partial u}{\partial t} = \frac{1}{2}\frac{\partial^2 u}{\partial x^2} + \frac{1}{1 + v^2},$$

$$\frac{\partial v}{\partial t} = \frac{1}{2}\frac{\partial^2 v}{\partial x^2} + \frac{1}{1 + u^2},$$

for $0 \leq x \leq 1$ and $0 \leq t \leq 0.2$. Our initial conditions are

$$u(x,0) = 1 + \tfrac{1}{2}\cos(2\pi x), \quad v(x,0) = 1 - \tfrac{1}{2}\cos(2\pi x),$$

Listing 12.5. *Function* bs.

```
function bs
%BS     Black-Scholes PDE.
%       Solves the transformed Black-Scholes equation.

m = 0;
r = 0.065;
sigma = 0.8;
k = r/(0.5*sigma^2);
a = log(2/5);
b = log(7/5);
t0 = 0;
tf = 5;

xmesh = linspace(a,b,40);
tspan = linspace(t0,tf,20);

sol = pdepe(m,@bspde,@bsic,@bsbc,xmesh,tspan,[],k);
u = sol(:,:,1);

mesh(xmesh,tspan,u)
xlabel('x','FontSize',12)
ylabel('t','FontSize',12)
zlabel('u','FontSize',12,'Rotation',0)

% --------------------------------------------------------
% Subfunctions.
% --------------------------------------------------------
function [c,f,s] = bspde(x,t,u,DuDx,k)
%BSPDE  Black-Scholes PDE.
c = 1;
f = DuDx;
s = (k-1)*DuDx-k*u;

% --------------------------------------------------------
function u0 = bsic(x,k)
%BSIC   Initial condition at t = t0.
u0 = max(exp(x)-1,0);

% --------------------------------------------------------
function [pa,qa,pb,qb] = bsbc(xa,ua,xb,ub,t,k)
%BSBC   Boundary conditions at x = a and x = b.
pa = ua;
qa = 0;
pb = ub - (7 - 5*exp(-k*t))/5;
qb = 0;
```

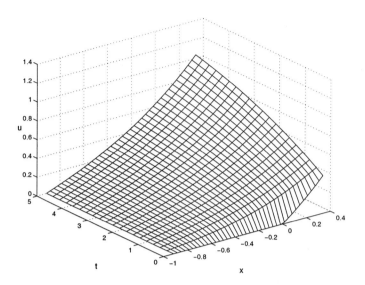

Figure 12.14. *Black–Scholes solution with* pdepe.

and our boundary conditions are

$$\frac{\partial u}{\partial x}(0,t) = \frac{\partial u}{\partial x}(1,t) = \frac{\partial v}{\partial x}(0,t) = \frac{\partial v}{\partial x}(1,t) = 0.$$

To put this into the framework of pdepe we write (u,v) as (u_1, u_2) and express the PDE as

$$\begin{bmatrix} 1 & 0 \\ 0 & 1 \end{bmatrix} \times \frac{\partial}{\partial t} \begin{bmatrix} u_1 \\ u_2 \end{bmatrix} = \frac{\partial}{\partial x} \begin{bmatrix} \frac{1}{2}\partial u_1/\partial x \\ \frac{1}{2}\partial u_2/\partial x \end{bmatrix} + \begin{bmatrix} 1/(1+u_2^2) \\ 1/(1+u_1^2) \end{bmatrix}.$$

The function mbiol in Listing 12.6 solves the PDE system. Note that the output arguments c, f, s, pa, qa, pb and qb in the subfunctions mbpde and mbbc are 2-by-1 arrays, because there are two PDEs in the system. The solutions plotted with surf can be seen in the upper part of Figure 12.15. It follows from [33, Ex. 11.5] that the energy

$$E(t) = \frac{1}{2} \int_0^1 \left[\left(\frac{\partial u}{\partial x} \right)^2 + \left(\frac{\partial v}{\partial x} \right)^2 \right] dx$$

decays exponentially to zero as $t \to \infty$. To verify this fact numerically, we use simple finite differences and quadrature in mbiol to approximate the energy integral. (Alternatively, the function pdeval could be used to obtain approximations to $\partial u/\partial x$ and $\partial v/\partial x$.) The resulting plot of $E(t)$ is given in the lower part of Figure 12.15.

Further examples of pdepe in use can be found in doc pdepe. We note that pdepe is designed to solve a subclass of small systems of parabolic and elliptic PDEs to modest accuracy. If your PDE is not suitable for pdepe then the Partial Differential Equation Toolbox might be appropriate.

Listing 12.6. *Function* mbiol.

```
function mbiol
%MBIOL    Reaction-diffusion system from mathematical biology.
%         Solves the PDE and tests the energy decay condition.

m = 0;
xmesh = linspace(0,1,15);
tspan = linspace(0,0.2,10);
sol = pdepe(m,@mbpde,@mbic,@mbbc,xmesh,tspan);
u1 = sol(:,:,1);
u2 = sol(:,:,2);

subplot(221)
surf(xmesh,tspan,u1)
xlabel('x','FontSize',12)
ylabel('t','FontSize',12)
title('u_1','FontSize',16)

subplot(222)
surf(xmesh,tspan,u2)
xlabel('x','FontSize',12)
ylabel('t','FontSize',12)
title('u_2','FontSize',16)

% Estimate energy integral.
dx = xmesh(2) - xmesh(1);  % Constant spacing.
energy = 0.5*sum( (diff(u1,1,2)).^2 + (diff(u2,1,2)).^2, 2)/dx;
subplot(212)
plot(tspan',energy)
xlabel('t','FontSize',12)
title('Energy','FontSize',16)

% ------------------------------------------------------------------
% Subfunctions.
% ------------------------------------------------------------------
function [c,f,s] = mbpde(x,t,u,DuDx)
c = [1; 1];
f = DuDx/2;
s = [1/(1+u(2)^2); 1/(1+u(1)^2)];

% ------------------------------------------------------------------
function u0 = mbic(x);
u0 = [1+0.5*cos(2*pi*x); 1-0.5*cos(2*pi*x)];

% ------------------------------------------------------------------
function [pa,qa,pb,qb] = mbbc(xa,ua,xb,ub,t)
pa = [0; 0];
qa = [1; 1];
pb = [0; 0];
qb = [1; 1];
```

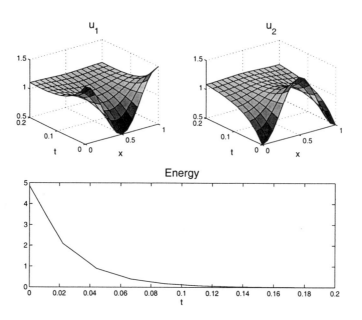

Figure 12.15. *Reaction-diffusion system solution with* pdepe.

Multidimensional integrals are another whole multidimensional bag of worms.
— WILLIAM H. PRESS, SAUL A. TEUKOLSKY,
WILLIAM T. VETTERLING and BRIAN P. FLANNERY,
Numerical Recipes in FORTRAN (1992)

Perhaps the crudest way to evaluate $\int_y^x f(u)du$
is to plot the graph of $f(u)$ on uniformly squared paper
and then count the squares that lie inside the desired area.
This method gives numerical integration its other name:
numerical quadrature.
Another way, suitable for chemists,
is to plot the graph on paper of uniform density,
cut out the area in question, and weigh it.
— WILLIAM M. KAHAN, *Handheld Calculator Evaluates Integrals* (1980)

The options vector is optional.
— LAWRENCE F. SHAMPINE and MARK W. REICHELT,
The MATLAB ODE Suite (1997)

Just about any BVP can be formulated for solution with bvp4c.
— LAWRENCE F. SHAMPINE, JACEK KIERZENKA and MARK W. REICHELT,
Solving Boundary Value Problems for Ordinary
Differential Equations in MATLAB with bvp4c (2000)

Chapter 13
Input and Output

In this chapter we discuss how to obtain input from the user, how to display information on the screen, and how to read and write text files. Note that textual output can be captured into a file (perhaps for subsequent printing) using the `diary` command, as described on p. 29. How to print and save figures is discussed in Section 8.4.

13.1. User Input

User input can be obtained with the `input` function, which displays a prompt and waits for a user response:

```
>> x = input('Starting point: ')
Starting point: 0.5
x =
    0.5000
```

Here, the user has responded by typing "0.5", which is assigned to x. The input is interpreted as a string when an argument `'s'` is appended:

```
>> mytitle = input('Title for plot: ','s')
Title for plot: Experiment 2
mytitle =
Experiment 2
```

The function `ginput` collects data via mouse clicks. The command

```
[x,y] = ginput(n)
```

returns in the vectors x and y the coordinates of the next n mouse clicks from the current figure window. Input can be terminated before the nth mouse click by pressing the return key. One use of `ginput` is to find the approximate location of points on a graph. For example, with Figure 8.7 in the current figure window, you might type `[x,y] = ginput(1)` and click on one of the places where the curves intersect. As another example, the first two lines of the Bezier curve example on p. 85 can be replaced by

```
axis([0 1 0 1])
[x,y] = ginput(4);
P = [x';y'];
```

Now the control points are determined by the user's mouse clicks.

The `pause` command suspends execution until a key is pressed, while `pause(n)` waits for n seconds before continuing. Typical use of `pause` is between plots displayed in sequence. It is also used in conjunction with the `echo` command for M-files intended for demonstration; to see an example, type `type census`.

13.2. Output to the Screen

The results of MATLAB computations are displayed on the screen whenever a semi-colon is omitted after an assignment and the format of the output can be varied using the `format` command. But much greater control over the output is available with the use of several functions.

The `disp` function displays the value of a variable, according to the current `format`, without first printing the variable name and "=". If its argument is a string, `disp` displays the string. Example:

```
>> disp('Here is a 3-by-3 magic square'), disp(magic(3))
Here is a 3-by-3 magic square
     8     1     6
     3     5     7
     4     9     2
```

More sophisticated formatting can be done with the `fprintf` function. The syntax is `fprintf(format, list-of-expressions)`, where *format* is a string that specifies the precise output format for each expression in the list. In the example

```
>> fprintf('%6.3f\n', pi)
 3.142
```

the `%` character denotes the start of a format specifier requesting a field width of 6 with 3 digits after the decimal point and `\n` denotes a new line (without which subsequent output would continue on the same line). If the specified field width is not large enough MATLAB expands it as necessary:

```
>> fprintf('%6.3f\n', pi^10)
93648.047
```

The fixed point notation produced by `f` is suitable for displaying integers (using `%n.0f`) and when a fixed number of decimal places are required, such as when displaying dollars and cents (using `%n.2f`). If `f` is replaced by `e` then the digit after the period denotes the number of significant digits to display in exponential notation:

```
>> fprintf('%12.3e\n', pi)
   3.142e+000
```

When choosing the field width remember that for a negative number a minus sign occupies one position:

```
>> fprintf('%5.2f\n%5.2f\n',exp(1),-exp(1))
 2.72
-2.72
```

A minus sign just after the `%` character causes the field to be left-justified. Compare

```
>> fprintf('%5.0f\n%5.0f\n',9,103)
    9
  103
```

```
>> fprintf('%-5.0f\n%-5.0f\n',9,103)
9
103
```

The format string can contain characters to be printed literally, as the following example shows:

```
>> m = 5; iter = 11; U = orth(randn(m)) + 1e-10;

>> fprintf('iter = %2.0f\n', iter)
iter = 11

>> fprintf('norm(U''*U-I) = %11.4e\n', norm(U'*U - eye(m)))
norm(U'*U-I) = 8.4618e-010
```

Note that, within a string, '' represents a single quote.

To print % and \ use \% and \\ in the format string. Another useful format specifier is g, which uses whichever of e and f produces the shorter result:

```
>> fprintf('%g %g\n', exp(1), exp(20))
2.71828 4.85165e+008
```

Various other specifiers and special characters are supported by fprintf, which behaves similarly to the C function of the same name; see doc fprintf.

If more numbers are supplied to be printed than there are format specifiers in the fprintf statement then the format specifiers are reused, with elements being taken from a matrix down the first column, then down the second column, and so on. This feature can be used to avoid a loop. Example:

```
>> A = [30 40 60 70];
>> fprintf('%g miles/hour = %g kilometers/hour\n', [A; 8*A/5])
30 miles/hour = 48 kilometers/hour
40 miles/hour = 64 kilometers/hour
60 miles/hour = 96 kilometers/hour
70 miles/hour = 112 kilometers/hour
```

The function sprintf is analogous to fprintf but returns its output as a string. It is useful for producing labels for plots. A simpler to use but less versatile alternative is num2str: num2str(x,n) converts x to a string with n significant digits, with n defaulting to 4. For converting integers to strings, int2str can be used. Here are three examples, the second and third of which make use of string concatenation (see Section 18.1).

```
>> n = 16;
>> err_msg = sprintf('Must supply a %d-by-%d matrix', n, n)
err_msg =
Must supply a 16-by-16 matrix

>> disp(['Pi is given to 6 significant figures by ' num2str(pi,6)])
Pi is given to 6 significant figures by 3.14159

>> i = 3;
>> title_str = ['Result of experiment ' int2str(i)]
title_str =
Result of experiment 3
```

13.3. File Input and Output

A number of functions are provided for reading and writing binary and formatted text files; type `help iofun` to see the complete list.

We show by example how to write data to a formatted text file and then read it back in. Before operating on a file it must be opened with the `fopen` function, whose first argument is the filename and whose second argument is a file permission, which has several possible values including `'r'` for read and `'w'` for write. A file identifier is returned by `fopen`; it is used in subsequent read and write statements to specify the file. Data is written using the `fprintf` function, which takes as its first argument the file identifier. Thus the code

```
A = [30 40 60 70];
fid = fopen('myoutput','w');
fprintf(fid,'%g miles/hour = %g kilometers/hour\n', [A; 8*A/5]);
fclose(fid);
```

creates a file `myoutput` containing

```
30 miles/hour = 48 kilometers/hour
40 miles/hour = 64 kilometers/hour
60 miles/hour = 96 kilometers/hour
70 miles/hour = 112 kilometers/hour
```

The file can be read in as follows.

```
>> fid = fopen('myoutput','r');
>> X = fscanf(fid,'%g miles/hour = %g kilometers/hour')
X =
    30
    48
    40
    64
    60
    96
    70
   112
>> fclose(fid);
```

The `fscanf` function reads data formatted according to the specified format string, which in this example says "read a general floating point number (`%g`), skip over the string ' miles/hour = ', read another general floating point number and skip over the string ' kilometers/hour'. The format string is recycled until the entire file has been read and the output is returned in a vector. We can convert the vector to the original matrix format using

```
>> X = reshape(X,2,4)'
X =
    30    48
    40    64
    60    96
    70   112
```

Alternatively, a matrix of the required shape can be obtained directly:

```
>> X = fscanf(fid,'%g miles/hour = %g kilometers/hour',[2 inf]);
>> X = X'
X =
      30    48
      40    64
      60    96
      70   112
```

The third argument to `fprintf` specifies the dimensions of the output matrix, which is filled column by column. We specify `inf` for the number of columns, to allow for any number of lines in the file, and transpose to recover the original format.

Binary files are created and read using the functions `fread` and `fwrite`. See the online help for details of their usage.

Make input easy to prepare and output self-explanatory.
— BRIAN W. KERNIGHAN and P. J. PLAUGER,
The Elements of Programming Style (1978)

Output is almost like input but it's not input, it's output.
To correlate the output with the input and
to verify that the input was put in correctly,
it's a good idea to output the input along with the output.
— ROGER EMANUEL KAUFMAN, *A FORTRAN Coloring Book* (1978)

On two occasions I have been asked [by members of Parliament],
"Pray, Mr. Babbage,
if you put into the machine wrong figures,
will the right answers come out?"
I am not able rightly to apprehend
the kind of confusion of ideas
that could provoke such a question.
— CHARLES BABBAGE

Chapter 14
Troubleshooting

14.1. Errors and Warnings

Errors in MATLAB are of two types: syntax errors and runtime errors. A syntax error is illustrated by

```
>> for i=1#10, x(i) = 1/i; end
??? for i=1#10, x(i) = 1/i; end
            |
Error: Missing variable or function.
```

Here a # has been typed instead of a colon and the error message pinpoints where the problem occurs. If an error occurs in an M-file then the name of the M-file and the line on which the error occurred are shown. If you move the cursor onto the error message and press the enter key then the M-file is opened in the MATLAB Editor/Debugger (see Section 7.2) and the cursor is placed on the line containing the error.

A runtime error occurs with the script fib in Listing 14.1. The loop should begin at i = 3 to avoid referencing x(0). When we run the script, MATLAB produces an informative error message:

```
>> fib
??? Index into matrix is negative or zero.

Error in ==> FIB.M
On line 4  ==>     x(i) = x(i-1) + x(i-2);
```

When an error occurs in a nested sequence of M-file calls, the history of the calls is shown in the error message. The first "Error in" line is the one describing the M-file in which the error is located.

MATLAB's error messages are sometimes rather unhelpful and occasionally misleading. It is perhaps inevitable with such a powerful language that an error message does not always make it immediately clear what has gone wrong. We give a few examples illustrating error messages generated for reasons that are perhaps not obvious.

• "end" expected, "End of Input" found. This message indicates a missing end, which is usually easy to correct. The message is produced by the following code, which is one way of implementing the sign function (MATLAB's sign):

```
if x > 0
   f = 1;
else if x == 0
   f = 0;
else
```

Listing 14.1. *Script* `fib` *that generates a runtime error.*

```
%FIB            Fibonacci numbers.
x = ones(50,1);
for i = 2:50
    x(i) = x(i-1) + x(i-2);
end
```

```
    f = -1;
  end
```

The problem is an unwanted space between `else` and `if`. MATLAB (correctly) interprets the `if` after the `else` as starting a new `if` statement and then complains when it runs out of `end`s to match the `if`s.

• `Undefined function or variable`. Several commands, such as `clear`, `load` and `global`, take a list of arguments separated by spaces. If a comma is used in the list it is interpreted as separating statements, not arguments. For example, the command `clear a,b` clears `a` and prints `b`, so if `b` is undefined the above error message is produced.

• `Matrix must be square`. This message is produced when an attempt is made to exponentiate a nonsquare matrix, and can be puzzling. For example, it is generated by the expression `(1:5)^3`, which was presumably meant to be an elementwise cubing operation and thus should be expressed as `(1:5).^3`.

• `At least one operand must be scalar`. This message is generated when elementwise exponentiation is intended but `^` is typed instead of `.^`, as in `(1:5)^(1:5)`.

• `Missing operator, comma, or semicolon`. This message can be produced by a typing error, for example in response to `hlp qr` or `typ peaks`.

Many functions check for error conditions, issuing an error message and terminating when one occurs. For example:

```
>> mod(3,sqrt(-2))
??? Error using ==> mod
Arguments must be real.
```

In an M-file this behavior can be achieved with the `error` command:

```
if ~isreal(arg2), error('Arguments must be real.'), end
```

produces the result just shown when `arg2` is not real.

The function `warning`, like `error`, displays its string argument, but execution continues instead of stopping. The reason for using `warning` rather than displaying a string with `disp` (for example) is that the display of warning messages can be controlled via certain special string arguments to `warning`. In particular, `warning('off')` or `warning off` turns off the display of warning messages and `warning('on')` or `warning on` turns them back on again. See `help warning` for further options. If you change the `warning` state in an M-file it is good practice to save the old state and restore it before the end of the M-file, as in the following example:

```
warns = warning;
warning('off')
```

```
    . . .
    warning(warns)
```

The most recent error and warning messages can be recalled with the `lasterr` and `lastwarn` functions.

14.2. Debugging

Debugging MATLAB M-files is in principle no different to debugging any other type of computer program, but several facilities are available to ease the task. When an M-file runs but does not perform as expected it is often helpful to print out the values of key variables, which can be done by removing semicolons from assignment statements or adding statements consisting of the relevant variable names.

When it is necessary to inspect several variables and the relations between them the `keyboard` statement is invaluable. When a `keyboard` statement is encountered in an M-file execution halts and a command line with the special prompt K>> appears. Any MATLAB command can be executed and variables in the workspace can be inspected or changed. When keyboard mode is invoked from within a function the visible workspace is that of the function. The command `dbup` changes the workspace to that of the calling function or the main workspace; `dbdown` reverses the effect of `dbup`. Typing `return` followed by the return key causes execution of the M-file to be resumed. The `dbcont` command has the same effect. Alternatively, the `dbquit` command quits keyboard mode and terminates the M-file.

Another way to invoke keyboard mode is via the debugger. Typing

```
    dbstop at 5 in foo
```

sets a breakpoint at line 5 of `foo.m`; this causes subsequent execution of `foo.m` to stop just before line 5 and keyboard mode to be entered. A listing of `foo.m` with line numbers is obtained with `dbtype foo`. Breakpoints are cleared using the `dbclear` command.

We illustrate the use of the debugger on the script `fib` discussed in the last section (Listing 14.1). Here, we set a breakpoint on a runtime error and then inspect the value of the loop index when the error occurs:

```
    >> dbstop if error
    >> fib
    ??? Index into matrix is negative or zero.

    Error in ==> FIB.M
    On line 4  ==>      x(i) = x(i-1) + x(i-2);

    K>> i
    i =
         2
    K>> dbquit
    >>
```

MATLAB's debugger is a powerful tool with several other features that we do not describe here. In addition to the command line interface to the debugger illustrated above, an Editor/Debugger window is available that provides a visual interface (see Section 7.2).

A useful tip for debugging is to execute

```
>> clear all
```

and one of

```
>> clf
>> close all
```

before executing the code with which you are having trouble. The first command clears variables and functions from memory. This is useful when, for example, you are working with scripts because it is possible for existing variables to cause unexpected behavior or to mask the fact that a variable is accessed before being initialized in the script. The other commands are useful for clearing the effects of previous graphics operations.

14.3. Pitfalls

We give some suggestions to help avoid pitfalls particular to MATLAB.

- If you use functions i or j for the imaginary unit, make sure that they have not previously been overridden by variables of the same name (clear i or clear j clears the variable and reverts to the functional form). In general it is not advisable to choose variable names that are the names of MATLAB functions. For example, if you assign

  ```
  >> rand = 1;
  ```

  then subsequent attempts to use the rand function generate an error:

  ```
  >> A = rand(3)
  ???  Index exceeds matrix dimensions.
  ```

  In fact, MATLAB is still aware of the function rand, but the variable takes precedence, as can be seen from

  ```
  >> which -all rand
  rand is a variable.
  rand is a built-in function.
  C:\MATLAB\toolbox\matlab\elmat\rand.m   % Shadowed
  ```

- Confusing behavior can sometimes result from the fact that max, min and sort behave differently for real and for complex data—in the complex case they work with the absolute values of the data. For example, suppose we compute the following 4-vector, which should be real but has a tiny nonzero imaginary part due to rounding errors:

  ```
  e =
     4.0076e+000 -2.7756e-016i
    -6.2906e+000 +3.8858e-016i
    -2.9444e+000 +4.9061e-017i
     9.3624e-001 +1.6575e-016i
  ```

To find the most negative element we need to use `min(real(e))` rather than `min(e)`:

```
>> min(e)
ans =
   9.3624e-001 +1.6575e-016i

>> min(real(e))
ans =
  -6.2906e+000
```

- Mathematical formulae and descriptions of algorithms often index vectors and matrices so that their subscripts start at 0. Since subscripts of MATLAB arrays start at 1, translation of subscripts is necessary when implementing such formulae and algorithms in MATLAB.

The road to wisdom?
Well, it's plain and simple to express:
Err
and err
and err again
but less
and less
and less.
— PIET HEIN, *Grooks* (1966)

Beware of bugs in the above code;
I have only proved it correct, not tried it.
— DONALD E. KNUTH[7] (1977)

Test programs at their boundary values.
— BRIAN W. KERNIGHAN and P. J. PLAUGER,
The Elements of Programming Style (1978)

By June 1949 people had begun to realize that
it was not so easy to get a program right as had at one time appeared...
The realization came over me with full force that
a good part of the remainder of my life was going to be spent in
finding errors in my own programs.
— MAURICE WILKES, *Memoirs of a Computer Pioneer* (1985)

---

[7] See `http://www-cs-faculty.stanford.edu/~knuth/faq.html`

Chapter 15
Sparse Matrices

A sparse matrix is one with a large percentage of zero elements. When dealing with large, sparse matrices, it is desirable to take advantage of the sparsity by storing and operating only on the nonzeros. MATLAB has a `sparse` data type that stores just the nonzero entries of a matrix together with their row and column indices. In this chapter we will use the term "sparse matrix" for a matrix stored in the `sparse` data type and "full matrix" for a matrix stored in the (default) `double` data type.

15.1. Sparse Matrix Generation

Sparse matrices can be created in various ways, several of which involve the `sparse` function. Given a t-vector `s` of matrix entries and t-vectors `i` and `j` of indices, the command `A = sparse(i,j,s)` defines a sparse matrix `A` of dimension `max(i)`-by-`max(j)` with `A(i(k),j(k)) = s(k)`, for `k=1:t` and all other elements zero. Example:

```
>> A = sparse([1 2 2 4 4],[3 1 4 2 4],1:5)
A =
    (2,1)        2
    (4,2)        4
    (1,3)        1
    (2,4)        3
    (4,4)        5
```

MATLAB displays a sparse matrix by listing the nonzero entries preceded by their indices, sorted by columns. A sparse matrix can be converted to a full one using the `full` function:

```
>> B = full(A)
B =
     0     0     1     0
     2     0     0     3
     0     0     0     0
     0     4     0     5
```

Conversely, a full matrix `B` is converted to the sparse storage format by `A = sparse(B)`. The number of nonzeros in a sparse (or full) matrix is returned by `nnz`:

```
>> nnz(A)
ans =
     5
```

After defining `A` and `B`, we can use the `whos` command to check the amount of storage used:

```
>> whos
  Name      Size            Bytes  Class

   A        4x4                80  sparse array
   B        4x4               128  double array
```

Grand total is 21 elements using 208 bytes

The matrix B comprises 16 double precision numbers of 8 bytes each, making a total of 128 bytes. The storage required for a sparse n-by-n matrix with nnz nonzeros is 8*nnz + 4*(nnz+n+1) bytes, which includes the nnz double precision numbers plus some 4-byte integers.

The sparse function accepts three extra arguments. The command

```
A = sparse(i,j,s,m,n)
```

constructs an m-by-n sparse matrix; the last two arguments are necessary when the last row or column of A is all zero. The command

```
A = sparse(i,j,s,m,n,nzmax)
```

allocates space for nzmax nonzeros, which is useful if extra nonzeros, not in s, are to be introduced later, for example when A is generated column by column.

A sparse matrix of zeros is produced by sparse(m,n) (both arguments must be specified), which is an abbreviation for sparse([],[],[],m,n,0).

The sparse identity matrix is produced by speye(n) or speye(m,n), while the command spones(A) produces a matrix with the same sparsity pattern as A and with ones in the nonzero positions.

The arguments that sparse would need to reconstruct an existing matrix A via sparse(i,j,s,m,n) can be obtained using

```
[i,j,s] = find(A);
[m,n] = size(A);
```

The function spdiags is an analogue of diag for sparse matrices. The command A = spdiags(B,d,m,n) creates an m-by-n matrix A whose diagonals indexed by d are taken from the columns of B. This function is best understood by looking at examples. Given

```
B =
     1     2     0
     1     2     3
     0     2     3
     0     2     3
d =
    -2     0     1
```

we can define

```
>> A = spdiags(B,d,4,4)
A =
   (1,1)          2
   (3,1)          1
```

```
      (1,2)          3
      (2,2)          2
      (4,2)          1
      (2,3)          3
      (3,3)          2
      (3,4)          3
      (4,4)          2

>> full(A)
ans =
      2       3       0       0
      0       2       3       0
      1       0       2       3
      0       1       0       2
```

Note that the subdiagonals are taken from the leading parts of the columns of B and the superdiagonals from the trailing parts. Diagonals can be extracted with spdiags: [B,d] = spdiags(A) recovers B and d above. The next example sets up a particular tridiagonal matrix:

```
>> n = 5; e = ones(n,1);
>> A = spdiags([-e 4*e -e],[-1 0 1],n,n);
>> full(A)
ans =
      4      -1       0       0       0
     -1       4      -1       0       0
      0      -1       4      -1       0
      0       0      -1       4      -1
      0       0       0      -1       4
```

Random sparse matrices are generated with sprand and sprandn. The command A = sprand(S) generates a matrix with the same sparsity pattern as S and with nonzero entries uniformly distributed on $[0, 1]$. Alternatively, A = sprand(m,n,density) generates an m-by-n matrix of a random sparsity pattern containing approximately density*m*n nonzero entries uniformly distributed on $[0, 1]$. With four input arguments, A = sprand(m,n,density,rc) produces a matrix for which the reciprocal of the condition number is about rc. The syntax for sprandn is the same, but random numbers from the normal (0,1) distribution are produced.

An invaluable command for visualizing sparse matrices is spy, which plots the sparsity pattern with a dot representing a nonzero; see the plots in the next section.

A sparse array can be distinguished from a full one using the logical function issparse (there is no "isfull" function); see Table 6.1.

15.2. Linear Algebra

MATLAB is able to solve sparse linear equation, eigenvalue and singular value problems, taking advantage of sparsity.

As for full matrices, the backslash operator \ can be used to solve linear systems. The effect of x = A\b when A is sparse is as follows. If A is square then the same operations as in the full case are performed (see Section 9.2.1), except that a reordering is used in the LU or Cholesky factorization to try to reduce the computation and storage and no warning message is produced if A is nearly singular. If A is rectangular then QR factorization is used; a rank deficiency test is performed based on the diagonal elements of the triangular factor.

To compute or estimate the condition number of a sparse matrix condest should be used (see Section 9.1), as cond and rcond are designed only for full matrices.

The lu function for LU factorization and the chol function for Cholesky factorization behave in a similar way for sparse matrices as for full matrices. The same factorizations are produced (using partial pivoting in the case of LU factorization), but the computations are done using sparse data structures. The lu function has one option not present in the full case: lu(A,thresh) sets a pivoting threshold thresh, which must lie between 0 and 1. The pivoting strategy requires that the pivot element have magnitude at least thresh times the magnitude of the largest element below the diagonal in the pivot column. The default is 1, corresponding to partial pivoting, and a threshold of 0 forces no pivoting.

Since lu and chol do not pivot for sparsity (that is, they do not use row or column interchanges in order to try to reduce the cost of the factorizations), it is advisable to consider reordering the matrix before factorizing it. A full discussion of reordering algorithms is beyond the scope of this book, but we give some examples.

We illustrate reorderings with the Wathen matrix:

```
A = gallery('wathen',8,8);
subplot(121), spy(A), subplot(122), spy(chol(A))
```

The spy plots of A and its Cholesky factor are shown in Figure 15.1. Now we reorder the matrix using the symmetric reverse Cuthill–McKee permutation and refactorize:

```
r = symrcm(A);
subplot(121), spy(A(r,r)), subplot(122), spy(chol(A(r,r)))
```

Note that all the reordering functions return an integer permutation vector rather than a permutation matrix (see Section 21.3 for more on permutation vectors and matrices). The spy plots are shown in Figure 15.2. Finally, we try the symmetric minimum degree ordering:

```
m = symmmd(A);
subplot(121), spy(A(m,m)), subplot(122), spy(chol(A(m,m)))
```

The spy plots are shown in Figure 15.3. For this matrix the minimum degree ordering leads to the sparsest Cholesky factor—the one with the least nonzeros. Another reordering function is symamd, the symmetric approximate minimum degree ordering, which for this example produces an even sparser Cholesky factor.

For LU factorization, possible reorderings include

```
p = colamd(A); p = colmmd(A); p = colperm(A);
```

after which A(:,p) is factorized.

In the QR factorization [Q,R] = qr(A) of a sparse rectangular matrix A the orthogonal factor Q can be much less sparse than A, so it is usual to try to avoid explicitly forming Q. When given a sparse matrix and one output argument, the qr function returns just the upper triangular factor R: R = qr(A). When called as [C,R] = qr(A,B), the matrix C = Q'*B is returned along with R. This enables an overdetermined system Ax = b to be solved in the least squares sense by

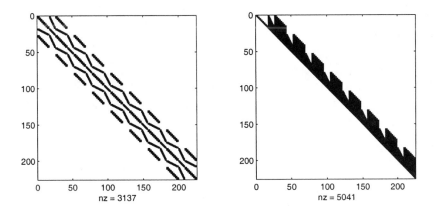

Figure 15.1. *Wathen matrix (left) and its Cholesky factor (right).*

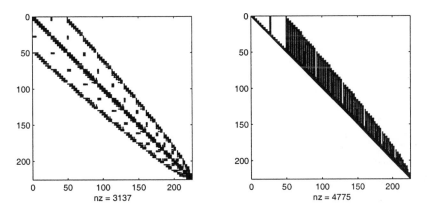

Figure 15.2. *Wathen matrix (left) and its Cholesky factor (right) with symmetric reverse Cuthill–McKee ordering.*

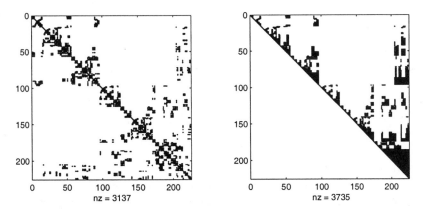

Figure 15.3. *Wathen matrix (left) and its Cholesky factor (right) with symmetric minimum degree ordering.*

```
[c,R] = qr(A,b);
x = R\c;
```

The backslash operator (A\b) uses this method for rectangular A.

The iterative linear system solvers in Table 9.1 are also designed to handle large sparse systems. See Section 9.8 for details of how to use them. Sparse eigenvalue and singular value problems can be solved using eigs and svds, which are also described in Section 9.8.

> *How much of the matrix must be zero for it to be considered sparse*
> *depends on the computation to be performed,*
> *the pattern of the nonzeros,*
> *and even the architecture of the computer.*
> *Generally, we say that a matrix is sparse*
> *if there is an advantage in exploiting its zeros.*
> — I. S. DUFF, A. M. ERISMAN and J. K. REID,
> *Direct Methods for Sparse Matrices* (1986)

> *Sparse matrices are created explicitly rather than automatically.*
> *If you don't need them, you won't see them mysteriously appear.*
> — *The MATLAB EXPO: An Introduction to MATLAB,*
> *SIMULINK and the MATLAB Application Toolboxes* (1993)

> *An objective of a good sparse matrix algorithm should be:*
> *The time required for a sparse matrix operation should be*
> *proportional to the number of arithmetic operations on nonzero quantities.*
> *We call this the "time is proportional to flops" rule;*
> *it is a fundamental tenet of our design.*
> — JOHN R. GILBERT, CLEVE B. MOLER and ROBERT S. SCHREIBER,
> *Sparse Matrices in MATLAB: Design and Implementation* (1992)

Chapter 16
Further M-Files

16.1. Elements of M-File Style

As you use MATLAB you will build up your own collection of M-files. Some may be short scripts that are intended to be used only once, but others will be of potential use in future work. Based on our experience with MATLAB we offer some guidelines on making M-files easy to use, understand, and maintain.

In Chapter 7 we explained the structure of the leading comment lines of a function, including the H1 line. Adhering to this format and fully documenting the function in the leading comment lines is vital if you are to be able to reuse and perhaps modify the function some time after writing it. A further benefit is that writing the comment lines forces you to think carefully about the design of the function, including the number and ordering of the input and output arguments.

It is helpful to include in the leading comment lines an example of how the function is used, in a form that can be cut and pasted into the command line (hence function names should not be given in capitals). MATLAB functions that provide such examples include `fzero`, `meshgrid`, `null` and `texlabel`.

In formatting the code, it is advisable to follow the example of the M-files provided with MATLAB, and to use

- spaces around logical operators and = in assignment statements,

- one statement per line (with exceptions such as a short `if`),

- indentation to emphasize `if`, `for`, `switch` and `while` structures (as provided automatically by MATLAB's Editor/Debugger—see Section 7.2),

- variable names beginning with capital letters for matrices.

Compare the code segment

```
if stopit(4)==1
% Right-angled simplex based on coordinate axes.
alpha=norm(x0,inf)*ones(n+1,1);
for j=2:n+1, V(:,j)=x0+alpha(j)*V(:,j); end
end
```

with the more readable

```
if stopit(4) == 1
   % Right-angled simplex based on coordinate axes.
   alpha = norm(x0,inf)*ones(n+1,1);
   for j=2:n+1
```

```
        V(:,j) = x0 + alpha(j)*V(:,j);
    end
end
```

In this book we usually follow these rules, occasionally breaking them to save space.

A rough guide to choosing variable names is that the length and complexity of a name should be proportional to the variable's scope (the region in which it is used). Loop index variables are typically one character long because they have local scope and are easily recognized. Constants used throughout an M-file merit longer, more descriptive names.

If you want to give someone else an M-file `myfun` that you have written, you also need to give them all the M-files that it calls that are not provided with MATLAB. This list can be determined in two ways. First, you can type `depfun('myfun')`, which returns a list of the M-files that are called by `myfun` or by a function called by `myfun`, and so on. More generally,

```
[Mfiles,builtins] = depfun('myfun')
```

returns lists of the M-files and the built-in functions that are used. Another way to obtain this information is with the `inmem` command, which lists all M-files that have been parsed into memory. If you begin by clearing all functions (`clear functions`), run the M-file in question and then invoke `inmem`, you can deduce which M-files have been called.

16.2. Profiling

MATLAB has a profiler that reports, for a given sequence of computations, how much time is spent in each line of each M-file, and how many times each M-file is called. Profiling has several uses.

- Identifying "hot spots"—those parts of a computation that dominate the execution time. If you wish to optimize the code then you should concentrate on the hot spots.

- Spotting inefficiencies, such as code that can be taken outside a loop.

- Revealing lines in an M-file that are never executed. This enables you to spot unnecessary code and to check whether your test data fully exercises the code.

To illustrate the use of the profiler, we apply it to MATLAB's `membrane` function (used on p. 93):

```
profile on
A = membrane(1,50);
profile report
profile off
```

The `profile report` command generates an html report that is displayed in the system's default Web browser. The part that deals with the `membrane` function itself (rather than the functions called by `membrane`) is:

```
membrane       C:\MATLAB\toolbox\matlab\demos\membrane.m
Time: 0.38 s    (100.0%)
Calls: 1
Self time: 0.05 s     (100.0%)

    Function: Time          Calls  Time/call
    membrane  0.38              1     0.380

    Parent functions:
    none

    Child functions:
    besselj   0.33  86.8%        4     0.083

    rot90     0.00   0.0%        1     0.000

100% of the total time in this function was spent on the following
lines:

          70:  t = sqrt(lambda)*r;
0.05 13% 71:  b1 = besselj(alf1,t);
0.06 16% 72:  b2 = besselj(alf2,t);
          73:  A = [b1(:,k1) b2(:,k2)];

          96:  S = zeros(m+1,mm);
0.05 13% 97:  r = sqrt(lambda)*r;
          98:  for j = 1:np
0.22 58% 99:      S = S + c(j) * besselj(alfa(j),r) .* ...
                  sin(alfa(j)*theta);
         100: end
```

The profile reveals that **membrane** spends most if its time evaluating Bessel functions. The "self time" is the time spent in **membrane** excluding the time spent in functions called by **membrane**. Note that the numbers followed by a colon are line numbers.

The command **profile plot** produces a bar graph in a figure window showing the M-files that took the most time. For the above example the plot is shown in Figure 16.1.

Next, consider the script **ops** in Listing 16.1. In order to compare the relative costs of the elementary operations +, -, *, / and the elementary functions sqrt, exp, sin, tan, we profiled the script down to the level of individual operators (see **help profile** for details of the various options of **profile**):

```
profile on -detail operator
ops
profile report
profile off
```

Part of the report is as follows:

Name	Time
tan	1.31 25.3%

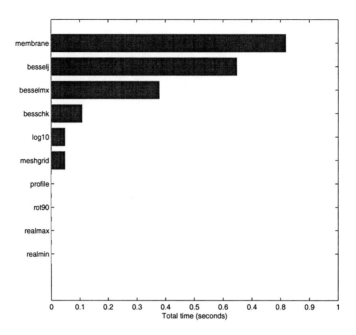

Figure 16.1. profile plot *for* membrane *example*.

```
exp      1.04 20.1%
sqrt     1.00 19.3%
sin      0.83 16.1%
./       0.33  6.4%
.*       0.22  4.3%
+        0.11  2.1%
-        0.05  1.0%
```

The precise results will vary with the computer. As expected, the exponential and trigonometric functions are much more costly than the four elementary operations.

Listing 16.1. *Script* ops.

```
%OPS    Profile this file to check costs of various elementary ops and funs.

rand('state',1), randn('state',1)
a = 100*rand(100);
b = randn(100);

for i = 1:100
    a+b;
    a-b;
    a.*b;
    a./b;
    sqrt(a);
    exp(a);
    sin(a);
    tan(a);
end
```

*I've become convinced that all compilers written from now on
should be designed to provide all programmers with feedback indicating
what parts of their programs are costing the most.*

— DONALD E. KNUTH, *Structured Programming with* go to *Statements* (1974)

*Instrument your programs.
Measure before making "efficiency" changes.*

— BRIAN W. KERNIGHAN and P. J. PLAUGER,
The Elements of Programming Style (1978)

*Arnold was unhappily aware that the complete Jurassic Park program contained
more than half a million lines of code,
most of it undocumented, without explanation.*

— MICHAEL CRICHTON, *Jurassic Park* (1990)

Chapter 17
Handle Graphics

The graphics functions described in Chapter 8 can produce a wide range of output and are sufficient to satisfy the needs of many MATLAB users. These functions are part of an object-oriented graphics system known as Handle Graphics that provides full control over the way MATLAB displays data. A knowledge of Handle Graphics is useful if you want to fine-tune the appearance of your plots, and it enables you to produce displays that are not possible with the existing functions. This chapter provides a brief introduction to Handle Graphics. More information can be found in [57].

17.1. Objects and Properties

Handle Graphics builds graphs out of objects organized in a hierarchy, as shown in Figure 17.1. The Root object corresponds to the whole screen and a Figure object to a figure window. Of the objects on the third level of the tree we will be concerned only with the Axes object, which is a region of the figure window in which objects from the bottom level of the tree are displayed. A figure window may contain more than one Axes object, as we will see in an example below. From the bottom level of the tree we will be concerned only with the Line, Surface and Text objects.

Each object has a unique identifier called a handle, which is a floating point number (sometimes an integer). The handle of the Root object is always 0. The handle of a Figure object is, by default, the figure number displayed on the title bar (but this can be changed). To use Handle Graphics you create objects and manipulate their properties by reference to their handles, making use of the `get` and `set` functions.

We begin with a simple example:

```
>> plot(1:10,'o-')
```

This produces the left-hand plot in Figure 17.2. Now we interactively investigate the objects comprising the plot, beginning by using the `findobj` function to obtain the handles of all the objects:

```
>> h = findobj
h =
         0
    1.0000
   73.0011
    1.0050
```

We know from the conventions that the first handle, 0, is that of the root, and the second, 1, is that of the figure. We can determine the types of all the objects that these handles represent using the `get` function:

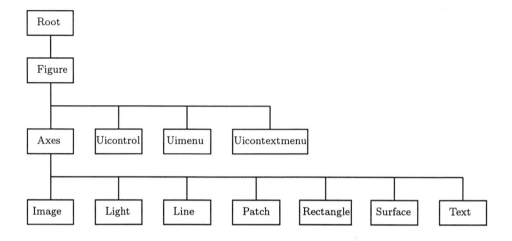

Figure 17.1. *Hierarchical structure of Handle Graphics objects.*

```
>> get(h,'type')
ans =
    'root'
    'figure'
    'axes'
    'line'
```

Thus h(3) is the handle to an Axes object and h(4) that to a Line object.

A handle provides access to the various properties of an object that govern its appearance. A list of properties can be obtained by calling the **set** function with the appropriate handle. For the Axes object the properties are illustrated by

```
>> set(h(3))
ALim
ALimMode: [ {auto} | manual ]
AmbientLightColor
Box: [ on | {off} ]
CameraPosition
CameraPositionMode: [ {auto} | manual ]
        ...
Visible: [ {on} | off ]
```

Here we have replaced about 80 lines of output with "...". The property names are listed one per line. For those properties that take string values the possible values are listed in square brackets; the default is enclosed in curly braces. For the Line object the properties are listed by

```
>> set(h(4))
Color
EraseMode: [ {normal} | background | xor | none ]
LineStyle: [ {-} | -- | : | -. | none ]
LineWidth
        ...
Visible: [ {on} | off ]
```

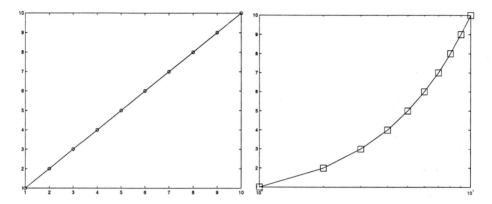

Figure 17.2. *Left: original. Right: modified by* set *commands.*

We see, for example, that the LineStyle property of the Line object has five possible values (those listed in Table 8.1 together with none, for use when only a marker is required) and the default is '-'. Full documentation of all object properties is available under the "Handle Graphics Object Properties" topic of the Help Browser. For direct access to the relevant help pages you can type doc name_props, where name is replaced by rootobject or by any of the names of objects below the root in Figure 17.1. Thus doc line_props displays information about Line object properties.

To obtain the allowable string values of a single property the property name is added as a second argument to set:

```
>> set(h(4),'Marker')
[ + | o | * | . | x | square | diamond | v | ^ | > | < | ...
pentagram | hexagram | {none} ]
```

Property values are assigned by providing set with the handle and pairs of property names and property values. Thus the command

```
>> set(h(4),'Marker','s','MarkerSize',16)
```

replaces the original 'o' marker by a square of size 16 in the line object in our example. It is only necessary to provide enough characters of the property name or value to uniquely identify it, so 's' above is equivalent to 'square', and any mixture of upper and lower case letters can be used. Next, we check the possible values of the XScale property for the Axes object:

```
>> set(h(3),'XScale')
[ {linear} | log ]
```

We set this property to log to make the x-axis scale logarithmic (as for semilogx):

```
set(h(3),'XScale','log')
```

The modified plot is shown on the right-hand side of Figure 17.2.

For a further example, we consider the following code, which produces Figure 17.3:

```
x = linspace(0,2*pi,35);

a1 = subplot(2,1,1);                % Axes object.
l1 = plot(x,sin(x),'x');            % Line object.

a2 = subplot(2,1,2);                % Axes object.
l2 = plot(x,cos(x).*sin(x));        % Line object.
tx2 = xlabel('x'); ty2 = ylabel('y'); % Text objects.
```

When the following code is executed it modifies properties of objects to produce Figure 17.4.

```
set(a1,'Box','off')                           % box off.
set(a1,'XTick',[])
set(a1,'YAxisLocation','right')
set(a1,'TickDir','out')
set(l1,'Marker','<')

set(a2,'Position',[0.2 0.15 0.65 0.35])
set(a2,'XLim',[0 2*pi])                        % xlim([0 2*pi]).
set(a2,'FontSize',14)
set(a2,'XTick',[0 pi/2 pi 2*pi])
set(a2,'XTickLabel','0|pi/2|pi|2pi')
set(a2,'XGrid','on')
set(a2,'XScale','log')
set(l2,'LineWidth',6)
set(tx2,'FontAngle','italic','FontSize',20)
set(ty2,'Rotation',0,'FontAngle','italic','FontSize',20)
```

Some of the effects of these set commands can be produced using commands discussed in Chapter 8, as indicated in the comments, or by appending property name-value pairs to argument lists of plot and text. For example, box off can be used in place of set(a1,'Box','off'), provided that the first Axes is current. However, certain effects can be conveniently achieved only by using set.

The properties altered here are mostly fairly self-explanatory. An exception is the Position property of Axes, which is specified by a vector of the form [left bottom width height], where left and bottom are the distances from the left edge and bottom edge, respectively, of the Figure window to the bottom left corner of the Axes rectangle, and width and height define the dimensions of the rectangle. The units of measurement are defined by the Units property, whose default is normalized, which maps the lower left corner of the figure window to $(0,0)$ and the upper right corner to $(1.0, 1.0)$. Note that tick labels do not support TeX notation, so we could not produce the symbol π in the x-axis labels specified by the XTickLabel property.

A counterpart to the set function is get, which queries the current values of properties. With just a handle as argument, get lists all the properties:

```
>> get(l1)
Color = [0 0 1]
EraseMode = normal
LineStyle = none
LineWidth = [0.5]
```

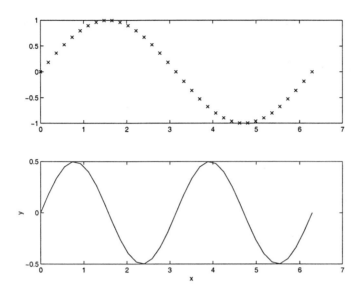

Figure 17.3. *Straightforward use of* subplot.

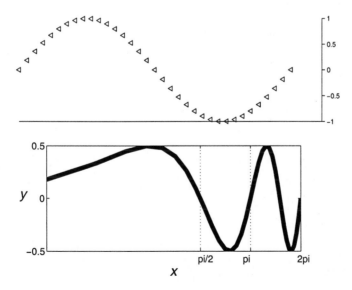

Figure 17.4. *Modified version of Figure* 17.3 *postprocessed using Handle Graphics.*

```
Marker = .
MarkerSize = [18]
          . . .
Visible = on
```

When invoked with a second argument specifying a property name, `get` lists just that value:

```
>> get(a3,'XTick')
ans =
       0    1.5708    3.1416    4.7124    6.2832
```

The `delete` function deletes an object with the specified handle. Thus `delete(l1)` removes the sine curve from the top plot in Figure 17.4 and `delete(tx2)` removes the x-axis label from the bottom plot.

Generally, if you plan to change the properties of an object after creating it then you should save the handle when you create it, as in the example above. However, handles of existing objects can be retrieved using `gca`, `gcf` and `gco`, which return the handles of the current Axes, the current Figure, and the current Object, respectively. In the following example we check the current and possible values of the `FontWeight` property for the current Axes and then change the property to `bold`:

```
>> get(gca,'FontWeight')
ans =
normal

>> set(gca,'FontWeight')
[ light | {normal} | demi | bold ]

>> set(gca,'FontWeight','bold')
```

The "current Object" whose handle is returned by `gco` is the object last clicked on with the mouse. Thus if we want to change the marker to '*' for the curve in the upper plot of Figure 17.4 we can click on the curve and then type

```
>> set(gco,'Marker','*')
```

In addition to setting graphics properties from the command line or in M-files it is possible to set them interactively using the Property Editor. The Property Editor is invoked on a particular graphic object by first enabling plot editing, by clicking on the plot editing icon in the figure window toolbar, and then double-clicking on the object. Experimenting with the Property Editor is an excellent way to learn about Handle Graphics.

The importance of the hierarchical nature of the Handle Graphics structure is not completely apparent in the simple examples described above. A particular object, say the Root, contains the handles of all its children, which makes it possible to traverse the tree structure, using `get(h,'Children')`, `get(h,'Parent')`, and the `findobj` and `findall` functions. Furthermore, it is possible to set default values for properties, and if these are set on a particular Axes, for example, they are inherited by all the children of that Axes. These aspects are beyond the scope of this book—see [57] for details.

Also beyond the scope of this book are MATLAB's Graphical User Interface (GUI) tools, described in [52] (type `help uitools` for a list of the relevant functions). However, we mention one GUI function that is of broad interest: `waitbar` displays a graphical bar in a window that can be used to show the progress of a computation. Its usage is illustrated by

```
h = waitbar(0,'Computing...')
for j = 1:n
  % Some computation ...
  waitbar(j/n) % Set bar to show fraction j/n complete.
end
close(h)
```

17.2. Animation

Two types of animation are possible in MATLAB. A sequence of figures can be saved and then replayed as a movie, and an animated plot can be produced by manipulating the XData, YData and ZData properties of objects. We give one example of each type. For further details see [57].

To create a movie, you draw the figures one at a time, use the `getframe` function to save each one as a pixel snapshot in a structure, and then invoke the `movie` function to replay the figures. Here is an example:[8]

```
clear  % Remove existing variables.
Z = peaks; surf(Z)
axis tight
set(gca,'nextplot','replacechildren')
disp('Creating the movie...')
for j = 1:11
    surf(cos(2*pi*(j-1)/10).*Z,Z)
    F(j) = getframe;
end
disp('Playing the movie...')
movie(F)
```

Figure 17.5 shows one intermediate frame from the movie. The `set` command causes all `surf` plots after the first to leave unaltered the Axes properties, such as `axis tight` and the grid lines. The movie is replayed n times with `movie(F,n)`. The amount of storage required by the movie depends on the window size but not on the contents of the window.

The second type of animation is most easily obtained using the functions `comet` and `comet3`. They behave like limited versions of `plot` and `plot3`, differing in that the plot is traced out by a "comet" consisting of a head (a circle), a body (in one color) and a tail (in another color). For example, try

```
x = linspace(-2,2,500);
y = exp(x).*sin(1./x);
comet(x,y)
```

---

[8]The fact that F in this example is not preallocated (cf. Section 20.2) does not cause any loss of efficiency. Since `getframe` returns a structure, F is a vector of `structs` and it is only pointers that need to be deallocated and reallocated.

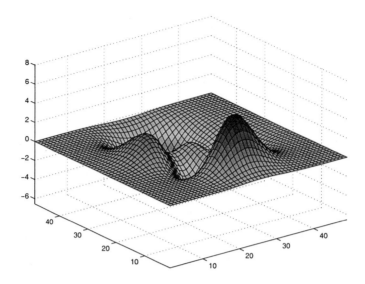

Figure 17.5. *One frame from a movie.*

We give a simple example to illustrate the principle used by comet. This example can be adapted for use in situations in which the data must be plotted as it is generated, as when solving a differential equation, for example (see the MATLAB demonstration function lorenz, mentioned at the end of Chapter 1).

```
x = linspace(-pi,pi,2000);
y = cos(tan(x))-tan(sin(x));
p = plot(x(1),y(1),'.','EraseMode','none','MarkerSize',5);
axis([min(x) max(x) min(y) max(y)])
hold on
for i=2:length(x)
    set(p,'XData',x(i),'YData',y(i))
    drawnow
end
hold off
```

This code creates a plot of just one point and then keeps redrawing the point by changing the XData and YData properties of the corresponding Line object. The key is to set the EraseMode property to none so that MATLAB does not erase existing objects when the plot is redrawn by the drawnow command. If EraseMode is set to background then the old point is erased as the new one is plotted, so a moving dot is seen. Figure 17.6 shows the final result. This figure is lower resolution than the others in the book because it was produced by using getframe to save the original figure, redisplaying it with image and then saving in the usual way. The reason we could not save the original figure directly is that it contains only one dot, the others being from unerased earlier plots.

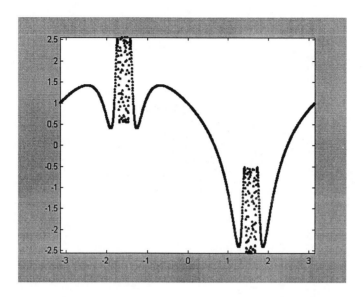

Figure 17.6. *Animated figure upon completion.*

17.3. Examples

In this section we give some practical examples of using Handle Graphics to create customized graphics.

MATLAB's choices of tick marks and axis limits are not always the most appropriate. The upper plot in Figure 17.7 shows the relative distance from IEEE single precision numbers $x \in [1, 16]$ to the next larger floating point number. The tick marks on the x-axis do not emphasize the important fact that interesting changes happen at a power of 2. The lower plot in Figure 17.7 (which is [30, Fig. 2.1]) differs from the upper one in that the following Handle Graphics commands were appended:

```
set(gca,'XTick',[1 2 4 8 16])
set(gca,'TickLength',[0.02 0.025])
set(gca,'FontSize',14);
```

The first set command specifies the location of the ticks on the x-axis and the second increases the length of the ticks (to 0.02 for 2D plots and 0.025 for 3D plots, in units normalized relative to the longest of the visible x-, y-, or z-axis lines). The last command sets a 14-point font size for the tick labels and axis labels.

Suppose that you wish to use a nonstandard font size (say, 16) throughout a Figure object. Explicitly setting the FontSize property for each Text object and each Axes is tedious. Instead, after creating the figure, you can type

```
h = findall(gcf,'type','text'); set(h,'FontSize',16)
h = findall(gcf,'type','axes'); set(h,'FontSize',16)
```

Note that using findobj in the first line would not produce any change to the xlabel, ylabel or title. The reason is that these text objects are created with the HandleVisibility property set to off, which makes them invisible to findobj, but not to findall. (Look at the code with type findall to gain some insight.)

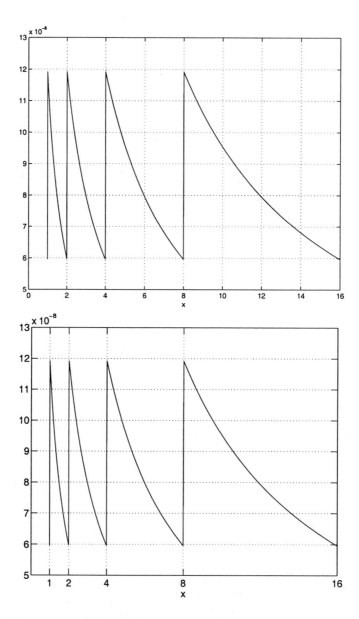

Figure 17.7. *Default (upper) and modified (lower) settings.*

For this reason, however, `findall` should be used with caution as it may expose to view handles that have intentionally been hidden by an application, so manipulating the corresponding objects could produce strange results.

The next example illustrates the use of a cell array (see Section 18.3) to specify the `YTickLabel` data and the `YDir` property to reverse the order of the y-axis values. The script file in Listing 17.1 produces Figure 17.8, which shows the most frequently used words of four letters or more, and their frequencies of occurrence, in a draft of this book.

Handle Graphics can be used to superimpose two different Axes, using the left y-axis for one set of data and the right y-axis for another. This is done by the code in Listing 17.2, which produces Figure 17.9. The comments in the code explain how it works. Note that the function `plotyy` automates this process of producing different left and right y-axes in the case of simple plots.

The final example illustrates how diagrams, as opposed to plots of data or functions, can be generated. The script file in Listing 17.3 produces Figure 17.10. It uses the `line` function, which is a low-level routine that creates a line object in the current Axes. Several of MATLAB's higher level graphics routines make use of `line`. The script also uses the `rectangle` function to draw a circle. The `Position` property of `rectangle` is a vector `[x y w h]` that specifies a rectangle of width `w` and height `h` with bottom left corner at the point `x`, `y`, all in Axes data units. The `Curvature` property determines the curvature of the sides of the rectangle, with extremes `[0 0]` for square sides and `[1 1]` for an ellipse. The `HorizontalAlignment` and `VerticalAlignment` text properties have been used to help position the text.

Listing 17.1. *Script* wfreq.

```
%WFREQ

% Cell array z stores the data:
z = {492, 'matrix'
     475, 'that'
     456, 'function'
     420, 'with'
     280, 'this'
     273, 'figure'
     261, 'example'
     226, 'which'
     201, 'functions'
     169, 'plot'
     158, 'using'
     154, 'file'
     150, 'command'
     140, 'from'
     135, 'vector'};
% Draw bar graph of first column of z.  CAT converts to column vector.
barh(cat(1,z{:,1}))
n = length(z);
set(gca,'YTick',1:n,'YTickLabel',z(:,2))
set(gca,'YDir','reverse')  % Reverse order of y-values.
ylim([0 n+1])
grid
```

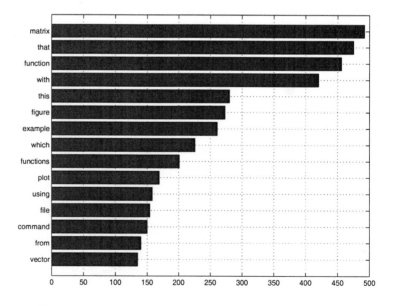

Figure 17.8. *Word frequency bar chart created by* wfreq.

Listing 17.2. *Script* garden *to produce Figure* 17.9.

```
%GARDEN

% Cols: Carrots|Broccoli|Green Beans|Cucumbers|Chard.  Rows are months.
Y = [0.4 0.3 0.0 0.0 0.9
     0.6 0.4 0.0 0.0 1.0
     0.7 0.8 0.3 0.2 1.2
     0.6 0.5 0.9 0.4 1.1
     0.4 0.4 0.7 0.6 0.9];

t = [13 15 22 24 18]; % Temperature.

b = bar(Y,'stacked');
ylabel('Yield (kg)'), ylim([0 4])

h1 = gca; % Handle of first axis.
set(h1,'XTickLabel','May|June|July|August|September')

% Create a second axis at same location as first and plot to it.
h2 = axes('Position',get(h1,'Position'));
p = plot(t,'Marker','square','MarkerSize',12,'LineStyle','-',...
           'LineWidth',2,'MarkerFaceColor',[.6 .6 .6]);
ylabel('Degrees (Celsius)')
title('Fran''s vegetable garden','FontSize',14)

% Align second x-axis with first and remove tick labels.
set(h2,'Xlim',get(h1,'XLim'),'XTickLabel',[])
% Locate second y-axis on right, make background transparent.
set(h2,'YAxisLocation','right','Color','none')

% Make second y-axis tick marks line up with those of first.
ylimits = get(h2,'YLim');
yinc = (ylimits(2)-ylimits(1))/4;
set(h2,'Ytick',[ylimits(1):yinc:ylimits(2)])

% Give legend the Axes handles and place top left.
legend([b,p],'Carrots','Broccoli','Green Beans','Cucumbers','Chard',...
             'Temperature',2)
```

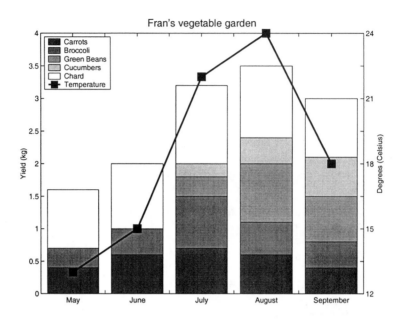

Figure 17.9. *Example with superimposed Axes created by script* garden.

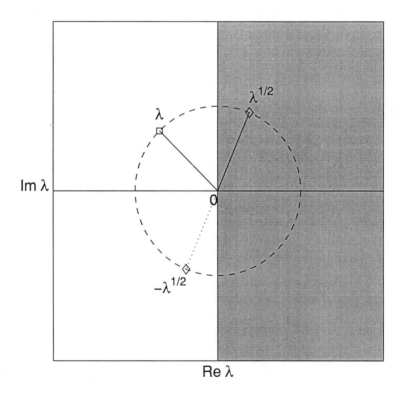

Figure 17.10. *Diagram created by* sqrt_ex.

Listing 17.3. *Script* sqrt_ex.

```
%SQRT_EX
% Script plotting a point on the unit circle and its two square roots,
% with the right half-plane shaded.

clear i                              % Ensure i is function, not variable.
z = -1+i; z = z/abs(z);              % Point z on unit circle.
s = sqrt(z);

h = axes('XLim',[-2 2],'YLim',[-2 2]); % Create Axes with specified range.

fill([0 2 2 0],[-2 -2 2 2],[.8 .8 .8]) % Shade right half-plane.
hold on

plot(z,'s','MarkerSize',8), line([0 real(z)],[0 imag(z)])
plot(s,'d','MarkerSize',8), line([0 real(s)],[0 imag(s)])
plot(-s,'d','MarkerSize',8), line([0 -real(s)],[0 -imag(s)],'LineStyle',':')

% Unit circle.
rectangle('Position',[-1,-1,2,2],'Curvature',[1,1],'LineStyle','--')
axis square

% Draw x- and y-axes through origin.
plot([-2 2], [0 0], '-'), plot([0 0], [-2 2], '-')
set(h,'XTick',[],'YTick',[])

xlabel('Re \lambda')
ylabel('Im \lambda','Rotation',0,'HorizontalAlignment','right')

text(real(z),imag(z)+0.2,'\lambda','HorizontalAlignment','center')
text(0,0,'0','HorizontalAlignment','right','VerticalAlignment','top')
text(real(s),imag(s)+0.2,'\lambda^{1/2}')
text(-real(s),-imag(s)-0.2,'-\lambda^{1/2}','HorizontalAlignment','right')
hold off

% Reset FontSize for all text.
g = findall(gcf,'type','text'); set(g,'Fontsize',16)
```

Words with most meanings in the Oxford English Dictionary:
1. set
⋮
6. get
— RUSSELL ASH, The Top 10 of Everything (1994)

Handle Graphics . . .
allows you to display your data and then
"reach in" and manipulate any part of the image you've created,
whether that means changing a color, a line style, or a font.
— *The MATLAB EXPO: An Introduction to MATLAB,*
SIMULINK and the MATLAB Application Toolboxes (1993)

The best designs . . .
are intriguing and curiosity-provoking,
drawing the viewer into the wonder of the data,
sometimes by narrative power,
sometimes by immense detail,
and sometimes by elegant presentation of simple but interesting data.
— EDWARD R. TUFTE, *The Visual Display of Quantitative Information* (1983)

Chapter 18
Other Data Types and Multidimensional Arrays

So far in this book we have identified two of MATLAB's fundamental data types (or classes): double and sparse. There are several others, including char, cell, struct, storage and function handle. The storage data types are for memory-efficient storage and are of use only in specialized situations. In this chapter we describe the char, struct and cell data types. All the fundamental types are, in general, multidimensional arrays; we describe multidimensional arrays in the second section.

If you want to determine the data type of an object you can use the class function, which provides the same information as the last column of the output from whos. For example,

```
>> class(pi)
ans =
double

>> class(speye(4))
ans =
sparse
```

You can also use the isa function to test whether a variable is of a particular class:

```
>> isa(rand(2),'double')
ans =
     1

>> isa(eye(2),'sparse')
ans =
     0
```

18.1. Strings

A string, or character array (char array), is an array of characters represented internally in MATLAB by the corresponding ASCII values. Consider the following example:

```
>> s = 'ABCabc'
s =
ABCabc
```

217

```
>> sd = double(s)
sd =
    65    66    67    97    98    99

>> s2 = char(sd)
s2 =
ABCabc

>> whos
  Name        Size          Bytes  Class

    s         1x6              12  char array
    s2        1x6              12  char array
    sd        1x6              48  double array

Grand total is 18 elements using 72 bytes
```

We see that a string can be specified by placing characters between single quotes or by applying the char function to an array of positive integers. Each character in a string occupies 2 bytes. Converting a string to a double array produces an array of ASCII values occupying 8 bytes per element; for example, double('A') is 65.

Strings can also be created by formatting the values of numeric variables, using int2str, num2str or sprintf, as described in Section 13.2.

MATLAB has several functions for working with strings. Function strcat concatenates two strings into one longer string. It removes trailing spaces but leaves leading spaces:

```
>> strcat('Hello',' world')
ans =
Hello world
```

A similar effect can be achieved using the square bracket notation:

```
>> ['Hello ' 'world']
ans =
Hello world
```

Two strings can be compared using strcmp: strcmp(s,t) returns 1 (true) if s and t are identical and 0 (false) otherwise. Function strcmpi does likewise but treats upper and lower case letters as equivalent. Note the difference between using strcmp and the relational operator ==:

```
>> strcmp('Matlab5','Matlab6')
ans =
     0

>> 'Matlab5' == 'Matlab6'
ans =
     1     1     1     1     1     1     0
```

The relational operator can be used only to compare strings of equal length and it returns a vector showing which characters match. To test whether one string is contained in another use findstr: findstr(s,t) returns a vector of indices of locations where the shorter string appears in the longer:

```
>> findstr('bc','abcd')
ans =
     2

>> findstr('abacad','a')
ans =
     1     3     5
```

A string can be tested for with logical function ischar.

Function eval executes a string containing any MATLAB expression. Suppose we want to set up matrices A1, A2, A3, A4, the pth of which is A - p*eye(n). Instead of writing four assignment statements this can be done in a loop using eval:

```
for p=1:4
    eval(['A', int2str(p), ' = A - p*eye(n)'])
end
```

When p = 2, for example, the argument to eval is the string 'A2 = A - p*eye(n)' and eval executes the assignment.

For more functions relating to strings see help strfun.

18.2. Multidimensional Arrays

Arrays of type double, char, cell and struct, but not sparse, can have more than two dimensions. Multidimensional arrays are defined and manipulated using natural generalizations of the techniques for matrices. For example we can set up a 3-by-2-by-2 array of random normal numbers as follows:

```
>> A = randn(3,2,2)
A(:,:,1) =
     0.8644     0.8735
     0.0942    -0.4380
    -0.8519    -0.4297
A(:,:,2) =
    -1.1027     0.1684
     0.3962    -1.9654
    -0.9649    -0.7443

>> whos
  Name       Size           Bytes  Class

  A          3x2x2             96  double array

Grand total is 12 elements using 96 bytes
```

Notice that MATLAB displays this three-dimensional array a two-dimensional slice at a time. Functions rand, randn, zeros and ones all accept an argument list of the form (n_1,n_2,...,n_p) or ([n_1,n_2,...,n_p]) in order to set up an array of dimension n_1-by-n_2-...-by-n_p. An existing two-dimensional array can have its dimensionality extended by assigning to elements in a higher dimension; MATLAB automatically increases the dimensions:

```
>> B = [1 2 3; 4 5 6];
>> B(:,:,2) = ones(2,3)
B(:,:,1) =
        1       2       3
        4       5       6
B(:,:,2) =
        1       1       1
        1       1       1
```

The number of dimensions can be queried using `ndims`, and the `size` function returns the number of elements in each dimension:

```
>> ndims(B)
ans =
     3

>> size(B)
ans =
     2       3       2
```

To build a multidimensional array by listing elements in one statement use the `cat` function, whose first argument specifies the dimension along which to concatenate the arrays comprising its remaining arguments:

```
>> C = cat(3,[1 2 3; 0 -1 -2],[-5 -3 -1; 10 5 0])
C(:,:,1) =
        1       2       3
        0      -1      -2
C(:,:,2) =
       -5      -3      -1
       10       5       0
```

Functions that operate in an elementwise sense can be applied to multidimensional arrays, as can arithmetic, logical and relational operators. Thus, for example, `B-ones(size(B))`, `B.*B`, `exp(B)`, `2.^B` and `B > 0` all return the expected results. The data analysis functions in Table 5.7 all operate along the first nonsingleton dimension by default and accept an extra argument `dim` that specifies the dimension over which they are to operate. For B as above, compare

```
>> sum(B)
ans(:,:,1) =
        5       7       9
ans(:,:,2) =
        2       2       2

>> sum(B,3)
ans =
        2       3       4
        5       6       7
```

Table 18.1. *Multidimensional array functions.*

`cat`	Concatenate arrays
`ndims`	Number of dimensions
`ndgrid`	Generate arrays for multidimensional functions and interpolation
`permute`	Permute array dimensions
`ipermute`	Inverse permute array dimensions
`shiftdim`	Shift dimensions
`squeeze`	Remove singleton dimensions

The transpose operator and the linear algebra operations such as `diag`, `inv`, `eig` and \ are undefined for arrays of dimension greater than 2; they can be applied to two-dimensional sections only.

Table 18.1 lists some functions designed specifically for manipulating multidimensional arrays.

18.3. Structures and Cell Arrays

Structures and cell arrays both provide a way to collect arrays of different types and sizes into a single array. They are MATLAB features of growing importance, used in many places within MATLAB. For example, structures are used by `spline` (p. 138), by `solve` in the next chapter (p. 229), and to set options for the nonlinear equation and optimization solvers (Section 11.2) and the differential equation solvers (Sections 12.2–12.3). Structures also play an important role in object-oriented programming in MATLAB (which is not discussed in this book). Cell arrays are used by the `varargin` and `varargout` functions (Section 10.3), to specify text in graphics commands (p. 101), and in the `switch-case` construct (Section 6.2).

We give only a brief introduction to structures and cell arrays here. See `help datatypes` for a list of functions associated with structures and cell arrays, and see [56] for a tutorial.

Suppose we want to build a collection of 4×4 test matrices, recording for each matrix its name, the matrix elements, and the eigenvalues. We can build an array structure `testmat` having three fields, `name`, `mat` and `eig`:

```
n = 4;
testmat(1).name = 'Hilbert';
testmat(1).mat = hilb(n);
testmat(1).eig = eig(hilb(n));
testmat(2).name = 'Pascal';
testmat(2).mat = pascal(n);
testmat(2).eig = eig(pascal(n));
```

Displaying the structure gives the field names but not the contents:

```
>> testmat
testmat =
1x2 struct array with fields:
    name
```

```
        mat
        eig
```

We can access individual fields using a period:

```
>> testmat(2).name
ans =
Pascal
```

```
>> testmat(1).mat
ans =
      1.0000      0.5000      0.3333      0.2500
      0.5000      0.3333      0.2500      0.2000
      0.3333      0.2500      0.2000      0.1667
      0.2500      0.2000      0.1667      0.1429
```

```
>> testmat(2).eig
ans =
      0.0380
      0.4538
      2.2034
     26.3047
```

For array fields, array subscripts can be appended to the field specifier:

```
>> testmat(1).mat(1:2,1:2)
ans =
      1.0000      0.5000
      0.5000      0.3333
```

Another way to set up the `testmat` structure is using the `struct` command:

```
testmat = struct('name',{'Hilbert','Pascal'},...
                 'mat',{hilb(n),pascal(n)}, ...
                 'eig',{eig(hilb(n)),eig(pascal(n))})
```

The arguments to the `struct` function are the field names, with each field name followed by the field contents listed within curly braces (that is, the field contents are cell arrays, which are described next). If the entire structure cannot be assigned with one `struct` statement then it can be created with fields initialized to a particular value using `repmat`. For example, we can set up a test matrix structure for five matrices initialized with empty names and zero matrix entries and eigenvalues with

```
>> testmat = repmat(struct('name',{''}, 'mat',{zeros(n)}, ...
                    'eig',{zeros(n,1)}),5,1)
testmat =
5x1 struct array with fields:
    name
    mat
    eig
```

```
>> testmat(5) % Check last element of structure.
ans =
```

```
    name: ''
     mat: [4x4 double]
     eig: [4x1 double]
```

For the benefits of such preallocation see Section 20.2.

Cell arrays differ from structures in that they are accessed using array indexing rather than named fields. One way to set up a cell array is by using curly braces as cell array constructors. In this example we set up a 2-by-2 cell array:

```
>> C = {1:3, pi; magic(2), 'A string'}
C =
    [1x3 double]    [  3.1416]
    [2x2 double]    'A string.'
```

Cell array contents are indexed using curly braces, and the colon notation can be used in the same way as for other arrays:

```
>> C{1,1}
ans =
     1     2     3

>> C{2,:}
ans =
     1     3
     4     2
ans =
A string.
```

The test matrix example can be recast as a cell array as follows:

```
clear testmat
testmat{1,1} = 'Hilbert';
testmat{2,1} = hilb(n);
testmat{3,1} = eig(hilb(n));
testmat{1,2} = 'Pascal';
testmat{2,2} = pascal(n);
testmat{3,2} = eig(pascal(n));
```

The clear statement is necessary to remove the previous structure of the same name. Here each collection of test matrix information occupies a column of the cell array, as can be seen from

```
>> testmat
testmat =
    'Hilbert'       'Pascal'
    [4x4 double]    [4x4 double]
    [4x1 double]    [4x1 double]
```

The celldisp function can be used to display the contents of a cell array:

```
>> celldisp(testmat)
testmat{1,1} =
Hilbert
```

```
testmat{2,1} =
      1.0000      0.5000      0.3333      0.2500
      0.5000      0.3333      0.2500      0.2000
      0.3333      0.2500      0.2000      0.1667
      0.2500      0.2000      0.1667      0.1429
testmat{3,1} =
      0.0001
      0.0067
      0.1691
      1.5002
testmat{1,2} =
Pascal
testmat{2,2} =
      1      1      1      1
      1      2      3      4
      1      3      6     10
      1      4     10     20
testmat{3,2} =
      0.0380
      0.4538
      2.2034
     26.3047
```

Another way to express the assignments to `testmat` above is by using standard array subscripting, as illustrated by

```
testmat(1,1) = {'Hilbert'};
```

Curly braces must appear on either the left or the right side of the assignment statement in order for the assignment to be valid.

When a component of a cell array is itself an array, its elements can be accessed using parentheses:

```
>> testmat{2,1}(4,4)
ans =
      0.1429
```

Although it was not necessary in our example, we could have preallocated the `testmat` cell array with the `cell` command:

```
testmat = cell(3,2);
```

After this assignment `testmat` is a 3-by-2 cell array of empty matrices.

Useful for visualizing the structure of a cell array is `cellplot`. Figure 18.1 was produced by `cellplot(testmat)`.

The functions `cell2struct` and `struct2cell` convert between cell arrays and structures, while `num2cell` creates a cell array of the same size as the given numeric array. The `cat` function, discussed in Section 18.2, provides an elegant way to produce a numeric vector from a structure or cell array. In our test matrix example, if we want to produce a matrix having as its columns the vectors of eigenvalues, we can type

```
cat(2,testmat.eig)
```

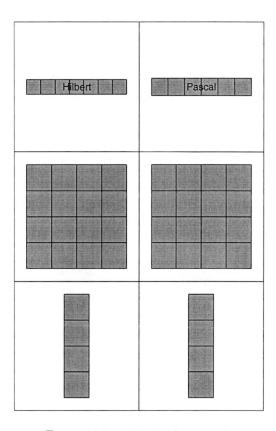

Figure 18.1. `cellplot(testmat)`.

for the structure `testmat`, or

    cat(2,testmat{3,:})

for the cell array `testmat`, in both cases obtaining the result

    ans =
        0.0001   0.0380
        0.0067   0.4538
        0.1691   2.2034
        1.5002   26.3047

Here, the first argument of `cat` causes concatenation in the second dimension, that is, columnwise. If this argument is replaced by 1 then the concatenation is row-wise and a long vector is produced. An example of this use of `cat` is in Listing 17.1, where it extracts from a cell array a vector that can then be plotted.

For many applications,
the choice of the proper data structure is really
the only major decision involved in the implementation;
once the choice has been made,
only very simple algorithms are needed.

— ROBERT SEDGEWICK, *Algorithms* (1988)

Chapter 19
The Symbolic Math Toolbox

The Symbolic Math Toolbox is one of the many toolboxes that extend the functionality of MATLAB, and perhaps the one that does so in the most fundamental way. The toolbox is provided with the MATLAB Student Version, but must be purchased as an extra with other versions of MATLAB. You can tell if your MATLAB installation contains the toolbox by issuing the `ver` command and seeing if the toolbox is listed.

The toolbox is based upon the Maple kernel, which performs all the symbolic and variable precision computations. Maple is a symbolic manipulation package produced by Waterloo Maple, Inc.

To obtain an overview of the functions in the toolbox type `help symbolic`.

19.1. Equation Solving

The Symbolic Math Toolbox defines a new datatype: a symbolic object, denoted by sym. Symbolic objects can be created with the `sym` and `syms` commands. Suppose we wish to solve the quadratic equation $ax^2 + bx + c = 0$. We define symbolic variables:

```
>> syms a b c x

>> whos
  Name      Size            Bytes  Class

  a         1x1               126  sym object
  b         1x1               126  sym object
  c         1x1               126  sym object
  x         1x1               126  sym object

Grand total is 8 elements using 504 bytes
```

The same effect can be achieved using

```
>> a = sym('a'); b = sym('b'); c = sym('c'); x = sym('x');
```

We recommend using the shorter `syms` form. Now we can solve the quadratic using the powerful `solve` command:

```
>> y = solve(a*x^2+b*x+c)
y =
[ 1/2/a*(-b+(b^2-4*a*c)^(1/2))]
[ 1/2/a*(-b-(b^2-4*a*c)^(1/2))]
```

MATLAB creates a 2-by-1 symbolic object y to hold the two solutions. We have used the shortest way to invoke `solve`. We could also have typed

```
>> y = solve('a*x^2+b*x+c=0');
>> y = solve(a*x^2+b*x+c,x);
```

Since we did not specify an equals sign, MATLAB assumed the expression we provided was to be equated to zero; if an equals sign is explicitly given then the whole expression must be placed in quotes. Less obvious is how MATLAB knew to solve for x and not one of the other symbolic variables. Since we did not provide a second argument specifying the unknown, MATLAB applied its findsym function to the expression a*x^2+b*x+c to determine the variable closest alphabetically to x, and solved for that variable. We can solve the same equation for a as follows:

```
>> solve(a*x^2+b*x+c,a)
ans =
-(b*x+c)/x^2
```

Suppose we now wish to check that the components of y really do satisfy the quadratic equation. We evaluate the quadratic at y, using elementwise squaring since y is a vector:

```
>> a*y.^2+b*y+c
ans =
[ 1/4/a*(-b+(b^2-4*a*c)^(1/2))^2+1/2*b/a*(-b+(b^2-4*a*c)^(1/2))+c]
[ 1/4/a*(-b-(b^2-4*a*c)^(1/2))^2+1/2*b/a*(-b-(b^2-4*a*c)^(1/2))+c]
```

The result is not displayed as zero, but we can apply the simplify function to try to reduce it to zero:

```
>> simplify(ans)
ans =
[ 0]
[ 0]
```

It is characteristic of all symbolic manipulation packages that postprocessing is often required to put the results in the most useful form.

Having computed a symbolic solution, a common requirement is to evaluate it for numerical values of the parameters. This can be done using the subs function, which replaces all occurrences of symbolic variables by specified expressions. To find the roots of the quadratic $x^2 - x - 1$ (cf. p. 136) we can type

```
>> a = 1; b = -1; c = -1;
>> subs(y)
ans =
    1.6180
   -0.6180
```

When given one symbolic argument the subs command returns that argument with all variables replaced by their values (if any) from the workspace. Alternatively, subs can be called with three arguments in order to assign values to variables without changing those variables in the workspace:

```
>> subs(y, {a, b, c}, {1, -1, -1})
ans =
    1.6180
   -0.6180
```

Note that the second and third arguments are cell arrays (see Section 18.3).

Simultaneous equations can be specified one at a time to the `solve` function. In general, the number of solutions cannot be predicted. There are two ways to collect the output. As in the next example, if the same number of output arguments as unknowns is supplied then the results are assigned to the outputs (alphabetically):

```
>> syms x y
>> [x,y] = solve('x^2+y^2 = 1','x^3-y^3 = 1')
x =
[                  0]
[                  1]
[ -1+1/2*i*2^(1/2)]
[ -1-1/2*i*2^(1/2)]
y =
[                 -1]
[                  0]
[  1+1/2*i*2^(1/2)]
[  1-1/2*i*2^(1/2)]
```

Alternatively, a single output argument can be provided, in which case a structure (see Section 18.3) containing the solutions is returned:

```
>> S = solve('y = 1/(1+x^2)','y = 1.001 - 0.5*x')
S =
    x: [3x1 sym]
    y: [3x1 sym]

>> [S.x(1), S.y(1)]
ans =
[ 1.0633051173985148109357033343229, .46934744130074259453214833283854]
```

The fields of the structure have the names of the variables, and in this example we looked at the first of the three solutions. This example illustrates that if `solve` cannot find a symbolic solution it will try to find a numeric one. The number of digits computed is controlled by the `digits` function described in Section 19.4; the default is 32 digits.

When interpreting the results of symbolic computations the precedence rules for arithmetic operators need to be kept in mind (see Table 4.1). For example:

```
>> syms a b
>> b=a/2
b =
1/2*a
```

Parentheses are not needed around the 1/2, since `/` and `*` have the same precedence, but we are used to seeing them included for clarity.

The `sym` and `syms` commands have optional arguments for specifying that a variable is real or positive:

```
syms x real, syms a positive
```

Both statuses can be cleared with

```
syms x a unreal
```

The information that a variable is real or positive can be vital in symbolic computations. For example, consider

```
>> syms p x y
>> y = ((x^p)^(p+1))/x^(p-1);
>> simplify(y)
ans =
(x^p)^p*x
```

The Symbolic Math Toolbox assumes that the variables x and p are complex and is unable to simplify y further. With the additional information that x and p are positive, further simplification is obtained:

```
>> syms p x positive
>> simplify(y)
ans =
x^(p^2+1)
```

19.2. Calculus

The Symbolic Math Toolbox provides symbolic integration and differentiation through the int and diff functions.

Here is a quick test that the MATLAB authors use to make sure that the Symbolic Math Toolbox is "online":

```
>> int('x')
ans =
1/2*x^2
```

Note that the constant of integration is always omitted. A more complicated example is

```
>> int('sqrt(tan(x))')
ans =
1/2*tan(x)^(1/2)/(cos(x)*sin(x))^(1/2)*cos(x)*2^(1/2)*(pi-...
acos(sin(x)-cos(x)))-1/2*2^(1/2)*log(cos(x)+2^(1/2)*...
tan(x)^(1/2)*cos(x)+sin(x))
```

This answer is easier to read if we "prettyprint" it:

```
>> pretty(ans)

              1/2          1/2
        tan(x)    cos(x) 2      (pi - acos(sin(x) - cos(x)))
    1/2 ---------------------------------------------------
                                         1/2
                          (cos(x) sin(x))

              1/2                  1/2        1/2
        - 1/2 2    log(cos(x) + 2      tan(x)    cos(x) + sin(x))
```

Note that we have not defined x to be a symbolic variable, so the argument to int must be enclosed in quotes. Alternatively we can define syms x and omit the quotes.

Definite integrals $\int_a^b f(x)\,dx$ can be evaluated by appending the limits of integration a and b. Here is an integral that has a singularity at the left endpoint, but which nevertheless has a finite value:

```
>> int('arctan(x)/x^(3/2)',0,1)
ans =
-1/2*pi+1/2*2^(1/2)*log(2+2^(1/2))-1/2*2^(1/2)*log(2-2^(1/2))+...
1/2*2^(1/2)*pi
```

The answer is exact and is rather complicated. We can convert it to numeric form:

```
>> double(ans)
ans =
    1.8971
```

It is important to realize that symbolic manipulation packages cannot "do" all integrals. This may be because the integral does not have a closed form solution in terms of elementary functions, or because it has a closed form solution that the package cannot find. Here is an example of the first kind:

```
>> int('sqrt(1+cos(x)^2)')
ans =
-(sin(x)^2)^(1/2)/sin(x)*EllipticE(cos(x),i)
```

The integral is expressed in terms of an elliptic integral of the second kind, which itself is not expressible in terms of elementary functions. If we evaluate the same integral in definite form we obtain

```
>> int('sqrt(1+cos(x)^2)',0,48)
ans =
30*2^(1/2)*EllipticE(1/2*2^(1/2))+...
2^(1/2)*EllipticE(-sin(48),1/2*2^(1/2))
```

and MATLAB can evaluate the elliptic integrals therein:

```
>> double(ans)
ans =
   58.4705
```

Next we give some examples of symbolic differentiation. We first set up the appropriate symbolic variables and so can omit the quotes from the argument to diff:

```
>> syms a x n
>> diff(x^2)
ans =
2*x

>> diff(x^n,2)
ans =
x^n*n^2/x^2-x^n*n/x^2

>> factor(ans)
```

```
ans =
x^n*n*(n-1)/x^2

>> diff(sin(x)*exp(-a*x^2))
ans =
cos(x)*exp(-a*x^2)-2*sin(x)*a*x*exp(-a*x^2)

>> diff(x^4*exp(x),3)
ans =
24*x*exp(x)+36*x^2*exp(x)+12*x^3*exp(x)+x^4*exp(x)
```

The result of the second differentiation needed simplifying; the simplify function does not help in this case so we used factor. In the second and last examples a second argument to diff specifies the order of the required derivative; the default is the first derivative.

Functions int and diff can both be applied to matrices, in which case they operate elementwise.

Differential equations can be solved symbolically with dsolve. The equations are specified by expressions in which the letter D denotes differentiation, with D2 denoting a second derivative, D3 a third derivative, and so on. The default independent variable is t. Initial conditions can optionally be specified after the equations, using the syntax y(a) = b, Dy(a) = c, etc.; if none are specified then the solutions contain arbitrary constants of integration, denoted C1, C2, etc. For our first example we take the logistic differential equation

$$\frac{d}{dt}y(t) = cy - by^2,$$

solving it first with arbitrary c and b and then with particular values of these parameters as an initial value problem:

```
>> syms b c y t
>> y = dsolve('Dy=c*y-b*y^2')
y =
c/(b+exp(-c*t)*C1*c)

>> y = dsolve('Dy=10*y-y^2','y(0)=0.01')
y =
10/(1+999*exp(-10*t))
```

We now check that the latter solution satisfies the initial condition and the differential equation:

```
>> subs(y,t,0)
ans =
    0.0100

>> res = diff(y,t)-(10*y-y^2)
res =
99900/(1+999*exp(-10*t))^2*exp(-10*t)-100/(1+999*exp(-10*t))+...
100/(1+999*exp(-10*t))^2

>> simplify(res)
```

```
ans =
0
```

Next we try to find the general solution to the pendulum equation, which we solved numerically on p. 150:

```
>> y = dsolve('D2theta + sin(theta) = 0')
Warning: Explicit solution could not be found; implicit solution
returned.
> In C:\MATLAB\toolbox\symbolic\dsolve.m at line 292
y =
[ -Int(1/(2*cos(a)+C1)^(1/2),a=''..theta)-t-C2=0,...
Int(1/(2*cos(a)+C1)^(1/2),a=''..theta)-t-C2=0]
```

No explicit solution could be found. If θ is small we can approximate $\sin\theta$ by θ, and in this case dsolve is able to find both general and particular solutions:

```
>> y = dsolve('D2theta + theta = 0')
y =
C1*cos(t)+C2*sin(t)

>> y = dsolve('D2theta + theta = 0','theta(0) = 1','Dtheta(0) = 1')
y =
cos(t)+sin(t)
```

Finally, we emphasize that the results from functions such as solve and dsolve need to be interpreted with care. For example, when we attempt to solve the differential equation $\frac{d}{dt}y = y^{2/3}$ we obtain

```
>> y = dsolve('Dy = y^(2/3)')
y =
1/27*t^3+1/3*t^2*C1+t*C1^2+C1^3
```

This is a solution for any value of the constant C1, but it does not represent all solutions: $y(t) = 0$ is another solution.

Taylor series can be computed using the function taylor:

```
>> syms x
>> taylor(log(1+x))
ans =
x-1/2*x^2+1/3*x^3-1/4*x^4+1/5*x^5
```

By default the Taylor series about 0 up to terms of order 5 is produced. A second argument specifies the required order and a third argument the point about which to expand:

```
>> pretty(taylor(exp(-sin(x)),3,1))

  exp(-sin(1)) - exp(-sin(1)) cos(1) (x - 1)


                                          2          2
        + exp(-sin(1)) (1/2 sin(1) + 1/2 cos(1) ) (x - 1)
```

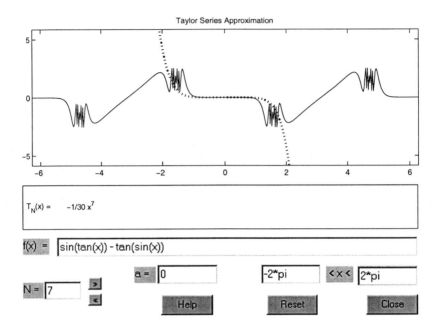

Figure 19.1. `taylortool` *window.*

Table 19.1. *Calculus functions.*

`diff`	Differentiate
`int`	Integrate
`limit`	Limit
`taylor`	Taylor series
`jacobian`	Jacobian matrix
`symsum`	Summation of series

A function `taylortool` provides a graphical interface to `taylor`, plotting both the function and the Taylor series. See Figure 19.1, which shows the interesting function $\sin(\tan x) - \tan(\sin x)$.

The Symbolic Math Toolbox contains some other calculus functions; see Table 19.1.

19.3. Linear Algebra

Several of MATLAB's linear algebra functions have counterparts in the Symbolic Math Toolbox that take symbolic arguments. To illustrate we take the numeric and symbolic representations of the 5-by-5 Frank matrix:

```
>> A_num = gallery('frank',5); A_sym = sym(A_num);
```

This illustrates a different usage of the `sym` function: to convert from a numeric datatype to symbolic form. Since the Frank matrix has small integer entries the

conversion is done exactly. In general, when given a floating point number as argument
sym tries to express it as a nearby rational number. For example:

```
>> t = 1/3; t, sym(t)
t =
    0.3333
ans =
1/3
```

Here, t is a floating point approximation to 1/3, whereas sym(t) exactly represents
1/3. For the precise rules used by sym, and details of arguments that allow control of
the conversion, see help sym.

Continuing our Frank matrix example we can invert the double array A_num in
the usual way:

```
inv(A_num)
ans =
      1.0000   -1.0000   -0.0000    0.0000         0
     -4.0000    5.0000   -1.0000   -0.0000         0
     12.0000  -15.0000    4.0000   -1.0000         0
    -24.0000   30.0000   -8.0000    3.0000   -1.0000
     24.0000  -30.0000    8.0000   -3.0000    2.0000
```

The trailing zeros show that the computed elements are not exactly integers. We can
obtain the exact inverse by applying inv to A_sym:

```
inv(A_sym)
ans =
[    1,   -1,    0,    0,    0]
[   -4,    5,   -1,    0,    0]
[   12,  -15,    4,   -1,    0]
[  -24,   30,   -8,    3,   -1]
[   24,  -30,    8,   -3,    2]
```

Here, MATLAB has recognized that inv is being called with a symbolic argument
and has invoked a version of inv that is part of the Symbolic Math Toolbox. The
mechanism that allows different versions of a function to handle different types of
arguments is called overloading. You can tell whether a given function is overloaded
from its help entry. Assuming the Symbolic Math Toolbox is present, help inv
produces

```
INV    Matrix inverse.
   INV(X) is the inverse of the square matrix X.
   A warning message is printed if X is badly scaled or
   nearly singular.

   See also SLASH, PINV, COND, CONDEST, NNLS, LSCOV.

   Overloaded methods
      help sym/inv.m
```

As indicated, to obtain help for the version of inv called for a symbolic argument we
type help sym/inv. We have already used an overloaded function in this chapter:
diff in the previous section.

Just as for numeric matrices, the backslash operator can be used to solve linear systems with a symbolic coefficient matrix. For example, we can compute the (5,1) element of the inverse of the Frank matrix with

```
>> [0 0 0 0 1]*(A_sym\[1 0 0 0 0]')
ans =
24
```

For a symbolic argument the `eig` function tries to compute the exact eigensystem. We know from Galois theory that this is not always possible in a finite number of operations for matrices of order 5 or more. For the 5-by-5 Frank matrix `eig` succeeds:

```
>> e = eig(A_sym)
e =
[                                              1]
[ 7/2+1/2*10^(1/2)+1/2*(55+14*10^(1/2))^(1/2)]
[ 7/2+1/2*10^(1/2)-1/2*(55+14*10^(1/2))^(1/2)]
[ 7/2-1/2*10^(1/2)+1/2*(55-14*10^(1/2))^(1/2)]
[ 7/2-1/2*10^(1/2)-1/2*(55-14*10^(1/2))^(1/2)]

>> double(e)
ans =
     1.0000
    10.0629
     0.0994
     3.5566
     0.2812
```

As we noted in the example in Section 9.7, the eigenvalues come in reciprocal pairs. To check we can type

```
>> [e(2)*e(3); e(4)*e(5)]
ans =
[ (7/2+1/2*10^(1/2)+1/2*(55+14*10^(1/2))^(1/2))*...
[ (7/2-1/2*10^(1/2)+1/2*(55-14*10^(1/2))^(1/2))*...
```

Note that we have had to truncate the output. Attempting to simplify these expressions using `simplify` fails. Instead we use the function `simple`, which tries several different simplification methods and reports the shortest answer:

```
>> s = simple(ans)
s =
[ 1]
[ 1]
```

(If `simple(ans)` is typed without an output argument then all intermediate attempted simplifications are displayed.) Finally, while we computed the characteristic polynomial numerically in Section 9.7, we can now obtain it exactly:

```
>> poly(A_sym)
ans =
x^5-15*x^4+55*x^3-55*x^2+15*x-1
```

A complete list of linear algebra functions in the toolbox is given in Table 19.2.

Table 19.2. *Linear algebra functions.*

diag	Diagonal matrices and diagonals of matrix
tril	Extract lower triangular part
triu	Extract upper triangular part
inv	Matrix inverse
det	Determinant
rank	Rank
rref	Reduced row echelon form
null	Basis for null space (not orthonormal)
eig	Eigenvalues and eigenvectors
svd	Singular values and singular vectors
poly	Characteristic polynomial
expm	Matrix exponential
colspace*	Basis for column space
jordan*	Jordan canonical (normal) form

* Functions existing in Symbolic Math Toolbox only.

19.4. Variable Precision Arithmetic

In addition to MATLAB's double precision floating point arithmetic and symbolic arithmetic, the Symbolic Math Toolbox supports variable precision floating point arithmetic, which is carried out within the Maple kernel. This is useful for problems where an accurate solution is required and an exact solution is impossible or too time-consuming to obtain. It can also be used to experiment with the effect of varying the precision of a computation.

The function `digits` returns the number of significant decimal digits to which variable precision computations are carried out:

```
>> digits

Digits = 32
```

The default of 32 digits can be changed to n by the command `digits(n)`. Variable precision computations are based on the `vpa` command. The simplest usage is to evaluate constants to variable accuracy:

```
>> vpa(pi)
ans =
3.1415926535897932384626433832795

>> vpa(pi,50)
ans =
3.1415926535897932384626433832795028841971693993751
```

As the second command illustrates, `vpa` takes a second argument that overrides the current number of digits specified by `digits`. In the next example we compute e to 40 digits and then check that taking the logarithm gives back 1:

```
>> d = 40;
```

```
>> x = vpa('exp(1)',d)
x =
2.7182818284590452353602874713526624977557
```

```
>> vpa(log(x),d)
ans =
1.0000000000000000000000000000000000000
```

A minor modification of this example illustrates a pitfall:

```
>> y = vpa(exp(1),d)
y =
2.7182818284590455348848081484902650011787
```

```
>> vpa(log(y),d)
ans =
1.0000000000000001101889132838495
```

We omitted the quotes around `exp(1)`, so MATLAB evaluated `exp(1)` in double precision floating point arithmetic, converted that 16 digit result to 40 digits—thereby adding 24 meaningless digits—and then evaluated the exponential. In the original version the quotes enable `exp(1)` to pass through the MATLAB interpreter to be evaluated by Maple.

Variable precision linear algebra computations are performed by calling functions with variable precision arguments. For example, we can compute the eigensystem of `pascal(4)` to 32 digits by

```
>> [V,E] = eig(vpa(pascal(4))); diag(E)
ans =
[ .38016015229139947237513500399910e-1]
[     26.304703267097871286055226455525]
[     .45383455002566546509718436703856]
[     2.2034461676473233016100756770374]
```

19.5. Other Features

The Symbolic Math Toolbox contains many other functions, covering Fourier and Laplace transforms, special functions, conversions, and pedagogical tools. Of particular interest are functions that provide access to Maple (these are not available with the Student Edition). Function `mfun` gives access to many special functions for which MATLAB M-files are not provided; type `mfunlist` to see a list of such functions. Among these functions are the Fresnel integrals; thus commands of the form

```
x = mfun('FresnelC',t); y = mfun('FresnelS',t);
```

provide another way to evaluate the Fresnel spiral in Figure 12.2. More generally, function `maple` sends a statement to the Maple kernel and returns the result. Maple help on Maple function `mfoo` can be obtained by typing `mhelp mfoo`.

The `maple` command is used in the following example, in which we obtain a definite integral that evaluates to the Catalan constant; we use Maple to evaluate the constant, since it is not known to MATLAB.

```
>> int('log(x)/(1+x^2)',0,1)
ans =
-Catalan

>> maple('evalf(Catalan)')
ans =
.91596559417721901505460351493238
```

Useful functions for postprocessing are `ccode`, `fortran` and `latex`, which produce C, Fortran and LaTeX representations, respectively, of a symbolic expression.

I'm very good at integral and differential calculus,
I know the scientific names of beings animalculous;
In short, in matters vegetable, animal, and mineral,
I am the very model of a modern Major-General.
— WILLIAM SCHWENCK GILBERT, *The Pirates of Penzance. Act 1* (1879)

Maple will sometimes "go away" for quite a while to do its calculations.
— ROB CORLESS, *Essential Maple* (1995)

The particular form obtained by applying an analytical integration method
may prove to be unsuitable for practical purposes.
For instance, evaluating the formula may be
numerically unstable (due to cancellation, for instance) or even
impossible (due to division by zero).
— ARNOLD R. KROMMER and CHRISTOPH W. UEBERHUBER,
Computational Integration (1998)

Maple has bugs. It has always had bugs ...
Every other computer algebra system also has bugs,
often different ones,
but remarkably many of these bugs are seen
throughout all computer algebra systems,
as a result of common design shortcomings.
Probably the most useful advice I can give for dealing with this is
be paranoid.
Check your results at least two ways (the more the better).
— ROB CORLESS, *Essential Maple* (1995)

Chapter 20
Optimizing M-Files

Most users of MATLAB find that computations are completed fast enough that execution time is not usually a cause for concern. Some computations, though, particularly when the problems are large, require a significant time and it is natural to ask whether anything can be done to speed them up. This chapter describes some techniques that produce better performance from M-files. They all exploit the fact that MATLAB is an interpreted language with dynamic memory allocation. Another approach to optimization is to compile rather than interpret MATLAB code. The MATLAB Compiler, available from The MathWorks as a separate product, translates MATLAB code into C and compiles it with a C compiler. External C or Fortran codes can also be called from MATLAB via the MEX interface; see [54], [55].

Vectorization, discussed in the first section, has benefits beyond simply increasing speed of execution. It can lead to shorter and more readable MATLAB code. Furthermore, it expresses algorithms in terms of high-level constructs that are more appropriate for high-performance computing.

MATLAB's profiler is a useful tool when you are optimizing M-files, as it can help you decide which parts of the code to optimize. See Section 16.2 for details.

All timings in this chapter are for a 500Mhz Pentium III.

20.1. Vectorization

Since MATLAB is a matrix language, many of the matrix-level operations and functions are carried out internally using compiled C or assembly code and are therefore executed at near optimum efficiency. This is true of the arithmetic operators *, +, -, \, / and of relational and logical operators. However, `for` loops are executed relatively slowly. One of most important tips for producing efficient M-files is to avoid `for` loops in favor of vectorized constructs, that is, to convert `for` loops into equivalent vector or matrix operations. Consider the following example:

```
>> n = 5e5; x = randn(n,1);
>> tic, s = 0; for i=1:n, s = s + x(i)^2; end, toc
elapsed_time =
    8.3500

>> tic, s = sum(x.^2); toc
elapsed_time =
    0.0600
```

In this example we compute the sum of squares of the elements in a random vector in two ways: with a `for` loop and with an elementwise squaring followed by a call to sum. The latter vectorized approach is two orders of magnitude faster.

The `for` loop in Listing 10.2 on p. 128 can be vectorized, assuming that f returns a vector output for a vector argument. The loop and the statement before it can be replaced by

```
x = linspace(0,1,n);
p = x*f(1) + (x-1)*f(0);
max_err = max(abs(f(x)-p));
```

For a slightly more complicated example of vectorization, consider the inner loop of Gaussian elimination applied to an n-by-n matrix A, which can be written

```
for i = k+1:n
    for j = k+1:n;
        A(i,j) = A(i,j) - A(i,k)*A(k,j)/A(k,k);
    end
end
```

Both loops can be avoided, simply by deleting the two `for`s and `end`s:

```
i = k+1:n;
j = k+1:n;
A(i,j) = A(i,j) - A(i,k)*A(k,j)/A(k,k);
```

The approximately $(n - k)^2$ scalar multiplications and additions have now been expressed as one matrix multiplication and one matrix addition. With n = 300 and k = 1 we timed the two-loop code at 3.46 seconds and the vectorized version at 0.11 seconds—again vectorization yields a substantial improvement.

The next example concerns premultiplication of a matrix by a Givens rotation in the (j, k) plane, which replaces rows j and k by linear combinations of themselves. It might be coded as

```
temp = A(j,:);
A(j,:) = c*A(j,:) - s*A(k,:);
A(k,:) = s*temp + c*A(k,:);
```

By expressing the computation as a single matrix multiplication we can shorten the code and dispense with the temporary variable:

```
A([j k],:) = [c -s; s c] * A([j k],:);
```

The second version is approximately twice as fast for n = 500.

Try to maximize the use of built-in MATLAB functions. Consider, for example, this code to assign to `row_norm` the ∞-norms of the rows of A:

```
for i=1:n
    row_norms(i) = norm(A(i,:), inf);
end
```

It can be replaced by the single statement

```
row_norms = max(abs(A),[],2);
```

(see p. 54), which is shorter and runs much more quickly. Similarly, the factorial $n!$ is more quickly computed by `prod(1:n)` than by

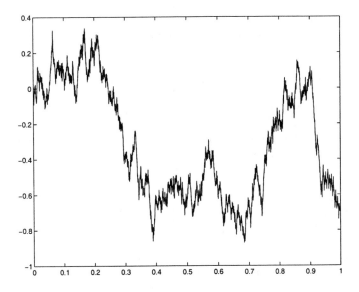

Figure 20.1. *Approximate Brownian path.*

```
p = 1; for i = 1:n, p = p*i; end
```

(in fact, there is a MATLAB function `factorial` that uses `prod` in this way).

As a final example, we start with the following code to generate and plot an approximate Brownian (standard Wiener) path [40], which produces Figure 20.1.

```
randn('state',20)
N = 1e4; dt = 1/N;
w(1) = 0;
for j = 2:N+1
    w(j) = w(j-1) + sqrt(dt)*randn;
end
plot([0:dt:1],w)
```

This computation can be speeded up by preallocating the array `w` (see the next section) and by computing `sqrt(dt)` outside the loop. However, we obtain a more dramatic improvement by vectorizing with the help of the cumulative sum function, `cumsum`:

```
randn('state',20)
N = 1e4; dt = 1/N;
w = sqrt(dt)*cumsum([0;randn(N,1)]);
plot([0:dt:1],w)
```

This produces Figure 20.1 roughly 10 times more quickly than the original version.

20.2. Preallocating Arrays

One of the attractions of MATLAB is that arrays need not be declared before first use: assignment to an array element beyond the upper bounds of the array causes

MATLAB to extend the dimensions of the array as necessary. If overused, this flexibility can lead to inefficiencies, however. Consider the following implementation of a recurrence:

```
% x has not so far been assigned.
x(1:2) = 1;
for i=3:n, x(i) = 0.25*x(i-1)^2 - x(i-2); end
```

On each iteration of the loop, MATLAB must increase the length of the vector x by 1. In the next version x is preallocated as a vector of precisely the length needed, so no resizing operations are required during execution of the loop:

```
% x has not so far been assigned.
x = ones(n,1);
for i=3:n, x(i) = 0.25*x(i-1)^2 - x(i-2); end
```

With $n = 1e4$, the first piece of code took 5.88 seconds and the second 0.38 seconds, showing that the first version spends most of its time doing memory allocation rather than floating point arithmetic.

Preallocation has the added advantage of reducing the fragmentation of memory resulting from dynamic memory allocation and deallocation.

You can preallocate an array structure with `repmat(struct(...))` and a cell array with the `cell` function; see Section 18.3.

20.3. Miscellaneous Optimizations

Suppose you wish to set up an n-by-n matrix of 2s. The obvious assignment is

```
A = 2*ones(n);
```

The n^2 floating point multiplications can be avoided by using

```
A = repmat(2,n);
```

The `repmat` approach is much faster for large n. This use of `repmat` is essentially the same as assigning

```
A = zeros(n); A(:) = 2;
```

in which scalar expansion is used to fill A.

There is one optimization that is automatically performed by MATLAB. Arguments that are passed to a function are not copied into the function's workspace *unless* they are altered within the function. Therefore there is no memory penalty for passing large variables to a function provided the function does not alter those variables.

20.4. Case Study: Bifurcation Diagram

For a practical example of optimizing M-files we consider a problem from nonlinear dynamics. We wish to examine the long-term behavior of the iteration

$$y_k = F(y_{k-1}), \quad k \geq 2, \quad y_1 \text{ given},$$

Listing 20.1. *Script* bif1.

```
%BIF1 Bifurcation diagram for modified Euler/logistic map.
%      Computes a numerical bifurcation diagram for a map of the form
%      y_k = F(y_{k-1}) arising from the modified Euler method
%      applied to a logistic ODE.
%
%      Slow version using multiple for loops.

for h = 1:0.005:4
    for iv = 0.2:0.5:2.7
        y(1) = iv;
        for k = 2:520
            y(k) = y(k-1) + h*(y(k-1)+0.5*h*y(k-1)*(1-y(k-1)))*...
                   (1-y(k-1)-0.5*h*y(k-1)*(1-y(k-1)));
        end
        plot(h*ones(20,1),y(501:520),'.'), hold on
    end
end

title('Modified Euler/logistic map','FontSize',14)
xlabel('h'), ylabel('last 20 y')
grid on, hold off
```

where the function F is defined by

$$F(y) = y + h \left(y + \tfrac{1}{2} hy(1-y) \right) \left(1 - y - \tfrac{1}{2} hy(1-y) \right).$$

Here $h > 0$ is a parameter. (This map corresponds to the midpoint or modified Euler method [69] with stepsize h applied to the logistic ODE $dy(t)/dt = y(t)(1-y(t))$ with initial value y_1.) For a range of h values and for a few initial values, y_1, we would like to run the iteration for a "long time", say as far as $k = 500$, and then plot the next 20 iterates $\{y_i\}_{i=501}^{520}$. For each h on the x-axis we will superimpose $\{y_i\}_{i=501}^{520}$ onto the y-axis to produce a so-called bifurcation diagram.

Choosing values of h given by 1:0.005:4 and using initial values 0.2:0.5:2.7 we arrive at the M-file bif1.m in Listing 20.1. This is a straightforward implementation that uses three nested **for** loops and does not preallocate the array y before the first time around the inner loop. Figure 20.2 shows the result.

The M-file bif2.m in Listing 20.2 is an equivalent, but much faster, implementation. Two of the loops have been removed and a single **plot** command is used. Here, we stack the iterates corresponding to all h and y_1 values into one long vector, and use elementwise multiplication to perform the iteration simultaneously on the components of this vector. The array Ydata, which is used to store the data for the plot, is preallocated to the correct dimensions before use. The vectorized code produces Figure 20.2 about 200 times more quickly than the original version.

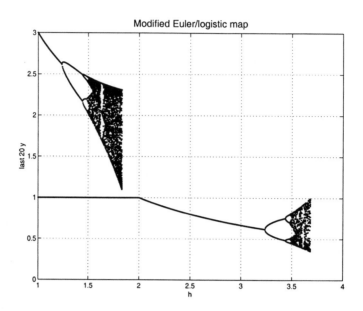

Figure 20.2. *Numerical bifurcation diagram.*

Listing 20.2. *Script* bif2.

```
%BIF2 Bifurcation diagram for modified Euler/logistic map.
%      Computes a numerical bifurcation diagram for a map of the form
%      y_k = F(y_{k-1}) arising from the modified Euler method
%      applied to a logistic ODE.
%
%      Fast, vectorized version.

h = (1:0.005:4)';
iv = [0.2:0.5:2.7];
hvals = repmat(h,length(iv),1);
Ydata = zeros((length(hvals)),20);
y = kron(iv',ones(size(h)));

for k=2:500
   y = y + hvals.*(y+0.5*hvals.*y.*(1-y)).*(1-y-0.5*hvals.*y.*(1-y));
end
for k=1:20
   y = y + hvals.*(y+0.5*hvals.*y.*(1-y)).*(1-y-0.5*hvals.*y.*(1-y));
   Ydata(:,k) = y;
end

plot(hvals,Ydata,'.')
title('Modified Euler/Logistic Map','FontSize',14)
xlabel('h'), ylabel('last 20 y'), grid on
```

Entities should not be multiplied unnecessarily.
— WILLIAM OF OCCAM (c. 1320)

Life is too short to spend writing for loops.
— *Getting Started with MATLAB* (1998)

In our six lines of MATLAB,
not a single loop has appeared explicitly,
though at least one loop is implicit in every line.
— LLOYD N. TREFETHEN and DAVID BAU, III, *Numerical Linear Algebra* (1997)

Make it right before you make it faster.
— BRIAN W. KERNIGHAN and P. J. PLAUGER,
The Elements of Programming Style (1978)

A useful rule-of-thumb is that the
execution time of a MATLAB function is
proportional to the number of statements executed,
no matter what those statements actually do.
— CLEVE B. MOLER, *MATLAB News & Notes* (Spring 1996)

Chapter 21
Tricks and Tips

Our approach in this book has been to present material of interest to the majority of MATLAB users, omitting topics of more specialized interest. In this chapter we relax this philosophy and describe some tricks and tips that, while of limited use, can be invaluable when they are needed and are of general interest as examples of more advanced MATLAB matters.

21.1. Empty Arrays

The empty matrix [], mentioned in several places in this book, has dimension 0-by-0. MATLAB allows multidimensional arrays with one or more dimensions equal to zero. These are created by operations such as

```
>> 1:0
ans =
   Empty matrix: 1-by-0

>> zeros(2,0)
ans =
   Empty matrix: 2-by-0

>> ones(1,0,3)
ans =
   Empty array: 1-by-0-by-3
```

Operations on empty arrays are defined by extrapolating the rules for normal arrays to the case of a zero dimension. Consider the following example:

```
>> k = 5; A = ones(2,k); B = ones(k,3); A*B
ans =
     5     5     5
     5     5     5

>> k = 0; A = ones(2,k); B = ones(k,3); A*B
ans =
     0     0     0
     0     0     0
```

Matrix multiplication A*B is defined in MATLAB whenever the number of columns of A equals the number of rows of B, even if this number is zero—and in this case the elements of the product are set to zero.

Empty arrays can facilitate loop vectorization. Consider the nested loops

```
for i = j-1:-1:1
    s = 0;
    for k=i+1:j-1
        s = s + R(i,k)*R(k,j);
    end
end
```

The inner loop can be vectorized to give

```
for i = j-1:-1:1
    s = R(i,i+1:j-1)*R(i+1:j-1,j);
end
```

What happens when i = j-1 and the index vector i+1:j-1 is empty? Fortunately R(i,i+1:j-1) evaluates to a 1-by-0 matrix and R(i+1:j-1,j) to a 0-by-1 matrix, and s is assigned the desired value 0. In versions of MATLAB prior to MATLAB 5 there was only one empty array, [], and the vectorized loop in this example did not work as intended.

21.2. Exploiting Infinities

The infinities inf and -inf can be exploited to good effect.

Suppose you wish to find the maximum value of a function f on a grid of points x(1:n) and f does not vectorize, so that you cannot write max(f(x)). Then you need to write a loop, with a variable fmax (say) initialized to some value at least as small as any value of f that can be encountered. Simply assign -inf:

```
fmax = -inf;
for i=1:n
    fmax = max(fmax, f(x(i)));
end
```

Next, suppose that we are given p with $1 \leq p \leq \infty$ and wish to evaluate the dual of the vector p-norm, that is, the q-norm, where $p^{-1} + q^{-1} = 1$. If we solve for q we obtain

$$q = \frac{1}{1 - 1/p}.$$

This formula clearly evaluates correctly for all $1 < p < \infty$. For $p = \infty$ it yields the correct value 1, since $1/\infty = 0$, and for $p = 1$ it yields $q = 1/0 = \infty$. So in MATLAB we can simply write norm(x,1/(1-1/p)) without treating the cases p = 1 and p = inf specially.

21.3. Permutations

Permutations are important when using MATLAB for data processing and for matrix computations. A permutation can be represented as a vector or as a matrix. Consider first the vector form, which is produced by (for example) the sort function:

```
>> x = [10 -1 3 9 8 7]
x =
    10    -1     3     9     8     7
```

```
>> [s,ix] = sort(x)
s =
    -1     3     7     8     9    10
ix =
     2     3     6     5     4     1
```

The output of sort is a sorted vector s and a permutation vector ix such that x(ix) equals s. To regenerate x from s we need the inverse of the permutation ix. This can be obtained as follows:

```
>> ix_inv(ix) = 1:length(ix)
ix_inv =
     6     1     2     5     4     3

>> s(ix_inv)
ans =
    10    -1     3     9     8     7
```

In matrix computations it is sometimes necessary to convert between the vector and matrix representations of a permutation. The following example illustrates how this is done, and shows how to permute the rows or columns of a matrix using either form:

```
>> p = [4 1 3 2]
p =
     4     1     3     2

>> I = eye(4);
>> P = I(p,:);
P =
     0     0     0     1
     1     0     0     0
     0     0     1     0
     0     1     0     0

>> A = magic(4)
A =
    16     2     3    13
     5    11    10     8
     9     7     6    12
     4    14    15     1

>> P*A
ans =
     4    14    15     1
    16     2     3    13
     9     7     6    12
     5    11    10     8
>> A(p,:)
ans =
```

```
          4      14      15       1
         16       2       3      13
          9       7       6      12
          5      11      10       8

>> A*P'
ans =
         13      16       3       2
          8       5      10      11
         12       9       6       7
          1       4      15      14
>> A(:,p)
ans =
         13      16       3       2
          8       5      10      11
         12       9       6       7
          1       4      15      14

>> p_from_P = (1:4)*P'
p_from_P =
          4       1       3       2
```

21.4. Rank 1 Matrices

A rank 1 matrix has the form $A = xy^*$, where x and y are both column vectors. Often we need to deal with special rank 1 matrices where x or y is the vector of all 1s. For y = ones(n,1) we can form A as an outer product as follows:

```
>> n = 4; x = (1:n)';   % Example choice of n and x.
>> A = x*ones(1,n)
A =
          1       1       1       1
          2       2       2       2
          3       3       3       3
          4       4       4       4
```

Recall that x(:,1) extracts the first column of x. Then x(:,[1 1]) extracts the first column of x twice, giving an n-by-2 matrix. Extending this idea, we can form A using only indexing operations

```
A = x(:,ones(n,1))
```

(This operation is known to MATLAB afficionados as "Tony's trick".) The revised code avoids the multiplication and is therefore faster.

Another way to construct the matrix is as

```
A = repmat(x,1,n);
```

21.5. Set Operations

Suppose you need to find out whether any element of a vector x equals a scalar a. This can be done using **any** and an equality test, taking advantage of the way that MATLAB expands a scalar into a vector when necessary in an assignment or comparison:

```
>> x = 1:5; a = 3;

>> x == a
ans =
     0     0     1     0     0

>> any(x == a)
ans =
     1
```

More generally, a might itself be a vector and you need to know how many of the elements of a occur within x. The test above will not work. One possibility is to loop over the elements of a, carrying out the comparison `any(x == a(i))`. Shorter and faster is to use the set function `ismember`:

```
>> x = 1:5; a = [-1 3 5];
>> ismember(a,x)
ans =
     0     1     1

>> ismember(x,a)
ans =
     0     0     1     0     1
```

As this example shows, `ismember(a,x)` returns a vector with ith element 1 if `a(i)` is in x and 0 otherwise. The number of elements of a that occur in x can be obtained as `sum(ismember(a,x))` or `nnz(ismember(a,x))`, the latter being faster as it involves no floating point operations. MATLAB has several set functions: see **help ops**.

21.6. Subscripting Matrices as Vectors

MATLAB allows a two-dimensional array to be subscripted as though it were one-dimensional, as we saw in the example of **find** applied to a matrix on p. 60. If A is m-by-n and j is a scalar then `A(j)` means the same as `a(j)`, where `a = A(:)`; in other words, `A(j)` is the jth element in the vector made up of the columns of A stacked one on top of the other.

To see how one-dimensional subscripting can be exploited suppose we wish to assign an n-vector v to the leading diagonal of an existing n-by-n matrix A. This can be done by

```
A = A - diag(diag(A)) + diag(v);
```

but this code is not very elegant or efficient. We can take advantage of the fact that the diagonal elements of A are equally spaced in the vector `A(:)` by writing

```
A(1:n+1:n^2) = v;
```

or

```
A(1:n+1:end) = v;
```

The main antidiagonal can be set in a similar way, by

```
A(n:n-1:n^2-n+1) = v;
```

For example,

```
>> A = spiral(5)
A =
        21      22      23      24      25
        20       7       8       9      10
        19       6       1       2      11
        18       5       4       3      12
        17      16      15      14      13

>> A(1:6:25) = -ones(5,1)
A =
        -1      22      23      24      25
        20      -1       8       9      10
        19       6      -1       2      11
        18       5       4      -1      12
        17      16      15      14      -1

>> A(5:4:21) = zeros(5,1)
A =
        -1      22      23      24       0
        20      -1       8       0      10
        19       6       0       2      11
        18       0       4      -1      12
         0      16      15      14      -1
```

One use of this trick is to shift a matrix by a multiple of the identity matrix: $A \leftarrow A - \alpha I$, a common operation in numerical analysis. This is accomplished with

```
>> A(1:n+1:end) = A(1:n+1:end)-alpha
```

21.7. Triangular and Symmetric Matrices

Some linear algebra functions perform different computations depending on the properties of their arguments. For example, when A is triangular MATLAB computes A\b by substitution, but when A is full it is first LU-factorized. The `eig` command performs the symmetric QR algorithm for symmetric arguments and the nonsymmetric QR algorithm for nonsymmetric arguments. If your matrix is known to be triangular or symmetric it usually makes sense to *enforce* the property in the presence of roundoff, in order to reduce computation and preserve mathematical properties. For example, the eigenvectors of a symmetric matrix can always be taken to be orthogonal and `eig` returns eigenvectors orthogonal to within rounding error when applied to a symmetric matrix. But if a matrix has a nonzero nonsymmetric part, however tiny, then `eig` applies the nonsymmetric QR algorithm and can return nonorthogonal eigenvectors:

```
>> A = ones(4); [V,D] = eig(A);   norm(V'*V-eye(4))
ans =
   3.9639e-016

>> Q = gallery('orthog',4,2); % Orthogonal matrix.
>> B = Q'*A*Q; norm(B-B')
ans =
   3.1683e-016

>> [V,D] = eig(B);   norm(V'*V-eye(4))
ans =
     0.5023
```

Here, the matrix B should be symmetric, but it is not quite symmetric because of rounding errors. There is no question of eig having performed badly here; even the exact eigenvector matrix is far from being orthogonal. In this situation it would normally be preferable to symmetrize B before applying eig:

```
>> C = (B + B')/2; [V,D] = eig(C);   norm(V'*V-eye(4))
ans =
   5.6514e-016
```

This discussion raises the question of how to test whether a matrix is symmetric or (upper) triangular. One possibility is to evaluate

```
norm(A-A',p), norm(A-triu(A),p)
```

taking care to use p=1 or p=inf, since the 1- and ∞-norms are much quicker to evaluate than the 2-norm. A better way is to use the logical expressions

```
isequal(A,A'), isequal(A,triu(A))
```

which do not involve any floating point arithmetic.

A technique is a trick that works.

— GIAN-CARLO ROTA

And none of this would have been any fun without MATLAB.

— NOËL M. NACHTIGAL, SATISH C. REDDY and LLOYD N. TREFETHEN,
How Fast are Nonsymmetric Matrix Iterations? (1992)

Appendix A
Changes in MATLAB

Recent releases of MATLAB have introduced many changes, which are documented in the Release Notes available from the Help Browser. The changes include new language features, new functions, and alterations to function names or syntax that require M-files to be rewritten for future compatibility. In this appendix we give a highly selective summary of changes introduced in versions 5.0 onwards of MATLAB. Our aim is to point out important changes that may be overlooked by users upgrading from earlier versions and that may cause M-files written for earlier versions to behave differently in MATLAB 6.

A.1. MATLAB 5.0

- New, improved random number generators introduced. Previously, the state of the random number generators was set with

    ```
    rand('seed',j), randn('seed',j)
    ```

    If this syntax is used now it causes the old generators to be used. The state should now be set with

    ```
    rand('state',j), randn('state',j)
    ```

A.2. MATLAB 5.3

Functions renamed as follows: fmin → fminbnd, fmins → fminsearch, nnls → lsqnonneg.

A.3. MATLAB 6

- Matrix computations based on LAPACK, rather than LINPACK as previously. MATLAB now takes advantage of Hermitian structure when computing the eigensystem of a complex Hermitian matrix, and of Hermitian definite structure when computing the eigensystem of a Hermitian definite generalized eigenvalue problem. Eigenvalues may be returned in a different order than with earlier versions of MATLAB, eigenvectors may be normalized differently, and the columns of unitary matrices may differ by scale factors of modulus unity.

- As a result of the switch to LAPACK, the flops function is no longer operative. (In earlier versions of MATLAB, flops provided a count of the total number of floating point operations performed.)

- Some of the arguments of the `eigs` function have changed (this function is now an interface to ARPACK rather than an M-file).

- The precedence of the logical `and` and `or` operators, which used to be the same, has been changed so that `and` has higher precedence (see p. 59).

- Function handles ("`@fun`") have been introduced for passing functions as arguments; they are preferred to the passing of function names in strings.

- The quadrature function `quad8` had been superseded by `quadl`. The default error tolerance for `quad` is now of order `eps` rather than 10^{-3}.

- The way in which the ODE solvers are called has been changed to exploit function handles (the "ODE file" format, documented in `help odefile`, is no longer used).

Appendix B
Toolboxes

A toolbox is a collection of functions that extends the capabilities of MATLAB in a particular area. The functions are normally collected in a single directory, are well documented, and include demonstrations.

In this book we have described one MATLAB toolbox: the Symbolic Math Toolbox. Many other toolboxes are marketed by The MathWorks. Table B.1 lists the Application Toolboxes; there are other toolboxes not in this category, for example related to the Simulink system. Various other toolboxes and M-files are freely available over the Internet.

Table B.1. *Application toolboxes marketed by The MathWorks.*

Area	Toolboxes
Signal and image processing	Frequency Domain System Identification, Higher-Order Spectral Analysis, Image Processing, Quantized Filtering, Signal Processing, Wavelet
Control design	Control System, Fuzzy Logic, LMI Control μ-Analysis and Synthesis, Model Predictive Control, Nonlinear Control Design Blockset, QFT Control Design, Robust Control, System Identification
General	Datafeed, Financial, Financial Time Series, GARCH, Mapping, NAG Foundation, Neural Network, Optimization, Partial Differential Equation, Spline, Statistics, Symbolic/Extended Symbolic Math

Appendix C
Resources

The first port of call for information about MATLAB resources should be the Web page of The MathWorks, at

http://www.mathworks.com

This Web page can be accessed from the Web menu item of the MATLAB desktop or by typing support at the command line. It includes FAQs (frequently asked questions), technical notes, a large collection of user-contributed M-files, a search facility, and details of MATLAB toolboxes.

The newsgroup comp.soft-sys.matlab is devoted to MATLAB. (Newsgroups can be read in various ways, including from Netscape.) It contains problems and solutions from MATLAB users, with occasional contributions from MathWorks employees.

Full contact details for The MathWorks can be obtained by typing info at the MATLAB prompt. For reference we give the details here:

```
The MathWorks, Inc.
3 Apple Hill Drive
Natick, MA 01760-2098 USA

Phone:             General:   +508-647-7000
                     Sales:   +508-647-7000
         Technical Support:   +508-647-7000

                       Fax:   +508-647-7101

                       Web:   www.mathworks.com
                 Newsgroup:   comp.soft-sys.matlab
                       FTP:   ftp.mathworks.com

E-mail:
         info@mathworks.com   Sales, pricing, and general information
      support@mathworks.com   Technical support for all products
          doc@mathworks.com   Documentation error reports
         bugs@mathworks.com   Bug reports
      service@mathworks.com   Order status, license renewals
      updates@mathworks.com   Microcomputer updates and subscriptions
       access@mathworks.com   MATLAB Access Program
      suggest@mathworks.com   Product enhancement suggestions
   news-notes@mathworks.com   MATLAB News & Notes Editor
      finance@mathworks.com   Financial products information
  connections@mathworks.com   MATLAB Connections Program
```

Glossary

Array Editor. A tool allowing array contents to be viewed and edited in tabular format.

Command History. A tool that lists MATLAB commands previously typed in the current and past sessions and allows them to be copied or executed.

Command Window. The window in which the MATLAB prompt >> appears and in which commands are typed. It is part of the MATLAB desktop.

Current Directory Browser. A browser for viewing M-files and other files and performing operations on them.

Editor/Debugger. A tool for creating, editing and debugging M-files.

FIG-file. A file with a .fig extension that contains a representation of a figure that can be reloaded into MATLAB.

figure. A MATLAB window for displaying graphics.

function M-file. A type of M-file that can accept input arguments and return output arguments and whose variables are local to the function.

Handle Graphics. An object-oriented graphics system that underlies MATLAB's graphics. It employs a hierarchical organization of objects that are manipulated via their handles.

Help Browser. A browser that allows you to view and search the documentation for MATLAB and other MathWorks products.

IEEE arithmetic. A standard for floating point arithmetic [32], to which MATLAB's arithmetic conforms.

LAPACK. A Fortran 77 library of programs for linear equation, least squares, eigenvalue and singular value computations [3]. Many of MATLAB's linear algebra functions are based on LAPACK.

Launch Pad. A window providing access to tools, demonstrations and documentation for MathWorks products.

M-file. A file with a .m extension that contains a sequence of MATLAB commands. It is of one of two types: a function or a script.

MAT-file. A file with a .mat extension that contains MATLAB variables. Created and accessed with the save and load commands.

MATLAB desktop. A user interface for managing files, tools, and applications associated with MATLAB.

MEX-file. A subroutine produced from C or Fortran code whose name has a platform-specific extension. It behaves like an M-file or built-in function.

script M-file. A type of M-file that takes no input or output arguments and operates on data in the workspace.

toolbox. A collection of M-files built on top of MATLAB that extends its capabilities, usually in a particular application area.

Workspace Browser. A browser that lists variables in the workspace and allows operations to be performed on them.

Bibliography

MATLAB documents marked "online version" are available from the MATLAB Help Browser.

[1] Forman S. Acton. *Numerical Methods That Work*. Harper and Row, New York, 1970. xviii+541 pp. Reprinted by Mathematical Association of America, Washington, D.C., with new preface and additional problems, 1990. ISBN 0-88385-450-3.

[2] D. E. Amos. Algorithm 644: A portable package for Bessel functions of a complex argument and nonnegative order. *ACM Trans. Math. Software*, 12(3):265–273, 1986. See also remark in same journal, 16 (1990), p. 404.

[3] E. Anderson, Z. Bai, C. H. Bischof, S. Blackford, J. W. Demmel, J. J. Dongarra, J. J. Du Croz, A. Greenbaum, S. J. Hammarling, A. McKenney, and D. C. Sorensen. *LAPACK Users' Guide*. Third edition, Society for Industrial and Applied Mathematics, Philadelphia, PA, USA, 1999. xxvi+407 pp. ISBN 0-89871-447-8.

[4] Russell Ash. *The Top 10 of Everything*. Dorland Kindersley, London, 1994. 288 pp. ISBN 0-7513-0137-X.

[5] Kendall E. Atkinson. *An Introduction to Numerical Analysis*. Second edition, Wiley, New York, 1989. xvi+693 pp. ISBN 0-471-50023-2.

[6] Kendall E. Atkinson. *Elementary Numerical Analysis*. Second edition, Wiley, New York, 1993. xiii+425 pp. ISBN 0-471-60010-5.

[7] Richard Barrett, Michael Berry, Tony F. Chan, James Demmel, June Donato, Jack Dongarra, Victor Eijkhout, Roldan Pozo, Charles Romine, and Henk van der Vorst. *Templates for the Solution of Linear Systems: Building Blocks for Iterative Methods*. Society for Industrial and Applied Mathematics, Philadelphia, PA, USA, 1994. xiii+112 pp. ISBN 0-89871-328-5.

[8] Jon L. Bentley. *More Programming Pearls: Confessions of a Coder*. Addison-Wesley, Reading, MA, USA, 1988. viii+207 pp. ISBN 0-201-11889-0.

[9] James L. Buchanan and Peter R. Turner. *Numerical Methods and Analysis*. McGraw-Hill, New York, 1992. xv+751 pp. ISBN 0-07-008717-2, 0-07-112922-7 (international paperback edition).

[10] Robert M. Corless. *Essential Maple: An Introduction for Scientific Programmers*. Springer-Verlag, New York, 1995. xv+218 pp. ISBN 0-387-94209-2.

[11] Germund Dahlquist and Åke Björck. *Numerical Methods*. Prentice-Hall, Englewood Cliffs, NJ, USA, 1974. xviii+573 pp. Translated by Ned Anderson. ISBN 0-13-627315-7.

[12] Harold T. Davis. *Introduction to Nonlinear Differential and Integral Equations*. Dover, New York, 1962. xv+566 pp. ISBN 0-486-60971-5.

[13] James W. Demmel. *Applied Numerical Linear Algebra*. Society for Industrial and Applied Mathematics, Philadelphia, PA, USA, 1997. xi+419 pp. ISBN 0-89871-389-7.

[14] I. S. Duff, A. M. Erisman, and J. K. Reid. *Direct Methods for Sparse Matrices*. Oxford University Press, 1986. xiii+341 pp. ISBN 0-19-853408-6.

[15] Alan Edelman. Eigenvalue roulette and random test matrices. In *Linear Algebra for Large Scale and Real-Time Applications*, Marc S. Moonen, Gene H. Golub, and Bart L. De Moor, editors, volume 232 of *NATO ASI Series E*, Kluwer Academic Publishers, Dordrecht, The Netherlands, 1993, pages 365–368.

[16] Alan Edelman, Eric Kostlan, and Michael Shub. How many eigenvalues of a random matrix are real? *J. Amer. Math. Soc.*, 7(1):247–267, 1994.

[17] Mark Embree and Lloyd N. Trefethen. Growth and decay of random Fibonacci sequences. *Proc. Roy. Soc. London Ser. A*, 455:2471–2485, 1999.

[18] George E. Forsythe, Michael A. Malcolm, and Cleve B. Moler. *Computer Methods for Mathematical Computations*. Prentice-Hall, Englewood Cliffs, NJ, USA, 1977. xi+259 pp. ISBN 0-13-165332-6.

[19] Walter Gander and Walter Gautschi. Adaptive quadrature—revisited. *BIT*, 40(1): 84–101, 2000.

[20] John R. Gilbert, Cleve B. Moler, and Robert S. Schreiber. Sparse matrices in MATLAB: Design and implementation. *SIAM J. Matrix Anal. Appl.*, 13(1):333–356, 1992.

[21] Gene H. Golub and Charles F. Van Loan. *Matrix Computations*. Third edition, Johns Hopkins University Press, Baltimore, MD, USA, 1996. xxvii+694 pp. ISBN 0-8018-5413-X (hardback), 0-8018-5414-8 (paperback).

[22] Anne Greenbaum. *Iterative Methods for Solving Linear Systems*. Society for Industrial and Applied Mathematics, Philadelphia, PA, USA, 1997. xiii+220 pp. ISBN 0-89871-396-X.

[23] David F. Griffiths and Desmond J. Higham. *Learning LaTeX*. Society for Industrial and Applied Mathematics, Philadelphia, PA, USA, 1997. x+84 pp. ISBN 0-89871-383-8.

[24] E. Hairer and G. Wanner. *Analysis by Its History*. Springer-Verlag, New York, 1996. x+374 pp. ISBN 0-387-94551-2.

[25] E. Hairer and G. Wanner. *Solving Ordinary Differential Equations II: Stiff and Differential-Algebraic Problems*. Second edition, Springer-Verlag, Berlin, 1996. xv+614 pp. ISBN 3-540-60452-9.

[26] Leonard Montague Harrod, editor. *Indexers on Indexing: A Selection of Articles Published in* The Indexer. R. K. Bowker, London, 1978. x+430 pp. ISBN 0-8352-1099-5.

[27] Piet Hein. *Grooks*. Number 85 in Borgens Pocketbooks. Second edition, Borgens Forlag, Copenhagen, Denmark, 1992. 53 pp. First published in 1966. ISBN 87-418-1079-1.

[28] Nicholas J. Higham. Algorithm 694: A collection of test matrices in MATLAB. *ACM Trans. Math. Software*, 17(3):289–305, September 1991.

[29] Nicholas J. Higham. The Test Matrix Toolbox for MATLAB (version 3.0). Numerical Analysis Report No. 276, Manchester Centre for Computational Mathematics, Manchester, England, September 1995. 70 pp.

[30] Nicholas J. Higham. *Accuracy and Stability of Numerical Algorithms*. Society for Industrial and Applied Mathematics, Philadelphia, PA, USA, 1996. xxviii+688 pp. ISBN 0-89871-355-2.

[31] Francis B. Hildebrand. *Advanced Calculus for Applications*. Second edition, Prentice-Hall, Englewood Cliffs, NJ, USA, 1976. xiii+733 pp. ISBN 0-13-011189-9.

[32] *IEEE Standard for Binary Floating-Point Arithmetic, ANSI/IEEE Standard 754-1985*. Institute of Electrical and Electronics Engineers, New York, 1985. Reprinted in SIGPLAN Notices, 22(2):9–25, 1987.

[33] D. S. Jones and B. D. Sleeman. *Differential Equations and Mathematical Biology*. George Allen and Unwin, London, 1983. xii+339 pp. ISBN 0-04-515001-X.

[34] William M. Kahan. Handheld calculator evaluates integrals. *Hewlett-Packard Journal*, August:23–32, 1980.

[35] David K. Kahaner, Cleve B. Moler, and Stephen G. Nash. *Numerical Methods and Software*. Prentice-Hall, Englewood Cliffs, NJ, USA, 1989. xii+495 pp. ISBN 0-13-627258-4.

[36] Irving Kaplansky. Reminiscences. In *Paul Halmos: Celebrating 50 Years of Mathematics*, John H. Ewing and F. W. Gehring, editors, Springer-Verlag, Berlin, 1991, pages 87–89.

[37] Roger Emanuel Kaufman. *A FORTRAN Coloring Book*. MIT Press, Cambridge, MA, USA, 1978. ISBN 0-262-61026-4.

[38] C. T. Kelley. *Iterative Methods for Linear and Nonlinear Equations*. Society for Industrial and Applied Mathematics, Philadelphia, PA, USA, 1995. xiii+165 pp. ISBN 0-89871-352-8.

[39] Brian W. Kernighan and P. J. Plauger. *The Elements of Programming Style*. Second edition, McGraw-Hill, New York, 1978. xii+168 pp. ISBN 0-07-034207-5.

[40] Peter E. Kloeden and Eckhard Platen. *Numerical Solution of Stochastic Differential Equations*. Springer-Verlag, Berlin, 1992. xxxv+632 pp. ISBN 3-540-54062-8.

[41] G. Norman Knight. Book indexing in Great Britain: A brief history. *The Indexer*, 6 (1):14–18, 1968. Reprinted in [26, pp. 9–13].

[42] Donald E. Knuth. Structured programming with go to statements. *Computing Surveys*, 6(4):261–301, 1974. Reprinted in [44].

[43] Donald E. Knuth. *The TEXbook*. Addison-Wesley, Reading, MA, USA, 1986. ix+483 pp. ISBN 0-201-13448-9.

[44] Donald E. Knuth. *Literate Programming*. CSLI Lecture Notes Number 27. Center for the Study of Language and Information, Stanford University, Stanford, CA, USA, 1992. xv+368 pp. ISBN 0-9370-7380-6.

[45] Donald E. Knuth. *Digital Typography*. CSLI Lecture Notes Number 78. Center for the Study of Language and Information, Stanford University, Stanford, CA, USA, 1999. xv+685 pp. ISBN 0-57586-010-4.

[46] Arnold R. Krommer and Christoph W. Ueberhuber. *Computational Integration*. Society for Industrial and Applied Mathematics, Philadelphia, PA, USA, 1998. xix+445 pp. ISBN 0-89871-374-9.

[47] Jeffrey C. Lagarias. The $3x + 1$ problem and its generalizations. *Amer. Math. Monthly*, 92(1):3–23, 1985.

[48] Leslie Lamport. *LATEX: A Document Preparation System. User's Guide and Reference Manual*. Second edition, Addison-Wesley, Reading, MA, USA, 1994. xvi+272 pp. ISBN 0-201-52983-1.

[49] R. B. Lehoucq, D. C. Sorensen, and C. Yang. *ARPACK Users' Guide: Solution of Large-Scale Eigenvalue Problems with Implicitly Restarted Arnoldi Methods*. Society for Industrial and Applied Mathematics, Philadelphia, PA, USA, 1998. xv+142 pp. ISBN 0-89871-407-9.

[50] F. M. Leslie. Liquid crystal devices. Technical report, Institute Wiskundige Dienstverlening, Technische Universiteit Eindhoven, Eindhoven, The Netherlands, 1992.

[51] Tom Marchioro. Putting math to work: An interview with Cleve Moler. *Computing in Science and Engineering*, 1(4):10–13, Jul/Aug 1999.

[52] *Building GUIs with MATLAB*. The MathWorks, Inc., Natick, MA, USA. Online version.

[53] *Getting Started with MATLAB*. The MathWorks, Inc., Natick, MA, USA. Online version.

[54] *MATLAB Application Program Interface Guide*. The MathWorks, Inc., Natick, MA, USA. Online version.

[55] *MATLAB Application Program Interface Reference*. The MathWorks, Inc., Natick, MA, USA. Online version.

[56] *Using MATLAB*. The MathWorks, Inc., Natick, MA, USA. Online version.

[57] *Using MATLAB Graphics*. The MathWorks, Inc., Natick, MA, USA. Online version.

[58] Cleve B. Moler. Demonstration of a matrix laboratory. In *Numerical Analysis, Mexico 1981*, J. P. Hennart, editor, volume 909 of *Lecture Notes in Mathematics*, Springer-Verlag, Berlin, 1982, pages 84–98.

[59] Cleve B. Moler. Yet another look at the FFT. *The MathWorks Newsletter*, Spring 1992.

[60] Cleve B. Moler. MATLAB's magical mystery tour. *The MathWorks Newsletter*, 7(1): 8–9, 1993.

[61] K. W. Morton and D. F. Mayers. *Numerical Solution of Partial Differential Equations*. Cambridge University Press, 1994. 227 pp. ISBN 0-521-42922-6.

[62] Noël M. Nachtigal, Satish C. Reddy, and Lloyd N. Trefethen. How fast are nonsymmetric matrix iterations? *SIAM J. Matrix Anal. Appl.*, 13(3):778–795, 1992.

[63] Salih N. Neftci. *An Introduction to the Mathematics of Financial Derivatives*. Academic Press, San Diego, CA, USA, 1996. xxi+352 pp. ISBN 0-12-515390-2.

[64] Heinz-Otto Peitgen, Hartmut Jürgens, and Dietmar Saupe. *Fractals for the Classroom. Part One: Introduction to Fractals and Chaos*. Springer-Verlag, New York, 1992. xiv+450 pp. ISBN 0-387-97041-X.

[65] Heinz-Otto Peitgen, Hartmut Jürgens, and Dietmar Saupe. *Fractals for the Classroom. Part Two: Complex Systems and Mandelbrot Set*. Springer-Verlag, New York, 1992. xii+500 pp. ISBN 0-387-97722-8.

[66] E. Pitts. The stability of pendent liquid drops. Part 1. Drops formed in a narrow gap. *J. Fluid Mech.*, 59(4):753–767, 1973.

[67] William H. Press, Saul A. Teukolsky, William T. Vetterling, and Brian P. Flannery. *Numerical Recipes in FORTRAN: The Art of Scientific Computing*. Second edition, Cambridge University Press, 1992. xxvi+963 pp. ISBN 0-521-43064-X.

[68] Robert Sedgewick. *Algorithms*. Second edition, Addison-Wesley, Reading, MA, USA, 1988. xii+657 pp. ISBN 0-201-06673-4.

[69] Lawrence F. Shampine. *Numerical Solution of Ordinary Differential Equations*. Chapman and Hall, New York, 1994. x+484 pp. ISBN 0-412-05151-6.

[70] Lawrence F. Shampine, Richard C. Allen, Jr., and Steven Pruess. *Fundamentals of Numerical Computing*. Wiley, New York, 1997. x+268 pp. ISBN 0-471-16363-5.

[71] Lawrence F. Shampine, Jacek A. Kierzenka, and Mark W. Reichelt. Solving boundary value problems for ordinary differential equations in MATLAB with bvp4c. Manuscript, available at ftp://ftp.mathworks.com/pub/doc/papers/bvp/, 2000. 27 pp.

[72] Lawrence F. Shampine and Mark W. Reichelt. The MATLAB ODE suite. *SIAM J. Sci. Comput.*, 18(1):1–22, 1997.

[73] Gilbert Strang. *Introduction to Linear Algebra*. Wellesley-Cambridge Press, Wellesley, MA, USA, 1993. viii+472 pp. ISBN 0-9614088-5-5.

[74] Steven H. Strogatz. *Nonlinear Dynamics and Chaos: With Applications to Physics, Biology, Chemistry, and Engineering*. Addison-Wesley, Reading, MA, USA, 1994. xi+498 pp. ISBN 0-201-54344-3.

[75] Lloyd N. Trefethen and David Bau III. *Numerical Linear Algebra*. Society for Industrial and Applied Mathematics, Philadelphia, PA, USA, 1997. xii+361 pp. ISBN 0-89871-361-7.

[76] Edward R. Tufte. *The Visual Display of Quantitative Information*. Graphics Press, Cheshire, CT, USA, 1983. 197 pp.

[77] Edward R. Tufte. *Envisioning Information*. Graphics Press, Cheshire, CT, USA, 1990. 126 pp.

[78] Edward R. Tufte. *Visual Explanations: Images and Quantities, Evidence and Narrative*. Graphics Press, Cheshire, CT, USA, 1997. 158 pp. ISBN 0-9613921-2-6.

[79] Charles F. Van Loan. *Computational Frameworks for the Fast Fourier Transform*. Society for Industrial and Applied Mathematics, Philadelphia, PA, USA, 1992. xiii+273 pp. ISBN 0-89871-285-8.

[80] Charles F. Van Loan. Using examples to build computational intuition. *SIAM News*, 28:1, 7, October 1995.

[81] Charles F. Van Loan. *Introduction to Scientific Computing: A Matrix-Vector Approach Using MATLAB*. Prentice-Hall, Englewood Cliffs, NJ, USA, 2000. xi+367 pp. ISBN 0-13-949157-0.

[82] D. Viswanath. Random Fibonacci sequences and the number 1.3198824.... *Math. Comp.*, 69(231):1131–1155, 2000.

[83] Maurice V. Wilkes. *Memoirs of a Computer Pioneer*. MIT Press, Cambridge, MA, USA, 1985. viii+240 pp. ISBN 0-262-23122-0.

[84] Paul Wilmott, Sam Howison, and Jeff Dewynne. *The Mathematics of Financial Derivatives: A Student Introduction*. Cambridge University Press, 1995. xiii+317 pp. ISBN 0-521-49699-3.

Index

The 18th century saw the advent of the professional indexer.
He was usually of inferior status—a Grub Street hack—
although well-read and occasionally a university graduate.

— G. NORMAN KNIGHT, *Book Indexing in Great Britain: A Brief History* (1968)

I find that a great part of the information I have was acquired by
looking up something and finding something else on the way.

— FRANKLIN P. ADAMS

A suffix "t" after a page number denotes a table, "f" a figure, "n" a footnote, and "ℓ" a listing. Entries in typewriter font beginning with lower case letters are MATLAB functions; those beginning with capital letters are Handle Graphics property names.